A WEALTH OF EVIL

"Dumas brings an unusual sensitivity and clarity to this disturbing tale."
—*Publishers Weekly*

❖

"No holds barred. . . . Dumas shatters the myth of this suburban Shangri-la with his probing, uncompromising look. . . . The author's crisp, lean writing style lends the work its power. . . . A perfect example of what a treasure trove of research can become in the hands of a capable writer."
—*Book Page*

❖

"The authentic and definitive literary authority on the Martha Moxley murder."
—*Greenwich Times*

❖

"As good as it gets . . . a literary, reasoned, reflective analysis of the terrible case."
—*Toronto Globe & Mail*

A WEALTH OF EVIL:

The True Story of the Murder of Martha Moxley in America's Richest Community

Timothy Dumas

WARNER BOOKS

A Time Warner Company

Author's Note

I have changed a few names for privacy's sake. Even today, nearly a quarter century after "the date in question"—as police call October 30, 1975, in their reports—there are people who will agree to an interview only after a careful laying out of conditions. Spoken words in quotes come directly from interviews; spoken words not in quotes are reconstructions of dialogue; italics denote thoughts or my reconstruction of thoughts. All the material in this book comes from historical records, from hundreds of pages of police reportage, and from the dozens of interviews I have conducted over the years.

WARNER BOOKS EDITION

Copyright © 1998 by Timothy Dumas
All rights reserved.

Published by arrangement with Arcade Publishing

Cover design by Tony Russo

Warner Books, Inc.
1271 Avenue of the Americas
New York, NY 10020

Visit our Web site at
www.warnerbooks.com

 A Time Warner Company

Printed in the United States of America

First Paperback Printing: August 1999

10 9 8 7 6 5 4 3 2 1

For Maria, and for my mother and father

". . . wounds bodily and ghostly, great and small, go aching on, not ev'ry one commemorated. . . ."

—Thomas Pynchon
Mason & Dixon

"Under the charm of these rich I was as trusting and as stupid as a bird dog who wants to go out with any man with a gun. . . ."

—Ernest Hemingway
A Moveable Feast

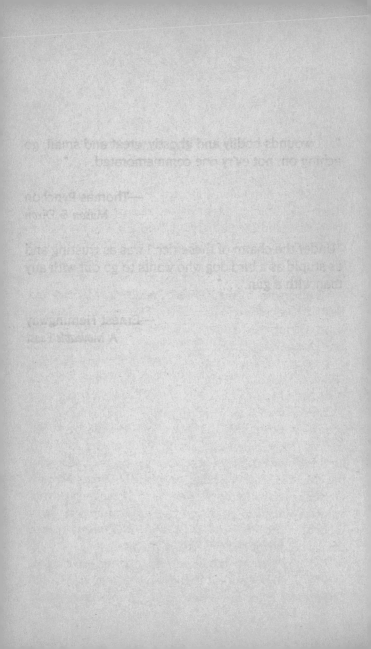

> wounds really and the character and small, go
> acting on not every one commemorated

—Thomas Pynchon
Mason & Dixon

> Under the charm of these men I was as trusting and
> as stupid as a bird dog who wants to go out with any
> man with a gun.

—Ernest Hemingway
A Moveable Feast

Acknowledgments

I am deeply indebted to Dorthy Moxley, John Moxley, Sheila McGuire, Christy Kalan, and the Fuchs family for their friendship and their trust. I am equally indebted to Steve Carroll, for his insight into the early stages of the Moxley investigation, and to Frank Garr, for his help as the story wore on in the nineties.

I also wish to thank Rock Stamberg, Michael and Beatriz Vasile, Mike White, David Dumas, John Dumas, Vinton McCabe, Tony Carvette, John Roberts, Jack and Donna Moffly, Cynthia Coulson, Frank Nicholson, Rod Lurie, Julia Chiappetta, Lawrence Fellows, Marjorie Horvitz, Samantha, Stephen Trent Seames, Adolfo Bezamat, Dominick Dunne, and the late Arthur Roth. Thanks also to Susan Richardson and Bill Finch at the Historical Society of the Town of Greenwich; to the staff of the Greenwich Library; and to the Library's Oral History Project, whose volumes on the collapse of the Mianus River Bridge and the United Nations Organization's attempted foray into Greenwich proved especially helpful. Another valuable source was Jerry Oppenheimer's book *The Other Mrs. Kennedy*, which details the history of the Skakel family.

Thanks also to Ed Novak for getting me started, and to Theresa Park for keeping me going, and to Fifi Oscard and Peter Sawyer. At Arcade Publishing, thanks to editor Tim Bent, who stood by me from beginning to end, to Richard and Jeannette Seaver for their faith in me, and to Phillipa Tawn, Cal Barksdale and Coates Bateman for all their hard work. At Warner, thanks to Susanna Einstein, Airié Dekidjiev, and Maureen Egen for believing that this story could occupy a wider universe.

A WEALTH
OF EVIL

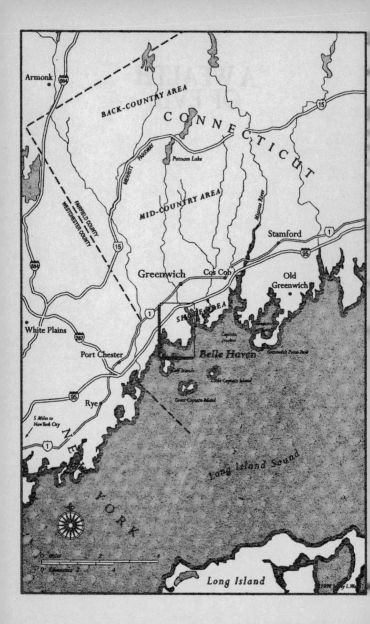

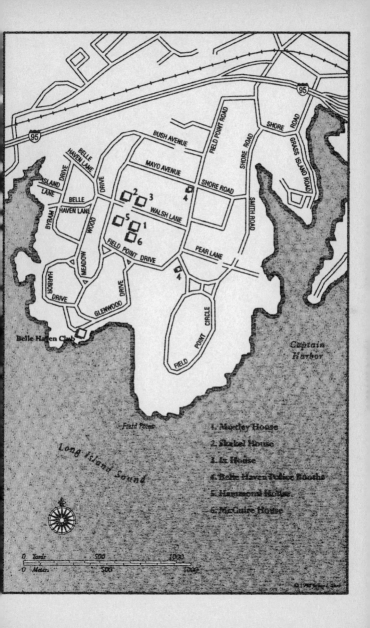

BUSH AVENUE

MAYO AVENUE

SHORE ROAD

WALSH LANE

PEAR LANE

BELLE HAVEN LANE

BELLE HAVEN LANE

ISLAND LANE

BYRAM

WOOD DRIVE

MEADOW DRIVE

GLENWOOD DRIVE

HARBOR DRIVE

FIELD POINT DRIVE

FIELD POINT ROAD

SHORE ROAD

SMITH ROAD

GRASS ISLAND ROAD

95

95

FIELD POINT CIRCLE

Belle Haven Club

Field Point

Long Island Sound

Captain Harbor

1. Moxley House
2. Skakel House
3. Ix House
4. Belle Haven Police Booths
5. Hammond House
6. McGuire House

0 Yards 500 1000
0 Miles 500 1000

Prologue

O<small>N THE NIGHT</small> of October 30, 1975, as the temperature plunged to freezing in the town of Greenwich, Connecticut, fifteen-year-old Martha Moxley started home through the dark. The distance from a neighbor's house to her own was not far, perhaps two hundred yards, but before she could cover it, a person unknown bludgeoned her to death with a woman's six iron.

Early the next afternoon—Halloween—a girl cutting across the Moxleys' lawn stumbled upon the corpse, lying beneath the low-hanging branches of a towering pine. The body was stripped bare below the waist, its head gashed and swollen and caked with blood. "It was a maniacal attack," Stephen Carroll, a retired Greenwich police detective, recalled many years afterward. "We were surprised later to find out that her hair was blond. We thought she was a redhead."

No person was ever arrested for the crime, much less convicted in a court of law. But a great many townspeople privately convicted a teenage nephew of Robert F. Kennedy. The man in question, Thomas Skakel, now lives peaceably in rural Massachusetts with his wife and two children. Another man on the scene that night, a promising schoolteacher named Ken Littleton, twice failed polygraph tests and slowly fell to pieces.

The Moxley investigation unfolded with nightmarish complexity. Some found it convenient to blame the local police force, whose usual work concerned drunken drivers and burglars, for flailing about clumsily in the deep waters of a murder investigation. Others murmured about a police cover-up. "It's upsetting to know the police didn't do the job they should have," John Moxley, Martha's brother, said years later. "But the realist in me says, 'How are they supposed to know how to solve a murder? You're in Greenwich, Connecticut. Stuff like this doesn't happen.'"

The Belle Haven peninsula, the part of town where Martha Moxley lived and died, posed special problems. This wealthy enclave on Long Island Sound was a distillation of the Greenwich image—remote, superior, and gorgeous. But underneath, Belle Haven was a place of considerable sorrow. Broken homes, alcoholism, and drug abuse were common in the 1970s, owing chiefly to hard partying and high-pressure business careers. "I must say, it was like alcoholics' row," one former Belle Haven resident, Cynthia Bjork, said. "I'd never seen so many alcoholics in my life!"

Belle Haven suffered a freakishly high incidence of premature deaths. Cancers, plane crashes, drug overdoses, and suicides took many residents in the bloom of their lives and multiplied the sorrow. And so, whether by circumstance or accident, Belle Haven came to seem a menagerie of eccentrics. On Halloween of 1975, as far as the police were concerned, a person worthy of suspicion dwelled in almost every house. "I couldn't get over it," Steve Carroll told me. "Oh my God—all this money, and these people had such problems."

Today Belle Haven seems scrubbed clean of those old problems. People don't drink as they once did, and there are new people with new money who have begun to tear down the old houses and build bigger ones. (One new Belle Haven palace under construction boasts a twenty-seven-car garage.) But Martha's death occurred at a precise time in the neighborhood's history, a time when the maze of personal crises was at its most baffling.

Meanwhile, the rest of Greenwich looked on in horror. Murder had struck in town before (most recently in 1973, when a despondent old man shot his wife and her French poodle), but there had been nothing as appalling and mysterious as this. Greenwich is a peaceful town—but also a secretive one. On certain days the air seems dense with secrets, which whirl around like autumn leaves in a storm. "Did you ever see the movie *Blue Velvet*?" Christy Kalan, who had been one of Martha's closest friends, asked me. "You have this nice peaceful town with all this *stuff* seething underneath. I think that's a lot like Greenwich. Everything seems so perfect on the surface—and that's just multiplied with all the money and all the high society—but beneath it there's all this junk going on."

This confounding atmosphere, as much as the failings of an untested police force, is why the Moxley investigation became so hard to navigate. The more information detectives amassed, the hazier the picture turned, until they found themselves adrift in a sea of clues. My own encounter with the case left me feeling as though I were standing on a hieroglyph discernible only from a bird's altitude, or chasing a squirrel in a room full of fog. Answers seemed close but never within reach.

My frustration did instill in me a degree of sympathy for the Greenwich police. Though they suffered the slings and arrows of a derisive pubic, they did not lose heart. Frank Garr, the only detective still investigating Martha's murder, said to me, "Anyone who's been on this case, going back to 1975, has not been able to let it go. It's not the kind of case that you come in and work, and at four o'clock you go home. Whether you did two years on it, two weeks on it, or two minutes on it, it was just something that got into you. I know *I'll* never let it go."

Born and raised in Greenwich, I was fourteen when Martha was murdered. Somehow this local cataclysm had, in my mind, wedded itself to the many strange events of that week: Mr. and Mrs. Joseph T. Quinlan, in a courtroom in Morristown, New Jersey, fighting for the right to remove their comatose daughter from life support; Generalissimo Franco lying on his deathbed in Madrid, bleeding from the stomach; Patty Hearst awaiting trial in a Redwood City, California, jail cell for her vexing role in the armed robbery of a San Francisco bank; New York City trembling on the brink of bankruptcy; a nuclear blast under the salt flats of Nevada that rattled chandeliers in Las Vegas and whose vibration was felt all the way to Sacramento.

Out in the world, the center was not holding, and now the chaos had finally infiltrated our little green world. The chill of that Halloween remains visceral for me, recalled in cells and sinew as much as in the cognitive brain.

Many years later, as I traveled the back roads of this story,

I kept recalling Nick Carraway, F. Scott Fitzgerald's bewildered narrator in *The Great Gatsby*. Nick imagines the fictional town of West Egg, on the north shore of Long Island—directly across the Sound from Greenwich—as a night scene by El Greco: "After Gatsby's death the East was haunted for me like that, distorted beyond my eyes' power of correction." That was how I felt as I pursued the story. Person after person would whisper in my ear some shining new detail, some glorious pearl, which would always crumble into dust.

There were elements—let's call them elements—who tried to silence talk of the Moxley murder, hoping it would evaporate like rain and fortunes. But as the years tumbled past, the case got bigger and bigger, like some science project run amok, until the image of the girl herself seemed to gaze down mutely upon the houses and trees and into the inscrutable heart of Greenwich.

Meanwhile, the elements, their datebooks crammed with golf games and tea luncheons, pretended Martha was not there; she was up in Putnam Cemetery or else in heaven; anywhere but there. Every time she had the bad manners to turn up in the newspapers or on television or merely in the air, the elements would murmur, "Oh no, not again. Haven't enough people been hurt by this?" Always the humanitarian pretense. And every time they said it, or thought it, or felt it, Martha's image distended even more.

And so her case wears on, telling more about the living than the dead.

Chapter One

Belle Haven

THE TOWN of Greenwich sits near the crook of Long Island Sound. Upon its landscape of soft green hills live sixty thousand bodies (and considerably fewer souls, the devil whispers), proud people who have done well in life.

On the Belle Haven peninsula they have done better than well. The peninsula juts a mile or so into the Sound, reaching out into the slate-gray water as if to detach itself from the rest of town. Strangers entering Belle Haven feel this detachment as keenly as they do a change in weather. They tighten their grip on their steering wheels, check their rearview mirrors for private police, and round the little white speed fences with edgy, excessive care.

Then, forgetting themselves, they slow at old mansions. They notice how some have turrets and gables that thrust through the tall trees. How others rest wearily, ponderously, as if subdued by centuries of Atlantic wear. It does not seem possible that some of the oldest-looking houses date only to the 1920s and that Belle Haven itself flowered as late as the 1880s.

A brochure from 1884 informs us:

> Of the many beautiful spots on the borders of Long Island Sound none is more beautiful that Greenwich, Connecticut. It possesses not only the charm of its natural advantages, which, without exaggeration, are innumerable, but is also of historic interest, some of the most exciting episodes of the Revolution having been enacted in its immediate vicinity.
>
> To come down to a later period, in our own times Greenwich has been widely known as a popular resort for the tired mortals of the busy metropolis, who find here in its delightful scenery and invigorating air all the needful appliances for the promotion of health, happiness and comfort, not to mention wealth.

Then the brochure wanders round to the lovely geography of Belle Haven itself, "grandly placed as it is upon a ridge, commencing with an elevation of one hundred and sixteen feet above tide-water, and sloping gradually to the water's edge. . . ." It tells of Belle Haven's salubrious breezes and the fine pitch at which its "sewage matter" is delivered into the depths of the Sound. It notes especially the talismanic qualities of health that Belle Haven living brings. Neither the man who originally owned the land, an obscure Dutch sea captain named Busch, nor any of his descendants, "has suffered in the slightest degree from malaria, chills or fever."

This is good news for the proposition at hand:

> The property on which Belle Haven is situated has recently passed into the hands of a small company of capitalists, whose

intention is to develop it into a Residence Park, and who will spare no expense to make it in all respects unequaled as a place of residence for summer or permanent location. . . .

Mission accomplished. Belle Haven rapidly became the most dazzling neighborhood in what was fast becoming one of the nation's wealthiest towns—a sanctuary for New York society, captains of industry, and other tired mortals of the busy metropolis.

By 1975 the mansions of Belle Haven are fading beauties, clinging to remnants of past glory. They are burdensome to keep up. Costly to make over. But their fusty grandeur adds a note of magic and mystery. "Belle Haven was the land of fairy tales," recalls Sheila McGuire, whose most vivid neighborhood memory happens to be a nightmare—but we'll get to that. "I'll tell you, there are hidden treasures in Belle Haven. It really was like Alice in Wonderland."

Other Belle Havenites tell me of mythical folk and haunted houses. "You know that house on Mayo Avenue, the small Victorian that's like the House of the Seven Gables?" asks Chip White, who lived down the street from Martha. "That was the Sutter house. Only, we called it the monkey house. It was haunted. The ghost wore long tennis whites. You'd see him glide behind the upstairs windows. When the new people moved in we asked, 'Did you see the tennis player?' and they said, 'Uhh, yeah.' "

Like much that I learned for this story, the tennis player turned out to be half truth, half invention. "I can tell you who the ghost in tennis whites was," says Sam Sutter, now a prosecutor in New Bedford, Massachusetts. "He was my father. Clifford Sutter. Fifth-best tennis player in the world in 1932. *He* was the ghost in tennis whites—but he wasn't dead."

Leaf Smashing

I'LL TELL YOU A GHOST STORY.

One day when the sky breathes gray and the leaves curl up like cold hands, an old yellow school bus smokes past the great houses of Greenwich and down the rain-slicked roads toward Long Island Sound. The bus chugs up Shore Road, breasts a long hill, squeaks to a halt in front of a tiny white guard booth with green shutters and a green roof. Upon the booth hangs a sign reading "Belle Haven. No Trespassing." The man in the booth waves a pale hand; leaves swim past his window like tropical fish. The bus gathers speed and rolls along under splendid bursts of color and into the heart of the Belle Haven peninsula.

The school bus runs through fading tunnels of yellow leaves. Past turreted Victorians, sulking Tudors, proud Georgian colonials, tile-roofed villas, self-conscious contemporaries—each the symbol of someone's dream. But for all their grandeur, these houses lack the elbow room they need. Few of them preside over more than two acres (far from the loose, farmy spaces of early Belle Haven), and this endows the peninsula with an opulent and eccentric density.

At the top of Walsh Lane, the door folds in like a concertina and two girls tumble out into the autumn air.

Martha Moxley and Sheila McGuire.

Wind blows. Leaves fatten against the sky, snap loose, and flutter earthward.

The girls seize upon the brightest ones on the damp road, deep-red maple, golden oak, and crush them under their shoes. Twirl on them like ballerinas. Their hair flies out as they sparkle down the lane, pressing the leaves into the black road and saying, "How pretty, how pretty, look, did you see this one, look at this one."

This joyful movement is their ode to the season, and they call it the Leaf-Smashing Dance.

Veils of leaves drop away from the great houses in flakes of gold. Mexicans are raking the leaves onto bolts of burlap, when the wind gusts and flings them all across the grass again. Martha brushes a leaf from her hair and smiles. Her hair shines bright gold. She blew in from San Francisco Bay fifteen months earlier. A California girl.

She has attended five schools in five years; lived in three neighborhoods and in two radically dissimilar states. For some, keeping upright in shifting terrain is an acquired skill, necessary for social survival. For Martha, this skill is inborn. Motion does not throw her. She thrives on it, instigates it, steers its course. Among a certain crowd of girls, whatever fun thing is happening has likely spun from the mind of Martha Moxley.

Consider tonight. Tonight is Mischief Night, the night before Halloween. Mischief Night is license to set free childish devils. Armed with toilet paper and shaving cream and eggs (M-80 firecrackers and baseball bats for real hellions), the youth of Greenwich scurry about in the dark, festooning the town with mischievous designs.

Tonight Martha Moxley will be among them.

Hey, Martha, look! When the leaves are down, the houses have faces. See? It looks like they're staring out at you!

People inside are looking out at us, crazy people with lots of booze and nothing to do.

The sun slips behind a roof, and the mansion eyes burn a dull orange. Pumpkin lanterns smirk through unlit holes. Crows sit fearlessly in the grass as Martha and Sheila send clouds of girls' laughter up into the air and stamp Walsh Lane with yellow and gold and red.

The girls turn in at Martha's house. Sheila goes on through the backyard to her own house, on the other side of the long brick garden wall. She does not take a good last look at Martha Moxley—there is no need; she will see her again tomorrow.

Mischief Night

DUSK. The sun sits low. Liquefies. Flames.

A man steps from the kitchen door of the Belle Haven Club, a beach and tennis club that is also the social axis of this neighborhood. The man is striding along, a cup of coffee raised to his chest. His fingers burn under a slanting plume of steam. He pauses in a rectangle of lighted lawn. At his back, the long sleek shining Sound goes dark and still, and he feels the cold air move through him.

Muffled voices leak out of the dining room and settle lightly on the water. The voices complain about the abrupt change in weather. The day before, October 29, the temperature hit seventy, and everyone opened windows to the faint bitter smell of decay. But this morning the people of the town rose to a killing frost that grayed their lawns and carved designs on their windows.

The man looks up. Night has come, moonlessly. The eastern sky is purple, black higher up, and the first stars hang overhead. Cloud traces track across the orange light of the west.

The man walks beyond the voices and becomes a vague

shape sliding past the tennis courts. He heads toward a 1970 Chevrolet Impala angled up against the seawall. Working-man's car. The Impala coughs, kicks to life. The man sips his coffee. He is ready to begin.

This dark, these trees, the anticipation of unrest—they are nothing to special police officer Charles Morganti. He has been hardened by his time in the jungles of Vietnam. Tonight the Belle Haven Association has hired him to keep watch over this gated patch of heaven. Piece of cake.

He rattles away from the club, climbing above the black water. His taillights advance into the tall trees and then vanish. Suddenly he feels it: a strangeness in the cooling air, a dreamlike quality that offends his sense of duty. Morganti later recalls, "It was dark. It was cold. There was a breeze going. But it was somehow very still too. You know how you get those still nights when you get down near the water? Like that. It felt strange, very strange, no doubt about it."

These qualities of night remind him of the air force base at Columbus, Mississippi. One night a guy on midnight duty hanged himself in a maintenance hangar. His limp body was found swaying gently from the upper deck. "Everybody who worked midnights after that was scared to go in there."

Now that feeling is coming round again.

And then things happen.

A car knocks down a speed fence on Otter Rock Drive and darts off in a swirl of lamp-lit leaves. Morganti steps uneasily from his patrol car and sets the fence upright. He stands on the roadside, alert. There are voices in the trees. He peers down Walsh Lane, a narrow, leafy street that dead-ends with a length of chain at Otter Rock.

"I saw a whole mob of kids down there. Twelve, thirteen, fourteen of them, by the Moxley house. Among those trees over where Martha was found. Kind of caught me strange. So I went walking down the drive toward them, to try to see what was going on, and they all came running out and they all ran over to the Skakel house."

Walsh Lane is lit by a streetlight that flickers and flickers as if under the burden of the dark. Morganti stops, shudders. "After I spotted those kids in the trees, I walked up Walsh Lane from Otter Rock to see if there was anybody still screwing around. You know how you walk into some area and it just gives you the willies? Two and a half years in Vietnam, not too many things got me scared. I pulled patrols in Vietnam, the whole bit. But you get a sixth sense, you know what I mean? So I walk up into that area and it just feels *weird*. I don't know what it was. I had two friends with me that night, Smith and Wesson. But all kidding aside, I felt really strange walking down that road. To this day, I don't know why."

He drives around the block and spies a man walking north on Field Point Road. The man is in his twenties, with blond hair and glasses. He has his head tucked into the collar of his fatigue jacket. *This guy looks out of place,* Morganti thinks. Morganti drifts over to the roadside and questions him. "I ask him if he lives in the neighborhood, and he says he lives down Walsh Lane. He's just out for a walk, he says. But I make a mental note to watch for him on my next sweep."

At about nine-thirty, Geoffrey Byrne, one of the children whom Morganti dispersed, starts home from the Skakel house. It is not far from there to the great dark Tudor in which he lives. He will walk across the Skakels' backyard to Walsh Lane, cross the front of the Ix house, then turn in at a wooded path that leads up to Mayo Avenue.

As he goes into the thickening trees, he hears heavy footfalls on the leaves, thumping rapidly toward him. He stops, but the steps keep coming, and so he flies through the trees, raising his arms against the black whips of bare branches, his long blond hair marking him like a white-tailed deer. He vaults over a low stone wall and sprints up a silvery lawn toward the mammoth silhouette of home. He touches against the back door; he does not remain outside to listen for the sound that is rushing through the trees.

As the clock nears ten, twelve-year-old Steven Skakel of 71 Otter Rock Drive wakes to the sound of screaming; Margaret Moore, fifteen, of 25 Walsh Lane, hears leaves rustling; Mr. and Mrs. Charles Gorman, of 21 Walsh Lane, hear the growling of an agitated dog; Morganti spies a big man, perhaps six feet tall and weighing two hundred pounds, with blond hair and dark-rimmed glasses, walking across the lawns of Otter Rock and vanishing between two houses. *The same darn guy,* he thinks, picturing the man he questioned earlier.

Ken Littleton, a teacher at the Brunswick School, a private boys' school in Greenwich, moved into the Skakel house that afternoon. He's a tall, thick-shouldered man with a square jaw and wire-frame glasses. After dinner, he ensconces himself in the master bedroom to watch the network premier of *The French Connection,* starring Gene Hackman.

The Skakels' Irish nanny, eighty-three-year-old Margaret Sweeney, calls upstairs.

"Mr. Littleton, would you please check into that fracas outside?" Littleton rises from his chair, keeping an eye on Popeye Doyle roughing up a stoolie in a bar. Then he goes downstairs. He opens the front door. The night is eerily still. He sees no kids, but he hears movement in the brush.

Robert Bjork, a prosecutor who works in New York City, is sitting in the library of his home on Otter Rock when he hears a collision outside his window—the speed fence—and the damaged car go beetling down the road. Soon he notices a Chevy parked in front of his house and goes outdoors to investigate. He finds Morganti. The two men chat for a moment, and then Bjork goes back inside.

Bjork has one piece of business to take care of before he turns in—corralling his springer spaniel, Mokui, and letting him out the back. Normally Mokui sniffs around, relieves himself, and paws at the door to be let in.

Tonight Mokui does not return.

Bjork steps outside and whistles. As he stands there, not even the floodlights illuminating his lawn can push back an invading presence. "It was an eerie night, bitter cold, wind blowing fiercely," Bjork remembers. A funny look comes over his face. "I had a sense of evil. That's the best way I can describe it."

The dog appears finally on the perimeter of the yard, a brushy patch that abuts the property of David and Dorthy Moxley. "He came from the junction point of our property and the Moxleys'. He was wavering in his step. He seemed disoriented and jumpy, whining a bit. Do you believe in the intelligence of animals? Well, that dog was trying to tell me something was wrong."

Bjork stares at the dog a moment and then beckons him toward the door, shutting it hard against the night. "I'm not a guy who's afraid of things. I'm not trying to be boastful or macho. That's just the way I am. But I can remember being very happy to get back inside the house."

The time is a few minutes past ten. Something has happened out there. You can feel it alive in the air, like the smell of lightning that has struck the earth.

Steven Hertig, twenty-three, lives across the street from the Skakels and three lots away from the Moxleys. Before he shuts off his bedroom light, at about eleven o'clock, he hears noises coming from the end of Walsh Lane. And now the night is winding down, all except for the high wind in the trees.

Sheila McGuire returns from a Halloween party at about midnight. She hustles up the long driveway in the dark. She pulls on the door. It's locked. This, in a night of oddities, isn't that odd.

"My mom and dad had a lot of kids and assumed sometimes we were all inside," Sheila recalls. "So I went through the ritual of throwing stones at the windows and banging on the door. I don't remember if I rang the doorbell. We'd had bad doorbells in the past, and I might have realized ringing would be futile. I ended up climbing in my dad's Mercury Brougham and lay there for a bit because it was so cold outside, and dark.

"I'd heard a door creak in back of our garage, a door to a little room we used to call the potting shed. I thought I heard it close. I didn't know whether it was a raccoon or what, but I wasn't going to meet up with it. I climbed in the car for shelter and so I wouldn't get the willies so bad."

Sheila is not a fearful girl. She cannot quite understand why she is afraid tonight.

"I used to leave my house at two o'clock in the morning, sneak through the woods, sneak through the neighbors' yards, throw rocks at someone's window, tell them to meet me someplace. Maybe we'd go down to the beach. But I don't remember having the willies outside at night, not before then. See, I'd been locked out before. And it was like, 'Oh, what a drag.' It wasn't anything to get spooked about."

The car gives no warmth. Sheila slides out the door and starts again with the stone throwing and the banging, until her mother, Elvira, comes to the door and lets her in. Sheila shakes off the night and goes up to her room.

As she drifts off to sleep, she thinks back on what she supposes was her pitiful performance that evening. She went to the Halloween party with a boy named David. She has a crush on him. The intensity of the crush is paralyzing—all the more so because Sheila does not think herself pretty. Even with her ash-white skin and tawny hair, she is unable to find a pleasing image in her mirror. Breasts too small. Hips too wide. Though no such image exists in the hard physics of glass and light.

Still, whatever makes her see what she sees also gives her that dark and watchful aspect, that hung-back look. She feels most at home on the edges of things.

Martha Moxley arranged her date. As the big day approached, the two of them felt pleased and conspiratorial; friendship blossomed. Now Sheila wants to tell Martha what a flop she was—the worst date in the world. She wants to hear Martha laugh and say, "Oh, Sheila, don't worry about it. He likes you!"

Martha always knows what to say.

At around two in the morning, Sheila wakes to find her mother standing in her bedroom. She's asking about Martha. Dorthy Moxley's on the phone, and she sounds worried. Does Sheila know anything? Did Martha go to the same Halloween party? No; no.

Sheila thought Martha had gone to her boyfriend's house to cook him dinner. Apparently she hadn't.

At four o'clock, the phone rings again. Mrs. Moxley is distraught; the police have been called. Well, it's Mischief Night, Sheila thinks. She imagines the revelers coming drowsily to rest in someone's playroom; in the morning all will be explained, if not forgiven. She rolls over and goes back to sleep.

The Killer

THE DOGS OF BELLE HAVEN shuck off their house-pet haze and rack their throats with feral noise.

A man's shadow works among the trees. There's another shadow too. That of a girl. Head turning, long hair tossed round her face as she registers alarm. The man raises something that glimmers like a wand. He strikes the girl once on the temple. She flies back beneath the branches of a willow tree and convulses upon roots and hardening earth.

A sunburst explodes before her eyes. Points of color skitter like water bugs upon the surface of a pond. Then there is nothing.

He is upon her again.

A German shepherd draws up, all teeth and reared shoulders. Its yellow eyes rock like marbles in the dark. Helen Ix, fifteen, leans against her window and listens, phone cradled in her neck. Was that Socks out there, making all that noise? *Jesus, listen to him.* She'll go find him, get him into the warm house.

The killer undoes the girl's jeans, claws them down below her knees, panties too, and squints at the little print flowers on them. He'll show her.

She lies there like a stone.

He wants her to move, but her spark has gone, faded out behind those pretty blue eyes. He collapses upon her; she cannot help him now. He curses and scrambles to his feet.

There's a low sound from the girl's throat.

He fishes for the weapon, straightens, rears back, levels it upon her skull. A storm of blows. But they are poorly directed, and some of them strike hard ground as well as flesh and bone. As one blow lands, a hunk of metal breaks loose and spins off into the leaves. He stares down at the shattered weapon in his hand: a golf club. He tosses it aside.

She shouldn't have made him do it. She shouldn't have made him crazy, the bitch, because this is what she gets. But she won't tell. She won't breathe a word.

He heaves up clouds of white breath. The dog across the street wails and gnashes its teeth, edges forward, shrinks back, something ancient stirring its blood.

He grabs her ankles and pulls her dead weight across the grass and then the driveway. She is wearing a blue down jacket, whose nylon fabric gives little resistance. He can pull her along like a sled. The inanimate world scrapes across her rosy face: pine needles, oak leaves, asphalt. He cannot see much—only her head bumping along the cold earth, the driveway, then the shimmer of her hair in the leaves.

The girl moans. He is stunned.

He lets go, stumbles back, trembles with rage. Branches that are bare and dark clatter in the gloom.

He lurches across the grass. *Where the fuck is it?* He finds it half buried in leaves. He grips the long headless shaft and runs back to where the girl lies pumping blood onto the grass. He raises the shaft and brings it down, but it keeps sliding off the back of her skull. He can't make it stick; the weapon is too long, too unwieldy.

He drops the shaft on the ground, clamps it under his foot, yanks up hard. Snap. Now he has the perfect weapon to finish her off—a steel shiv with a nice rubber grip.

Lights burn in the upstairs windows of the great house. Dorthy Moxley moves behind them, humming to herself, vaguely conscious of some distraction. Kids. Mischief Night.

She studies the window trim and runs a paintbrush around it, taking care not to touch the glass.

He drops to his knees, clutches her hair, and plunges the shaft into her neck. Rams it straight through the soft tissue. Strands of blond hair go in one side and out the other like needlework on a rag doll.

He stops, catches his breath. Blood pools heavily. He is tired, and his head begins to clear. He squeezes his eyes shut, brings a trembling hand to his brow, reaches down for the girl's ankles.

Looking up suddenly, he is seized by fright. Headlights? Voices? Wind in the trees?

Helen Ix starts out the door, appearing briefly in a halo of lamplight on her front steps. Does the killer see this? Clyne Shaw, the Ixes' nanny, perceives a tone of menace. Stay here, stay here, she commands the girl; there's something bad in that barking. Helen steps back inside, shutting the door against the cold.

Robert Bjork walks out his back door, a gray figure under floodlights, whistling for his dog. Maybe this is what the killer sees. Or headlights bobbing down the road, cutting a pale swath through the dark and turning in at the Hammond place. Or the outdoor lights of the Moxley house snapping on, washing the scene in bright yellow light, blowing him back to a darker place. All these things occur between about ten o'clock and twenty after. The killer runs for the cover of bushes until the threat passes, or until he dares to make for home.

But he's back.

He stumbles around for the shaft, crouches to retrieve it, but then his eyes wander to the body of the girl, whose skin shines in the darkness. This won't do. He must get her out of view of the street. He can't drag her body down the slope toward the Bjork and Hammond places because of the flood-lights, and he can't drag it to the thick undergrowth at the back edge of the Moxley property; he'd have to cross open lawn, in full view of the same houses.

The beating of the girl's heart slows, ceases. The wounds are severe. She has bled out quickly. The blood runs away from the body and does not soak it, save for strands of long hair, which have spilled forward. But the skin of the face has been harshly scraped upon the rough asphalt driveway.

The lights of the Moxley house make pale squares on the lawn. He drags the girl to the inky shadow of a ponderosa pine, a great breathing mass that is silvery black in the faint glow of the house lights.

Wide feathery boughs nod over the girl, loosely concealing her body and the evil work he has wrought upon it. He staggers about uncertainly. Where are all his broken pieces? He moves to search. He balks. And clutching the shaft, he hastens into the night.

Martha Moxley's last moments go roughly like that.

The following evening, over cocktails in Belle Haven libraries, people tell of the barking dogs. A linear progression of rough noise from Walsh Lane all the way down to Long Island Sound, where, some of them will presume a twelve-inch section of golf club axeled out over the dark water, made a small splash, and settled in the mud and silt off the Belle Haven peninsula.

As She Lay Dying

MANY YEARS LATER, under a hypnotist's spell, or when she is daydreaming on long afternoons, the precarious details of that night will float up from the depths of her memory. She will remember that while she was painting she heard voices—two or three, the agitated voices of young men down in her yard. "Commotion," she will say to me in a faraway tone. "That's the word that comes to mind."

In the hour of her daughter's murder, Dorthy dabs a window frame with off-white paint. Then she stops to listen to the commotion. Her brush is poised in the air. She thinks, *I wonder what the heck is going on out there*. She lays down the brush, walks into the bathroom, and angles her face to the window. Too dark to see. She turns on the outside lights but quickly reconsiders: *Oh, I can't do that; somebody will steal Martha's bicycle*.

The girl's brand-new yellow Schwinn sits on the screened porch. The girl herself lies bleeding into a bed of pine needles. Dorthy shuts off the lights, wraps her brushes in aluminum foil, and goes to take a shower.

Afterward, she descends the grand staircase, enters the library, switches on the eleven o'clock news. The front door swings open, and footsteps echo in the foyer. There, at last. Dorthy lets out a sigh.

Her son, John, appears in the doorway, and a puzzled look crosses her face. John before Martha? "Funny," she says, and sends John outside to take a look. He rolls his eyes, heads back out. He scouts around the yard. Returning without news or grave concern, he goes up to bed.

Dorthy sits and thinks. *This is a Thursday night, a school night. No school tomorrow, though—a teachers' conference or some such thing. Of course. That's it. The weekend has begun early, and Martha has found herself wrapped up in some will-o'-the-wisp party. But wait. The private school kids—Lord, most of the neighborhood—they* would *have* school. Hmm.

Dorthy tries to wave the thing away. *Well, this is Mischief Night. Perhaps Martha and her friends got carried away with some bit of . . . something. Or went in from the cold and fell asleep in front of somebody's fireplace. There. A simple, rational explanation.* Soon Martha will wake up, horrified at the hour, and slip home through the dark.

Dorthy allows herself to consider alcohol, or worse, and suddenly the bad feeling coils again inside her. But what can she do?

Fatigued from painting and from worry, she reclines on the window seat and drifts into a light sleep as the news chatters away in the background. Her sleep is troubled. She rises to consciousness as though from the bottom of a shadowy pool, and when she opens her eyes in the lamplight, she knows somehow that Martha has not come home. She checks her room anyway, seeing only the menagerie of stuffed animals upon Martha's neatly made bed. Panic takes hold.

Dorthy picks up the phone and commences to dial neighbors. It is something like two in the morning. Dorthy talks to the mothers of Martha's friends: Elvira McGuire, Nancy Ziluca, Joan Redmond, Barrie Fuchs—so many they blur together in her memory. All the mothers are relieved to find their children in bed; none have news of Martha. Dorthy talks to Marionna Hammond, next door, who will later complain to police that she had trouble getting back to sleep. Then Dorthy calls Helen Ix, from whom she learns that Martha was last seen with Tommy Skakel, one of the wild motherless brood who live down the lane. Dorthy talks both to Tommy and to Julie Skakel—at age eighteen, the surrogate mother of the family—three times or more. Tommy tells her he has no idea where Martha has gone; he himself said good night to her at nine-thirty. Julie suggests that Dorthy try their cousins the Terriens, who live out on Cliffdale Road, a winding, wooded road in the back country.

How peculiar, Dorthy thinks. *What on earth would Martha be doing way out there?*

Jimmy Terrien was among the congregation of teens at the Skakel house that night. But still. Jimmy's mother, Georgeann (whose sister is Ethel Kennedy), reaches groggily for the phone, battling sleep and a boozy bloodstream, and tries to tune in to the words streaming through the line.

The woman on the other end sounds frightened.

"Mrs. Terrien? Dorthy Moxley calling from Belle Haven. Sorry to trouble you. My daughter Martha hasn't come home yet. Julie Skakel said, well, to call you. I don't know why. Tommy Skakel was with her last."

Georgeann grumbles, "Oh, that darned kid. He's always getting into trouble." She hangs up, annoyed at having to go explore the grounds—*what the hell time is it anyway?*—but she pulls on her coat and totters down to the guesthouse.

Calling here and there into the dark, she finds only emptiness. *Where the heck is Jimmy?* Not in his bed. Not in the guesthouse. Seventeen years old, and nowhere to be found. Puzzled, her head spinning, she goes back to bed.

Down at police headquarters, the night has grown quiet. Some homeowners have called to complain of egged houses and battered mailboxes, but in the wee hours of the morning these indignant voices give way to night sounds, radio static, and the drone of fluorescent lighting. Patrolman Bill Oberdorster straightens when the telephone rings. He glances at the wall clock: 3:48 A.M. He listens closely to the woman's story and dispatches a car to Belle Haven.

Donald Merchant swings Car 51 onto the peninsula. Dorthy meets him at the door, quickly explaining that her husband, David, is in Atlanta on business and will not return until tomorrow night. So together the patrolman and the mother search the house, in case Martha has quietly slipped home and fallen asleep somewhere other than her own room. Nothing, anywhere.

Dorthy leads Officer Merchant to the basement. It looks as dark and as ancient as the catacombs of Rome. Merchant notices it's decorated for a Halloween party. "Martha's?" he asks. Dorthy nods. Merchant wonders; *Would a girl risk the wrath of her parents with a party in the offing?* The question forms itself into a small alarm.

Merchant goes around back, one hundred feet from where Martha's body lies, and vanishes, flashlight and all, into depths of black lawn. He reappears in the thin beam of his light, jiggling the door of a tiny cottage abutting the garden. The door creaks open. Nothing but tools, weed killer, fertilizer. He marches unknowingly past the corpse again on his way back to the house.

At this hour, on this night, the case of the missing Belle Haven girl is nothing more than a banal suburban drama, a thing that happens when parents' backs are turned. Surely the mystery will evaporate like frost at sunrise.

Yet Merchant is unable to shake off his apprehension. He radios for help. He and two other patrolmen loop around the peninsula's narrow, hedged-in lanes, purr past the darkened hulks of waterfront mansions, then drive out of Belle Haven and into the heart of Greenwich, the search for Martha Moxley growing colder every minute.

Finally, having found nothing, Merchant drives off to check a report of a parking meter knocked over down on Steamboat Road, near Greenwich Harbor.

Before long, the first light of Halloween Day pushes through the dingy windows of police headquarters. It is not customary to consider a person missing before twenty-four hours have elapsed. Yet Merchant scribbles his notes. Something tells him to get it down. Then he hands the notes over to Penny Monahan, a police secretary. At the top of Complaint No. D-20262, she types MISSING PERSON. She clack-clack-clacks:

At the above time and date Mrs. Dorothy [*sic*] Moxley, Walsh Lane, Greenwich, called headquarters and reported that her 15-year-old daughter was missing. Car 51 detailed.

Upon arrival at the scene the undersigned was met by the complainant who stated that her daughter Martha Moxley who was expected home at 9:30 p.m. 10/30/75 had not returned home. Mrs. Moxley further stated that Martha had gone out with a girlfriend and two young children to visit friends in the area. . . .

Mrs. Moxley then checked with the Skakel residence and was advised that Martha had left that residence at 9:30 p.m. stating that she was going home to do her homework. . . . Mrs. Moxley then called several more of Martha's friends and they all stated that they had not seen her last night. Headquarters [was] then notified that Martha Moxley, Age 15, 5-feet-5 Tall, Weighing 120 lbs., with long Blonde Hair and wearing a Blue Parka and blue dungarees, was missing from her home.

Car 44 with Ptlm. W. Carroll and M. McDermott then met the undersigned and both units made a search of the entire Belle Haven area. . . . This effort also met with negative results. The above officers then checked Grass Island and Bruce

Park also with negative results. Headquarters then dispatched a local alarm for Martha Moxley.

At 6:35 a.m. this date the undersigned called Mrs. Moxley and she advised that her daughter had not returned home and that she had called every friend of her daughter's known to her with negative results . . . her daughter was to have several friends over to her home for a party this evening. . . .

Merchant reads over what he has written. He considers that Mrs. Moxley probably knows her daughter well; that perhaps Martha is indeed a good girl, for whom disappearing is no act of bratty defiance; that the Moxleys themselves are not like all these chaotic and decadent rich. Still, you never know.

Some tangled story always seems to lie behind the one story people shovel you. Anyway, his shift is over. As the nine-to-fivers trickle into headquarters, soon to be devoured by chaos themselves, Merchant goes home.

Chapter Two

Halloween Dawns

SUNLIGHT STREAMS through the window of the Moxley library. Dorthy fell asleep there at some lonely hour, but it was a short and restless sleep. Now she lifts her head, apprehends the thing that bothers her, and the worry floods back.

She dresses, walks outside; the wind blows, leaves fly, the sky is an almost painful shade of blue. She cuts across the front lawn, past a pool of her daughter's blood. She passes within yards of where her daughter lies. Martha is behind the tree, whose top tilts and sways, but she is not visible from this patch of lawn. Dorthy walks down the driveway and out to the street.

She proceeds down to the end of Walsh Lane, turns right onto Otter Rock, and stands in front of the Skakel house. She is nervous. A mongrelly dog called Max will bark savagely if roused. Dorthy seeks no meeting with Max. Gingerly she approaches the front door of the pretty brick house, which seems to have been dusted with powdered sugar.

Michael Skakel answers. He is a wiry, kinetic boy of fifteen with a bright Irish face and a tousled mop of brown hair. Wet hair, Dorthy notes. Michael looks washed out, pale—shocked?

Dorthy explains her mission. Michael does not know about Martha.

There's a big tan camper parked in the driveway, over on the side of the house, by the brick arbor and the vines that wind around it. Dorthy considers that Martha likes beer. Perhaps Martha has drunk beer and fallen asleep in that big old camper. Michael peers out the door, then leads Dorthy down the walk. He opens the camper door, shrugs.

Dorthy walks away from the Skakel house, feeling defeated. She walks uncertainly up Walsh Lane, turns in at her driveway, and passes again the place where her daughter lies—wondering where on earth she could be.

Discovery

SHEILA MCGUIRE WALKS out in search of the lost girl. It is late morning and still no sign of Martha Moxley.

Martha lives on the other side of the high brick wall, in the mottled old villa with the English garden that all the neighborhood girls call "secret." It is sufficiently elaborate, with its walls and fountain and hedges, to hold secrets.

Sheila strolls through the dead leaves along the wall and down the path to a little stone teahouse. No Martha. She stands in the teahouse a moment and listens to the autumn wind hum through the peepholes. Then she unlatches the iron gate on the eastern wall and steps among the tangled raspberry bushes and sleeping flowers of the Moxley estate.

In these moments before the delicate architecture of her world collapses, Sheila's mind crowds with macabre notions. This is, after all, the season of dread, when life goes to sleep and spirits take to the wind.

The legend of the Belle Haven Masher comes alive to her. *What if he spirited Martha away, wrestled her down to the old granite pit by the water, where rats scurry up from the caves?* Legend has the Masher roaming the peninsula in a long white car, his face recessed in shadow. The only thing visible is the handle of his umbrella—an eagle's imperious head—which peeks outside the passenger-side window as the car floats past. Sheila herself has never quite seen the Masher but is certain she has run from his swift approach many times.

"Marrr-thaaa!"

Sheila pokes her head into the musty stillness of the potting shed.

Then she backs out, brushing aside the evil notions. In truth, Sheila believes Martha has fallen asleep at someone's house or, more disconcertingly, outside in the cold. Maybe, walking along in the dark, she smacked her head on a branch or something and got knocked out cold. What else could explain it? Or she'd drunk some beer and stumbled into a bush and gone to sleep. Something like that. Soon she would wake up and hurry home, and her mother—overjoyed, furious—would impose a suitably stiff penalty.

But it would all be over.

Sheila plans to work her way up the lawns of Belle Haven and meet Holly Fuchs between Mayo Avenue and Walsh Lane. Together they'll walk through the woods to the promontory at the edge of Belle Haven's northern border. The promontory looks down on Interstate 95. At night the kids go there to drink and smoke and watch the car lights congest at the tollbooth below Belle Haven. Still . . . Martha of all her friends knows better than to leave her mother in a panic. Mrs. Moxley spent the night calling all over town, her troubled voice waking people into the small hours. She called the McGuires twice.

Unknown to Sheila, Holly Fuchs is brought up short by a bad feeling as she nears Walsh Lane. Holly stops, stares fixedly across the tapestry of lawns and hedges, then turns back.

As Sheila advances, the dying look of things resurrects her sense of dread. Crows, bare trees, and bitter scents—these seasonal tokens rouse the darker reaches of her imagination.

Only short weeks ago, the peninsula was covered with sensuous green foliage. The gables and peaks of the great houses pushed through the leaves like pirate ships, dragging arbors full of flowers in their wakes. But when the leaves had fallen, it was as though something meant to be hidden was suddenly exposed. The great houses looked spare and lifeless as the sun fell into the crow-studded limbs of black trees.

"Marrr-thaaa!"

Sheila is into the Moxley yard. The grass is brittle underfoot. A chill drifts in off the Sound. Sheila's path gives onto a broad sweep of lawn, and the leaves that are lying there leap up as though disturbed by invisible hands.

To Sheila's right is the Moxley house and its English garden. To her left, the lawn falls away in a gentle slope. Straight ahead is a silvery-blue pine, towering above the house and everything else. Sheila heads down the slope; stops; something breaks the view of greens and browns and yellows, something under the pine.

Oh. Camping stuff. A pinkish egg-crate foam mattress, a

blue sleeping bag. People are always leaving them outside. She saw one just a couple of weeks ago in the Skakel yard.

Sheila steps forward. When she's upon the tree, still focusing on the foam mattress, she starts blinking. The stuff is trying to shape-shift into something else, something . . . ungraspable.

"All of a sudden the picture I was seeing was not what I was telling myself it was, but rather this incredibly horrific sight of this child that I knew well. And there was no escaping what was now before me."

Nightmare

"THERE'S A PART OF ME that can separate from this," Sheila McGuire says years later. She takes a breath and stares into the middle distance. "Martha was lying on her stomach, with her feet pointed toward the slope and her head pointed toward her house. She was wearing navy-blue pinwale corduroy jeans, and they were pushed down around her ankles and all bunched up. She was naked from the waist down. On her torso she had a navy L. L. Bean–style down jacket that had those Michelin Man puffs around them. I think her arms were up around her head. Her face was down.

"She had what I thought were scratches and gouges in her right hip: they were covered in blood and pine needles and debris. I was standing above her, so I had some view of her other side, but not as much as if I were standing there. On that side too, she'd been scratched from her hips down to her thighs, like this." Sheila claws the air as though making a screech on a blackboard. "And there was blood in her hair. Then the snapshot gets blurred in my head. I called her name a couple of times: 'Martha? Martha?' "

As she calls her friend's name, someone guns an engine. Sheila looks up. "I saw this silvery-blue sedan on Walsh Lane, driving hurriedly away—or so I felt at the time," Sheila says. "My fear escalated. I thought, Whoever did this to Martha is in that car, and now they know I've found her, and now they've seen me, and now they think I've seen them."

As Sheila swoons over Martha's body, Dorthy Moxley sits in her living room, a distracted host to three guests: Marilyn Pennington, Jeanne Wold, and Joan Redmond. The women sip coffee from white china cups and offer flimsy consolation. Fifteen is a funny age. You never can tell what crazy things they'll do at fifteen. But don't you worry, Dorthy—Martha will turn up any moment now.

This isn't like her, this isn't like Martha at all, Dorthy keeps telling the women. Martha is a responsible girl, a thoughtful girl. There must be something wrong.

The three visitors keep their own ideas to themselves. Martha has spent the night with a boy; perhaps she fell asleep and was ashamed to come home. And you had to consider drugs. All the kids were doing drugs now; you could see it sometimes in those dull, glassy eyes, those windowless faces. Why, Martha's probably sleeping off the damage in some creaky old carriage house.

Dorthy seems to be reading their thoughts. "I know Martha likes beer," she says, glancing up to see the women's reactions. She waves her hand in the air. "Oh, well. You know Martha. She's kind of a flirt."

Marilyn Pennington had planned to take her son to an art show up in Hartford, but when Dorthy called her early in the morning, the distress in her voice so plain, Marilyn sighed and changed her plans. She pulled up in the driveway—"with a clear view of the tree where Martha was later discovered"—and walked up to the great brooding villa. Jeanne Wold had already arrived; the maid, Teresa, was running a vacuum off in the background. "One thing that stands out vividly in my mind was Dorthy checking the time incessantly," Marilyn recalls. "The only clock was in the kitchen—apparently none of us had on watches—and we were sitting in the living room, a very long walk. I can still hear her heels clicking on the stone floor, back and forth, again and again."

Before Jeanne Wold went out the door of her house that morning, she'd talked on the phone with Joan Redmond, who was one of those Belle Haven neighbors awakened the night before by Dorthy's desperate voice. Joan's daughter Janey was among Martha's closest friends, but Joan had forbidden Janey to take part in the Mischief Night devilry; instead the girl attended a meeting of the Greenwich Red Cross.

Now, as morning blended into afternoon, Joan felt the worry overtake her, and she knew somehow that she must walk over to the Moxley house. Her worry was two-edged. Jeanne Wold, a diabetic, was going blind and had a weak heart. Would her body be able to bear whatever might come to pass? Joan Redmond headed out into the day at about noon, and the air was tense and cold and very quiet.

And so the women wait for it all to come clear. While they do so, the phone rings and rings, and on the other end are people whom Dorthy awakened on Mischief Night, Martha's friends and their parents, wanting an update, wanting news, wanting to be able to move on to the next thing. An expectant web has begun to stretch out across the town.

Dorthy in her distraction cannot track the flow of the conversation. Marilyn Pennington takes up phone duty. *Lord, it's*

Julie Skakel again. All morning long, Julie has been calling: "Is Martha home yet? No? Well, gee. I wonder what could have happened."

(Later, some think these calls from the Skakel house to be false concern; think that in those morning hours there was a squaring of stories, an aligning of alibis under the Skakel roof, perhaps even in the presence of Skakel lawyers. Others believe the Skakels are cursed again, doomed to have even their best intentions turned back on them.)

At some point the women grow so frustrated that they again call the police. They try to impress upon them the extraordinary nature of this event. Well, yes, Dorthy must admit, Martha stayed out late once, just a week ago, but they'd had quite a talk about that. The police listen—dubiously, the women think—but promise to send someone back to Belle Haven.

David Moxley calls from Atlanta and talks to Marilyn, who is still manning the phone. Word of Martha's disappearance has spread through the partners' meeting there, and occasionally someone phones to see if Martha has returned. Now Marilyn can only tell David that no, she hasn't returned, and there is no news.

As she hangs up, Marilyn begins to abandon her notion that whatever is unfolding is some childish thing, some adolescent lapse in judgment. There seems to be something else to it. The women stare out the living room's enormous picture window, watching the color trickle away from the trees.

Sheila lights out across the lawn. Her heart thumps in her chest like a trapped animal. She is flying now, kicking up a spray of leaves, yet she cannot reach the Moxleys' front door fast enough. She turns the corner, fixes the door in her sights, scrambles up the broad stone steps, and pounds, pounds, pounds.

"Let me in, let me in!" she cries. "I found Martha, I found Martha, please let me in!"

Why does nobody come to the door?

The women look up from their coffee. They glance briefly at one another, and then Marilyn Pennington gets up. Dorthy trails her to the front hall, with Joan Redmond and Jeanne Wold close behind.

Tears flow down the translucent skin of the girl on the doorstep. The women furrow their brows. "Sheila, Sheila, what is it?"

The girl trembles and shakes and is confused by all the women. The blond woman in front of her—is this Mrs. Moxley? No, *there* she is, a taut, expectant presence in the background.

"I found Martha, I found her!" Sheila bawls. "She's here on the property!"

"Where?"

"Under the big tree."

Dorthy fails to grasp the dire implications of this image, but deeper powers are at work, numbing her senses.

Sheila shakes so violently that the women sit her down at the foot of the stairs.

"Now, now. Is she all right?"

The women hover.

What is happening? What is real? Sheila tries to keep her world from spinning off its hinge.

"No," Sheila replies, setting her face. "But she will be. She'll be just fine. I think she's been raped or attacked by dogs." Then she says, "We'd better call 911."

Marilyn Pennington picks up the phone. Jeanne Wold wobbles out to the porch and takes a pill for her heart. Joan Redmond puts her hand on Dorthy's shoulder. "You'd better stay here." Dorthy nods and retreats to the living room. Joan and Sheila trek around the front of the house and angle off toward the backyard.

Suddenly Sheila draws up short.

She can neither absorb nor erase what she has seen; it is simply an image whose meaning has yet to detonate. When they near the pine tree, Sheila's knees buckle, and Joan proceeds without her. Sheila wraps herself in her arms and waits.

Joan raises her hand, sweeps aside a bough of pine, calls Martha's name. The girl is lying facedown, legs stretched out straight as though she has been dragged and then dropped in place. Joan bends down to look her over. Staring at the back of Martha's head, Joan sees that the girl is horribly wounded. She sees dried blood caked in the lovely blond hair.

Sheila thinks she sees Joan grab hold of Martha's hair, lift her head, gasp. Something like that.

I know what she sees. Sheila feels as though she wants to die.

But Joan has only touched the girl's exposed back. That is enough to tell. As Joan struggles to recover, she is hit by an awareness of someone watching her from afar. She believes she knows who it is. She rises unsteadily among the branches and turns back to the house. Dorthy Moxley is sitting on a yellow couch, staring into space, her hands resting lightly in her lap.

"Dorthy?" says Joan.

Dorthy does not look up. "Is she dead?"

Joan waits a beat. "I think she is."

Something Ominous

JUVENILE OFFICERS Millard Jones and Daniel Hickman pull up behind their favorite eatery: Johnny Moore's lunch wagon, an old red truck parked on the Post Road across from the abandoned Condé Nast Building, whose crumbling turrets rise above wild silvery weeds.

Jones and Hickman spent the morning cruising the waterfront, working inland from the shore, in search of the Belle Haven girl reported missing during the night. They had slowed and stopped and peered through the trees. But they found nothing save Mischief Night relics—dew-drenched tissue paper and globs of shaving cream. So they left the peninsula for Johnny Moore's.

They are eating sausage sandwiches in Car 22 when the radio hisses. An odd message. Call us right back, the voice instructs, but don't use the radio; use a call box. Jones and Hickman look at each other, set down their sandwiches, and walk up to the junction of the Post Road and Ferris Road. Hickman flips open the little red box and reaches Audrey Aidinis in the detective division.

Something's happened down at the Moxley place, but the facts are muddy. It sounds ominous, she tells them.

Hickman asks headquarters to patch him through to the residence. A woman picks up the phone, reports that the girl has been found in a thicket near the Moxley house. Hickman and Jones sprint back to the car. "The dispatcher said, 'Let us know what you got when you get there,' because he couldn't say on the air what it was," Hickman says in retrospect. "Man, we let out all the stops. Red lights, siren. We blew down that road."

Hickman's at the wheel. He and Jones blaze into Belle

Haven and jerk to a stop in the Moxleys' crescent driveway. There they come upon a curious scene. "Some folks were milling about the house, hysterical. I remember all this crying," Hickman says. "Mill Jones and I looked at each other and wondered what we had. Then a girl said, 'She's down there! Down there!' Crying her eyes out. We went bolting down the slope and came to a big tree. We split up, just on instinct; Jonesy went around this way and I went around that way. So I start going around, and then I put on my brakes: 'My God, Mill, over here!'"

Jones and Hickman stand over Martha Moxley in silence. Dry leaves skip across their thick black shoes and across the body of the girl. Mill Jones kneels to check the girl's pulse. There is none. Then they draw back and leave the girl as they found her, face pressed against the soft matted needles, lovely young body frozen in the death posture. Neither man ventures an opinion on what has occurred. They think, *A lunatic has mauled her to death with a blunt instrument. Or an ax of some kind.* They remain silent. To utter the thought is to admit to the presence of evil among them.

Hickman checks his watch. It's twelve-thirty in the afternoon. Jones lopes up to the house to phone for help. Hickman puffs up his cherub cheeks and stares down at the girl. Her body is rigid. The underside has purpled from the settling of blood. The back and legs are white as an egg. There is not the subtlest bloom of life. Hickman has never seen anything quite like it. Once, he was ordered to the house of a suicide. A young man had blown a hole through his skull. Hickman never forgot the way the boy and the rifle lay peacefully side by side.

But this girl was something else again. "It was the first sign of foul play I'd ever run across. I tell you, it sets your mind *racing*."

Hickman is a deeply spiritual man. Maybe this is why he can sense the devil's aura as he stands among the great houses. He tries to calm himself. He draws in some air, pushes it back out, the warm vapor sifting up through the pine needles like a ghost.

Mill Jones has disappeared around the corner of the house. Hickman's alone. His head swims. He would rather be anywhere else. Anywhere in the world but here.

Captain Thomas Keegan strides across the grass, detectives Stephen Carroll and Joe McGlynn close behind. Hickman backs to the edge of the scene.

Keegan, breathing hard, says, "What did you do here?" He's a handsome, moody man with dark straight hair and critical blue eyes.

"Nothing yet," Hickman replies.

Keegan bends to take the girl's pulse, confirming what her battered skull makes obvious.

At about this time, a slender young man with alert black eyes walks up the steps and into the house. Richard Danehower is the Moxley family doctor. He's been beeped out of a lecture downtown and given the Moxleys' phone number. "Marilyn Pennington wanted me to come to the house right away. I was sort of resistant, because she wasn't making it clear why I should come. Eventually I got her to tell me, and I guess there was some question as to whether Martha was still alive. They needed somebody to come and help make that decision." His voice grows soft. "And to present the facts to Dorthy."

Dr. Danehower glances around the living room. It's a bad scene, this scattered energy of grief. Then he goes out to where the men are gathered, and uneasily they make a space for him to approach the body. He looks the girl over. He inspects the worst of her wounds, a deep slicing chop near the crown of her head. "I could see that it had penetrated the skull, and I could see the dura mater layer of the brain through the injury. There was no motion. No life."

Dr. Danehower straightens, brushes the dirt from his knees, and heads back inside.

Dorthy sits pinned to the yellow couch, weeping quietly. Faces loom above her like masks out of the dark. Their mouths move and words come out, but they dissolve into meaningless sound. Dr. Danehower's face is before her now, but privately he is despairing the limitations of medical science: "There is no antidote to reality." Dorthy is thinking about the last time she saw Martha, fleeing into the night with her friends. She would be back early, she said. *Why didn't I just make Martha stay at home? I should have made her stay at home.* The hindsight will drive her mad if she lets it. She regrets having been on the phone as the big front door swung shut. It was no way to say goodbye.

The phone rings. Marilyn Pennington hears David Moxley's voice on the other end and closes her eyes. He's standing in an airport in Atlanta. "I kept telling him to please come back to Connecticut. He persisted in asking me why, and I kept begging him just to come."

She looks desperately around the room. She sees Dr. Danehower on his knees in front of Dorthy. Her husband, Lou, a coworker of David Moxley's, has arrived at the house, but he's gone outside with the police. There's no rescue. She braces.

"David finally asked, point-blank, 'Is she dead?' I pleaded with him to come back, but he kept asking the same question. I finally lost it. Sobbing, I replied, 'Yes'—the most heartbreaking thing I've ever done."

Going Numb

POLICE HUDDLE around the body. From a distance, Sheila stares down at the somber men, some of them in dark-blue uniforms, others in trench coats and windblown ties. They are not looking at Martha now but have begun to pad softly around the yard. Martha's invisible. *Why are they letting her stay there? Why aren't they taking her to the hospital? She needs help. Somebody go get her fixed.*

Since they are in no hurry, Sheila comes to understand that Martha's wounds are not mortal, not serious. *Clean her off, and she'll look much better.*

Sheila floats into the Moxley house. As she passes through the door, she hears a low, helpless moaning, the sound of women crying, but Sheila is numb to it, as she is to the tears falling down her own cheeks. She turns around and sees her mother standing in the foyer with her head tilted to one side, confusion scrawled on her brow.

"Are you okay?"

"Take me home."

The mother's eyes search her daughter's face. She sees that perhaps something is broken, but she lacks the necessary information.

"You found Martha? Where is she?"

Doesn't she hear me? Sheila thinks.

Sheila moves for the door, her mother following, and once again she enters the Halloween dreamscape: crows, leaves, sheet, body. Cops step through the grass like Easter egg hunters, their faces sewn shut in concentration.

Sheila circles wide around the great pine. The outline of Martha's body hugs the ground. *She must be cold. Unable to say so*. The cops are smoking and murmuring, and Sheila skims across the short bent grass, thinking, *This is torture. I can't walk past her again*. She and her mother move silently across the lawn. *Martha is under that sheet. Jesus, I can see her under that sheet. And those men, they're walking around, talking. Doing nothing*.

The fact of Martha's death works above her head like an aura, beyond the reach of consciousness. But other senses know. "I remember being just catatonic. I wanted to be like *I Dream of Jeannie,* just blink my eyes and cease to exist for a little while." And so with a great effort she directs her eyes away from the girl under the sheet and disappears behind the wall.

Mrs. McGuire brews her daughter a cup of tea. The girl sits in the kitchen, staring absently at the shivering trees—maples, oaks, ashes, lindens—at the pale light falling through them like lace. *I am not to say a word. That is what the police have told me. It is important that I am good. I will hold it in if it kills me*.

In truth, she doesn't know what she *could* say. Her mind has recorded an image. She does not understand it. She lowers her mouth to the steaming cup. Some terrible thing sleeps beneath the river of her thoughts. She can feel it down there, shifting around in the mud, and it makes her chest go tight and cold. "Part of me knew that this was a really big, terrible thing. But there was a part of me that infantilely wanted to think she'd just skinned a knee or been attacked by a dog. They would go give her some stitches, and then we'd all be laughing at the bus stop on Monday morning."

Mrs. McGuire goes off to answer the phone. It's Holly, asking for Sheila. "Sheila can't come to the phone right now," Mrs. McGuire says, and drops the phone in its cradle. She does not know what else to do.

Up on Mayo Avenue, Holly Fuchs stares at the phone, puzzled, afraid. She starts to cry. She knows intuitively that this has something to do with Martha. She calls out to her mother. Barrie Fuchs listens carefully and then dials the McGuire house. Mrs. McGuire tells Mrs. Fuchs that Sheila has found Martha, but says nothing more.

Sheila's muted awareness of the bad thing ends in alarm. Her friends Wright Ferguson and Tad Sisman are tramping up the driveway on the balls of their feet, necks thrust slightly forward, the rest of them hanging back involuntarily. They're headed for the great brick wall. Sheila rushes from her chair and presses her face to the window. *Are they looking for Martha? Have they heard something? Uh-oh. They're headed for the shortcut. They must not go through the wall.*

"Darling, we have to tell them," Mrs. McGuire says somberly.

Tell them what? What does her mother know?

Sheila bolts out the door and waves her arms in the air.

"I can't come out," she announces. "I found Martha. Yes, I found her. She's going to be okay, but you can't go over there."

The boys trundle back down the driveway.

While Lou Pennington is outside, making the official identification of Martha Moxley, his wife sits on the living room sofa, sorting through the shock. *The girl cannot be dead. Just last week she was more alive than any two people I know.*

"We had spent the previous Saturday at the Moxley home for dinner, just the four of us—David, Dorthy, Lou, and me—having one of Dorthy's fabulous meals in their baronial dining room," she recalls. "David had called to Martha and asked her to bring him a cigar. In she waltzed, wearing my full-length

mink coat, literally sweeping the floor with it, David's unlighted cigar in her mouth. It was the cutest sight imaginable."

And then a stranger memory impinges. Marilyn saw Martha
just a couple of days earlier at Greenwich High School, where
Marilyn is a volunteer tutor. "Hi, Martha!" she said brightly,
but the girl blew past her, preoccupied, oblivious, as if the two
had never met. Her last glimpse of Martha Moxley.

Marilyn shakes herself into the moment. Lou has come in,
pallid and shaken and loose-jointed. He was unprepared for
the violence of the image. It was a thing no person should see.
Then, after a short discussion with his wife, he goes back out,
to drive over to the high school and get John Moxley out of
football practice, get him and bring him home.

Greenwich High School is a sprawling complex of dark-red
brick slung across what once was a swampland called Ten
Acres. When the swamp froze in winter, the townspeople
would skate over the broad plane of ice, from the base of Put's
Hill to the gray trees in the distance. Now football players run
patterns across the cold grass that once was ice.

Someone walks out to deliver a message to Coach Ornato.
The coach listens intently and bows his head. Then he quietly
calls John Moxley over to the sideline and rests a hand on the
boy's padded shoulder. "Look. Something's happened at
home. Your family wants you home right away."

John feels a powerful wave of sickness pass through him.
It fills him with numbing awe and then lightness and then terror. Without changing clothes, he climbs into his Mustang and
drives to Belle Haven, passing Lou Pennington's car somewhere along the way.

Back on the football field, Coach Ornato gathers the team

around him and grimly announces that Martha Moxley was murdered during the night. Young mouths form the shape of bewilderment. There are a few soft gasps. All the proud shoulders, the long red line of them, seem to contract in the cool air; everything is still, except for leaves that ripple above a ridge on the western edge of the field.

They can all go home if they want, Ornato tells his charges, or they can stay and practice a bit. It's up to them. The coach scans the huddled throng. The players look around at one another. Nobody knows what to do; there are no rules for this. They stay and practice, but nothing is as it was.

Lou Pennington arrives at the edge of the field and discovers that John Moxley has left. He heads back to Belle Haven, driving as quickly as the law allows, maybe quicker. He wants to be able to steady John in his grief, since Dorthy has retreated to a place inside herself and Marilyn is braving all the muted cries that travel through the phone line.

David Moxley is in the air above the Eastern Seaboard, making his way home among the other travelers, all alone up in the clouds, feeling trapped and empty and not quite real.

Joan Redmond has begun to meditate on her own daughter. She wonders how she'll break the news to her and wonders too about the general safety of the neighborhood. She walks out of the Moxley house and away from the police cars with their flashing lights, away from the officers stringing yellow tape, and she hurries toward home.

John Moxley rounds onto Walsh Lane. He blinks hard and his head moves slightly backward. "There was a sea of police cars, crime tape," John says later. "It could be something you've never seen before in your life, but you walk into the picture and know exactly what it is. There was no question in my mind that this was a major police event that involved us somehow."

Martha. Something has happened to Martha.

Lou Pennington catches John on the front steps. There is only one way to do it. He looks him in the eyes and tells him that his sister has been killed.

"How?" John says. "Was she stabbed or something?"

"No. Hit with a golf club."

There's a wildness racing through John. Without warning, he takes a swing at Lou Pennington. Lou steps back quickly, and John runs inside the house, crying, "My sister, my sister!"

"I mean, the lights were on but nobody was home," John recalls. "Everything just shut down. I was in denial for years. Absolute denial. Just couldn't comprehend."

Golden Lady

EARLY IN THE AFTERNOON Holly Fuchs's sister Tori walks to her friend Tina Gaede's house, on Field Point Drive. They'll team up to search for Martha, as Holly and Sheila have done. As Tina slips on her coat, the phone rings.

Martha's been found.

They should feel relief but don't. There's something unsaid.

Tori races down three flights of stairs and hastens toward Martha's house. Police cars are everywhere, making her head spin and her heart race. Tori approaches the house, but officers vigorously wave her on. She sprints up the Skakels' backyard and into her own.

"They found Martha," she tells her mother. She's breathless and wild-eyed.

"What do you mean, they found her?"

"I saw all the police by her house. They wouldn't let me anywhere near."

Barrie Fuchs calls the Moxley house, and Joan Redmond answers. Joan feels the need to speak elliptically about the event and in her light midwestern drawl tells Barrie, "What Martha's got, I don't think she'll recover from."

It is all very muddy. The Fuchses do not know what to think. They get in the car and drive over to Walsh Lane, but they're met by Officer Dan Pendergast, who says, "Get that car out, get that car out." They hesitate and then leave.

Tori Fuchs seems tougher than her fifteen years should allow. She has grit and presence and a voice as bright as brass. She's the sort of girl you lean on in a crisis. Yet there's a well of tenderness deep inside her and she seems to guard it; sometimes feelings flow up and overwhelm her anyway.

She goes into the library of her house and sits on the couch and cries. The window looks out on the backyard to the Skakels' and across some hedges to the great somber facade of the Moxley house. There are distant flashing lights through the trees.

Yesterday afternoon on the school bus, Tori invited Martha to a party at Polly Weiss's house, in another part of town. They'd call each other later. Except they never did. *If only I had called,* Tori thinks. *Then maybe Martha would still be alive.*

"Martha and I go, 'Well, we'll talk later.' But Holly and I end up leaving, and I get there and I go, 'Oh my God. I never called her. I should have called her.' That wasn't like me. Then again, Martha hadn't called me, either.

"But I remember being there at Polly's and listening to this song. We would go over to Martha's house a lot of times after school and listen to albums. Stevie Wonder had just put out a new song called 'Golden Lady,' and we all thought it was great because it reminded us of Martha. She had such white-blond hair. And I remember being at Polly's and that song came on and I was just sitting there, listening to it, feeling very uncomfortable about it and very sad about it, and I remember looking at the clock and it was the exact time they say Martha died."

And so the next day Tori sits on the couch looking out the window and crying and waiting for news.

Late in the afternoon, light clouds shoal in from the west, covering a pale crescent moon.

Elvira McGuire feels overwhelmed. She doesn't know what to do. Her husband is out of town, she has six young girls to watch—with a murderer on the loose!—and now it has fallen to her to break the news to a daughter who is trying not to know. *How to do it?*

Mrs. Fuchs hits on a solution: Why don't we tell Sheila up here at our house? she says to Elvira. All the girls can be together that way. Share the grief.

And so the McGuires set out again into the neighborhood, which is being shut off from the rest of the world. They drive past the madness on Walsh Lane. The confusion of things seems mingled with the falling leaves. A kind of going to pieces. Mother and daughter mount the steps of the graceful yellow Victorian at 78 Mayo Avenue. The Fuchs house radiates benevolence and familial warmth. Five daughters, their mother, and a Saint Bernard live inside.

Sheila is intent on giving the news that Martha Moxley will make a full recovery. "I remember Holly and Tori were crying and crying and crying. I'm standing in their big foyer, and I'm like, 'Oh! You know, she's fine! The worst of it's over. She's been found, she's at the hospital, she's going to be fine. Don't cry about it.'"

Sheila tries to lift the girls from their sorrow. The Fuchs girls look up through little storms of tears. *What on earth is Sheila talking about?* There's a sick silence in the house. Holly and Tori go on crying and aching. They do not speak to Sheila. They do not know what to say.

"Sheila?" The girl turns around. It's Mrs. McGuire. She seems a great distance away, though she is only standing at the door, silhouetted against a pane of frosted glass. Her face is dark. "Martha's dead, honey."

Sheila shakes her head violently. "No way. No way. She's not."

The Fuchs girls are dumbfounded as Sheila wills her story forth. "She was alive when I found her. She wasn't dead. I didn't find her dead. She was just hurt."

After a painful silence, Mrs. McGuire says, "We've got to go home now. The police want to talk to you."

Mutely they leave the fractured scene. That is it, the moment of profound and irreversible change. Sheila says, "My life as I knew it was over."

The Bitch

IN BELLE HAVEN, an outsider feels crowded, fenced out, unwelcome. Now the neighborhood is crawling with outsiders, and it is the residents who feel unnerved.

Detectives fan out across lawns. Cops stroll the perimeter of the crime scene. They glance up at a scudding rib of clouds and shiver: it is cold when the sun disappears. Forensics men will arrive soon, pushing their way to the center of things.

Belle Haven residents stare from a distance as the chaos

spreads. Some stand out on their front lawns, arms folded defensively across their chests. Some stutter-step toward the crime scene, seeking a quick answer to what will become an enduring riddle.

After hearing the news, Peter Coomaraswamy, fifteen, drifts out of his house on Otter Rock. The night before, Mischief Night, he swiped a bottle of his parents' wine and went out with Chris Gentri. Between swigs they propelled water balloons at passing cars with a sort of slingshot. They did this from the chained-off end of Walsh Lane, down which, if sighted, they could safely escape.

Peter last saw Martha there at eight o'clock.

Now he walks up the road and turns in at 71 Otter Rock to see his friend Michael Skakel. Peter and Michael wander over to where the Skakel lawn meets Walsh Lane and stand at the edge of the picture. It unfolds into something disjointed, surreal. Reporters, people walking around, police going in and out of Martha's house. The disorder is quiet but stupefying. Everyone seems afraid of talking to everyone else.

Except for a radio reporter.

"This fucking bitch comes up to Michael and says, 'I hear your mother was a steak-choke victim,'" Peter tells me, years later. "Michael turned away and started crying. I'm sorry I didn't have the presence of mind to kick her in the ass."

I tell Peter Coomaraswamy that it was not Michael's mother, but an aunt, who choked to death. Michael's mother died of cancer. "I don't think so," he says. "Are you sure about that?"

"Yes."

There's a pregnant silence, and then he adds, "Well, if Michael was a violent person, he'd have smacked her. The fucking idiot."

Chapter Three

First Suspect

IN THE MIDAFTERNOON, police turn up two gleaming gifts in the grass. One is the metal head of a woman's six iron. The club head is buried among the paling leaves on the Moxleys' front lawn, and it is splotched with blood.

The second gift is found in the side yard, just beyond the driveway. It is an eighteen-inch section of shaft, resting in a thick puddle of blood. The blood has begun to congeal. When the police carefully extract the shaft, it is covered by a thin red film.

A third piece is unaccounted for. The handle. Detectives kick through the leaves, looking for it. Already the light is failing; they must find it soon. There ought to be a print on the handle, maybe blood, maybe skin and hair.

The police scarcely have time to consider the enormity of the crime. They are concentrating on the task at hand. Yet there is some waiting, too, and time to contemplate what has happened. Dan Hickman recalls, "We felt our turf had been infiltrated by the enemy. We would hear about this sort of thing happening in cities. But here in our own backyard? You felt protected here. You felt you weren't going to be violated. Who would do something like this in Greenwich?"

Who? That's what they all wonder. Theories get worked out behind closed doors. One of the first: the murderer is a stranger, a drifter who slipped down off Interstate 95. This stretch of I-95 is among the most heavily traveled roadways in the country. Anyone from anywhere could have waded through the roadside foliage and crept into the heart of Belle Haven.

All the residents have golf clubs. A kid has left one lying around. The killer picked it up. Hid among the trees. Waited for the young merrymakers to disband. There. Blond hair shining beneath a streetlamp. She's alone. He steps out of the shadow of the trees.

It gives comfort to believe this. Evil has blown onto this peninsula like weather, then moved on. It does not reside among these people, its face now returned to human form.

The drifter theory does not hold. Belle Haven is no accidental destination. You don't chance your way onto narrow, hemmed-in Walsh Lane in the dark; nor do you design to attack a girl in what the newspapers tomorrow will call "the heavily guarded and heavily patrolled Belle Haven" section of Greenwich.

Yet some persist in imagining a psychopath creeping down from the highway, or brazenly driving past the police booth at Belle Haven's entrance. What then? The night is cold and lonely. The killer doesn't know his way around. House lights are still ablaze. He manages to produce a golf club. He has rape, not murder, on his mind—but maybe the golf club will aid her compliance.

He moves upon her. She runs. Without thinking, he strikes her down. Instead of fleeing, he keeps beating her. He begins to drag her off—somehow he senses where to go—but stops to stab her through the neck. That finishes the job. Then he continues to the tree out toward the edge of the Moxley property.

Most of the neighbors don't buy it. The killer knows the geography too well. "There was no weird man lurking in the woods," says Chris Gentri, a contemporary of Martha's who went out on Mischief Night. "Whoever did it saw Martha that night, and she knew who it was. One of the people in that frickin' neighborhood did it. There was no guy who snuck in off the thruway behind Belle Haven." The police remain noncommittal. The *New York Times* will say:

> Deputy Chief Raymond E. Grant, Jr., whose 147-member force is more concerned with protecting Greenwich residents from outsiders than from each other, had bridled at the conviction widespread among residents that the killer had to have been a Belle Haven resident in order to have found his way past guard points and in and out of the narrow, winding, and dimly lit streets.
>
> "We have nothing to report," he said. "No leads, no motive, and no suspects from Belle Haven or anywhere else."

First orders: the police must trace the club to its owner. Start there and see what happens. The model is not a common one: Toney Penna. A men's golf champion of the thirties and forties who later went into the business of manufacturing golf equipment.

Keegan, the captain of detectives, has his men canvass the neighborhood. They begin to leave the Moxley estate in teams.

Off in a corner of the house, Jeanne Wold and Joan Redmond confer. "You've got to tell them about Edward," whispers Joan to Jeanne. But Jeanne is afraid. She is sick and going blind and afraid. With Joan at her elbow, she sidles up to Keegan and tells him about a young man named William Edward Hammond.

In April, Jeanne Wold tells Keegan, she'd been sitting in a chair on her porch when she heard strange noises around the corner. She rose and walked to a side entrance to investigate.

One set of doors had been opened. A dark-haired, sturdily built man was rattling the French doors to the living room, trying to open them. The man was Edward Hammond of 48 Walsh Lane.

"Edward, what on earth are you doing?" she asked the startled young man. He walked off without answering.

Hammond appeared on Jeanne Wold's front doorstep the next morning, bearing a peculiar excuse: he had wanted to see the Wolds' new dog. Jeanne Wold let it go. She believed Hammond to be a loner and a heavy drinker. She believed he had difficulty relating to women.

Six months later, she wonders whether he is also capable of unspeakable violence.

Meanwhile, Marilyn Pennington scrutinizes all who walk through the Moxleys' door. The scene resembles something out of Truman Capote's *In Cold Blood*. The residents of Holcomb, Kansas, reeling from the slaughter of the Herbert William Clutter family, draw fearfully inward:

At the time, not a soul in sleepy Holcomb heard them—four shotgun blasts that, all told, ended six human lives. But afterward, the townspeople, theretofore sufficiently unfearful of each other to seldom trouble to lock their doors, found fantasy re-creating them over and over again—those somber explosions that stimulated fires of mistrust in the glare of which many old neighbors viewed each other strangely, and as strangers.

Capote spent his adolescence in Greenwich, in a picture-book house by a pond. He wrote confident stories for *The Green Witch*, Greenwich High's literary magazine. He did not graduate with the class of 1942 because he would not go to gym class. In June of that year, he and his mother moved to New York City. Six years later, the publication of *Other Voices, Other Rooms* brought him fame, but Greenwich never figured much in his writing; to Capote, Greenwich was staid, conventional, smothering—a place from which a flamboyant homosexual must escape.

Edward Hammond gazes out the window of his house and sees the police cars hovering like bees. *Something's happening,* he thinks. *Something bad is happening on my street.*

Before long, Detectives Carroll and McGlynn call at 48 Walsh Lane, a white colonial house situated behind a row of hemlocks, where Hammond lives with his mother. Hammond sometimes makes a lousy impression on people. So it is with the detectives. Carroll recalls, "We thought, *Oh, man, this is him.* There were all kinds of skin magazines. And this was sick: he would masturbate in condoms and then put the condoms back in his closet. Joe and I were like, 'Let's get somebody down here right now.' "

Hammond, twenty-six, is tall and good-looking enough for some Belle Haven mothers to think him a fine catch for their daughters. But he appears to be uninterested. He is a Yale graduate and a veteran of the army, which taught him to speak

Chinese. One year ago, he left the service. Now he attends Columbia Business School but shows scant interest in his courses.

Perhaps he is not strange, only grieving. His father died in 1973, and since then he has lost himself in the bottle. He moved into a neighbor's house, a gorgeous Victorian down the street, but he kept getting into the liquor cabinet and the neighbor had to ask him to leave. He moved back up to Walsh Lane.

The detectives read him his rights and quietly escort him to a squad car. On the night of the murder, he was home alone, watching television. *The French Connection*. Not much of an alibi, he knows. He sits in the back of the police car, nervously watching the hum of activity at the Moxley house and wondering what these impassive men want of him. He has been cooperative. What can they want of him? They have taken scrapings from under his fingernails and strands of his longish dark hair. They have taken his clothes:

> One pair men's beige-colored corduroy pants. Blood stain left upper leg.
> One men's red knitted sweater, color red. Unknown type stain on chest area.
> One pair of men's brown leather topsider shoes. Moccasin type boat shoe.
> One blue men's shirt, size 17-34, "Alexander." Bearing unknown stains . . .
> One men's red crushed velvet material bathrobe . . .

Marionna Hammond appears during her son's interrogation ("interview," the police benignly call it) in the Greenwich police department's detective bureau. She looks sad and drawn.

There is little Hammond can tell the detectives. He was home alone while his mother dined at the Belle Haven Club. *Home alone*. He knows it sounds bad, but hell, it's true. Hammond finishes giving his statement, and then the police take the mother and son home.

Afterward, they seal up Edward's clothes in evidence bags and send them to the state lab. They have a suspect. They wait. Will the blood on his corduroys speak to them? They think it will, and they think they know what it will say.

What the Skakels Said

THE SKAKEL HOUSEHOLD waits, expectant.

Cops are canvassing the neighborhood. They've locked up Belle Haven as tight as Fort Knox. It is only a matter of time before they haunt the last place Martha Moxley was seen alive.

A couple of strapping, poker-faced detectives cover the two hundred yards between the Moxley and Skakel houses with purposeful strides. It is three o'clock in the afternoon. Two hours of light, then the sun will drop into the trees. Then Halloween.

Detective Jim Lunney's red hair and beard tell accurately of fire, of impatience. The man beside him, genial, even-tempered Ted Brosko, calls Lunney "Mr. Breach of Peace." Lunney comes off as rough and hard-nosed, but underneath is something else. Something you couldn't get close to. Something incongruous, suggesting intellectual curiosity. He's a talented artist. He speaks precisely and well—when he wants or needs to, such as in court. Yet he can come off as a mean,

mean bastard. So he's been paired with a guy who can smooth him out. Teddy Brosko.

At the Skakels' house, Martha's last minutes receive definition. Julie Skakel tells the detectives that they all went to dinner the night before at the Belle Haven Club. Ten of them. Julie and her brothers; a cousin named Jimmy Terrien; Andrea Shakespeare, a friend; and Ken Littleton, the tutor who had moved into the Skakel house that afternoon.

Their father, Rushton Skakel, has gone hunting in the Vermont woods. And anyway, when he's home he is not present. He sits alone, drinking, lost in the memory of his wife, dead of cancer at forty-one. This Julie does not divulge. It is sufficient to say that her father has gone away, is often away, hires a man "to keep an eye on the family." Hence Mr. Littleton.

The group left the club close to nine o'clock and walked home up Otter Rock Drive through the dark. At home they gathered in the family room to watch TV.

Ten minutes went by. Michael Skakel says he saw three figures moving outside the windows: Helen Ix, Martha Moxley, and Geoffrey Byrne. Michael motioned them around to the back door, and they walked the length of the house and crossed a brick patio to the open door, where Michael waited. They walked through the kitchen and out a door that led to the driveway. Michael and the three visitors hopped into the family Lincoln: Michael and Martha in front, Helen and Geoffrey in back.

Tommy is a wiry-strong boy of seventeen, his great frizz of light-brown hair forcefully parted over his left eye. He tells the detectives that he went out to the car to retrieve a cassette tape and, seeing the others, joined them. The time was about nine-twenty. He squeezed in next to Martha Moxley; the detectives learn, but fail to report, that Tommy explored

Martha's thigh; that she kept brushing the hand away. Michael is the source of this information.

Young Rush, nineteen, John, sixteen, and Jimmy Terrien, seventeen, appeared outside and commandeered the Lincoln. They must take Jimmy home to Sursum Corda—Lift Up Our Hearts—a strange and lovely neo-Gothic palace in the back country, as Greenwichites call the wooded hills north of the Merritt Parkway.

The time was nine-twenty-five. Tommy, Martha, Geoffrey, and Helen climbed out of the car, but Michael went off with the others to Sursum Corda. Helen and Geoffrey said they were going home, headed across the lawn toward the Ix house, and disappeared into the night. For reasons unknown, Martha did not go with them but stayed behind with Tommy Skakel.

Perhaps she enjoyed the attention. The attention of boys was new and important now that she was slender and strong and fifteen; and her bright blond hair drew them like bees.

Here the story of events breaks into versions. Tommy Skakel's is this: he said good night, and Martha went off into the backyard, heading toward Walsh Lane and home. It was about nine-thirty. Tommy went inside through the kitchen, and as he was walking through the house he heard the door-bell ring.

Tommy opened the front door, to find Andrea Shakespeare standing there. Julie was about to take her home, but she had forgotten the keys and sent Andrea back for them. Maybe this happened, maybe it didn't. Maybe it happened in some other sequence.

Ken Littleton had gone up to Mr. Skakel's room to unpack and watch *The French Connection.*

This is the skeletal story Lunney and Brosko extract, but it will grow and change over time. At about ten-thirty, or slightly before, Tommy appeared in the doorway and sat down to watch the famous chase scene with Littleton. Tommy seemed neither harried nor disheveled. Except for his tie, which he'd removed, he wore the same clothes he'd worn to dinner: a blue Oxford-cloth shirt, Khakis, and Topsiders.

As Lunney and Brosko make ready to leave, they pass a storage bin on the first floor, where assorted golf clubs are kept. They see something that stops them cold. They see a five iron. A Toney Penna.

They know it may be the first big break in the case, and will try to collect it when Rush Skakel has returned from hunting wild game.

Late in the Afternoon

DETECTIVES SEARCH through the Hammond house. They don't bother with a search warrant. In the 1970s, in a town that still fancies itself small, evidence gathering is an almost neighborly affair.

There is a paper that gives police permission to search the premises without a warrant. Marionna Hammond signs it.

Police go through the house and retrieve an odd assortment of items:

> one box of Trojans, 3 empty, 2 unused, one used (brown)
> two empty bottles of Schweppes Bitter Lemon
> one piece of cardboard
> one empty Crest toothpaste box
> five empty Marlboro boxes

one deposit slip, Putnam Trust Co., name William E.
   Hammond
one Yale vs. Cornell football stub, dated 10–25–75
one note Things I Gotta Do
one news clipping, 9–11–75 on *The Guns of Autumn*

They go through trash cans, hampers, closets, washing machine, and dryer, and put arbitrary items in evidence bags:

one 75 watt light bulb, GE soft white and container
one Pantyhose advertisement
tissues, lipstick blotted
graying hair, small amount
two cigarette butts, Marlboro

Detectives take all of it away, even the kitchen garbage, which they scour through, then discard, "due to the fact that it was decomposing."

All in all, a thorough performance. They believe they might have their man.

Meanwhile, the red stain on Edward's beige corduroys that so intrigued them turns out to be not blood but food.

The rumor, as the years unfold, will be that Belle Haven residents threw up a wall of silence. It is not as clear as that. Some try to help. In their zeal, they point nervously to William Edward Hammond. At ten o'clock on Halloween, Robert Bjork's wife, Cynthia, calls the police. Unnerved by the prospect of living next door to a murderer, she describes Hammond as lonely, a little odd, a heavy drinker.

One day during the summer, Edward appeared at her door, reeking of alcohol, and asked to borrow a saw. They strolled through the yard, talking, and Edward mentioned that there was much brush to cut away. "And somehow the conversation turned to sunbathing."

"He was a voyeur," Mrs. Bjork tells me years later. "He liked to watch."

Cynthia Bjork is a beautiful woman, slender and blonde. Because of this, she attracted considerable notice when she moved to Belle Haven in the spring of 1975. It would be a normal thing for a young man to want to watch her. But she says it's true that Hammond seemed odd. "I didn't deal with him very much. Theirs was such a sad house."

The following night, Hammond's name clicks off the tongues of other neighbors. The Proctors, Jim and June, tell police that Hammond's an alcoholic. Marionna spoke to them, despairing of it. He doesn't socialize. Is seen only at his mother's side. Seems strange in his actions. The Proctors offer this without prompting or provocation, but give no specifics.

The Wolds and the Bjorks remember Hammond at the Moxleys' house six days before the murder. A neighborhood cocktail party. He was off away from the crowd, in the kitchen, having a conversation with Martha Moxley.

Great significance is accorded unremarkable actions. Hammond has taken on a malevolent cast. Joan Redmond also attended the Moxleys' cocktail party. "I felt I was looking at the face of the devil," she tells me. "He showed no emotion at all, as though he was looking right through you."

Her impression of Hammond has not dulled over time. She knows he was alone on Mischief Night. She wonders if he was drunk or hiding among the hemlocks and clutching a golf club. Wonders if it was Hammond who chased Geoffrey Byrne through the woods. Wonders if Martha Moxley was next to cross his path. "I think he was out there drunk, chasing around."

One thing. Edward does not drink in the fall of 1975. He's taking Antabuse, an oral drug that deters drinking alcohol by making you so nauseated that you vomit.

Yet with the small chorus of Belle Havenites breathing his name, and no other suspects materializing, police go after him with gusto. And find . . . nothing. No police record. No strange tales from his past. Nobody who even disliked him. He was simply a shy young man in great pain.

Belle Havenites who actually knew him—contemporaries whom the police have not managed to interview—scoff at the idea of Hammond as a killer.

"A quiet soul" is how his neighbor Chip White describes him. "I believe it was about the time his dad died that he absolutely fell apart. Just got lost."

"He was a good guy who went through a tough time," his friend Dan Connor, of Belle Haven, says. "He could never have done it. No way."

Halloween

THE STATE POLICE ARRIVE at the Moxley house after sundown. They lug powerful searchlights down from a truck and beam them across blue lawn and gray trees to the faded walls of the old house.

It is Halloween. Small children in sheets and masks trot along the lanes swinging unfilled sacks. Grim-faced parents stay near them, and so do police officers, ten paces back, their flashlights aglow.

Martha's body has lain out in the cold all day. At five-thirty Charlie Danks from the Reilly-Gallagher funeral home eases his hearse past the trick-or-treaters of Belle Haven and into the Moxley driveway. The place looks preposterous, lit up like a Hollywood movie set, extras weaving about the lawn, as if in search of a diva's lost earring.

Police load the shrouded figure into the hearse. Officer James Gleason hops in with Danks, and the two of them drive Martha up to Greenwich Hospital, where they'll wheel her to the morgue and lay her on a refrigerated slab. Tomorrow Elliot Gross, the state medical examiner, will perform an autopsy.

David Moxley arrives home from the airport. Today is his forty-fourth birthday, but nobody remembers this now. He moves through his lighted yard and through the door to the room where his wife sits weeping. David himself is stoic. "David was clearly stunned but never wept in our presence," Marilyn Pennington remembers. "I think it was just impossible for him to let down." Lou Pennington watches David toil at emotion management. "Why don't you just go out back and scream your lungs out, get it out of your system!"

But David shakes him off. That is not his manner of grief. Instead he asks pointed questions, his hard blue eyes demanding an honest account, whatever the price in pain. Now he wants to know about Martha's wounds.

Lou stares at the floor.

Marilyn says, "Neither David nor Dorthy had seen Martha, and Lou had. Lou went to great lengths to protect them from the knowledge of how she looked. The Moxleys were such good friends. They'd been hurt horribly, and we didn't want them hurt any more. So when David asked Lou point-blank how Martha looked, poor Lou tried to downplay the truth."

The phone rings all evening: calls of anguished condolence. Most are from friends and relatives. One is from a stranger named Irving Grossman. Repeatedly he has the operator cut in, claiming emergency, only to offer his "condolence." He speaks quickly and oddly and is hard to understand. When asked to slow down, he says "why?" He goes on to claim friendship with a Reverend Snow, who is an adviser to President Ford. The Moxleys never do talk to him, and the messages that friends take get discarded. Police try to track down Grossman—he seems to live in the Bronx—but cannot.

The night wears on. There is not much to say. No talk of justice yet with the fact of Martha's death still trying to penetrate these rooms.

John McCreight's on the phone for David.

John McCreight? David thinks as he walks to the phone.

McCreight is an associate of David's at Touche, Ross, the accounting firm where he works. David does not know McCreight well. He's short and solid, with curly brown hair and a brashly confident manner. He came to Touche from the Apollo space program in 1968 and made partner in a record four years. He'd been circulating about the Midwest until this year but spent so much time in the field that he'd been a stranger even to his Touche, Ross colleagues in the Detroit office.

McCreight calls himself "Columbo in a slightly better raincoat." He had studied Detroit's escalating homicide rate and then revamped the city's police department. The murder rate quickly dropped off. So when he heard about the murder of his boss's daughter, he pictured the scene, pictured the overburdened machinery of the local police department, imagined interviewing officers at the scene of the crime. He'd been through it all before.

"David," he tells Moxley, "they're never going to be able to solve this. Let me get you some help."

David glances out the library window. "The place is alive with people. The state police are here, the town police are here. The place is all lighted up. There's a lab vehicle out front."

"I understand what's there, David. But I repeat: they're never going to be able to solve this alone."

McCreight knows that town police lack what it takes to solve murders. They have neither practice nor experience. "It would be like you or me walking in and doing brain surgery," McCreight tells me. Homicide investigation is like no other aspect of police work. It is a subtle science practiced by men who are part detective, part animal; part reason, part instinct. McCreight knows you can't entrust a job like this to men who investigate shopliftings at the A&P.

"I think we're okay," David says.

McCreight thinks to press his point a little harder, but he holds his tongue. "Okay, David. But don't forget me. I'm here."

The neighborhood grows dark, save for the wash of light over the Moxley estate. In Belle Haven and all over Greenwich, people lock up their houses and lie in the dark, listening for sounds. "I felt so strongly there was somebody in my backyard," Barrie Fuchs says. "I'll never forget—I wanted to take a bath at night, and I literally couldn't do it without support." Her daughter Holly adds, "That was such a big house. We never locked it and we didn't even have keys to some of the doors. Five girls, the doors all open, and a murderer, probably in our neighborhood."

The police investigation will not soon find a focus, and as the hours rush past, as the evidence recedes into nature's design, as suspects firm up their alibis, and as police grasp at distant possibilities, David Moxley will reconsider John McCreight's offer.

He calls after a couple of weeks and tells him, "We're in trouble."

But now, catastrophically, it is too late. "After a couple of days, it gets much harder to solve a homicide—by several orders of magnitude," McCreight tells me. "It's like a half gallon of ice cream you bring home from the supermarket. You put it on the counter and it's hard as a rock. It's ice cream. But it doesn't take long for it to be nothing."

Big News

THE MURDER of Martha Moxley lands on the front pages of all the New York newspapers, even the staid *New York Times*: GREENWICH GIRL, 15, BLUDGEONED TO DEATH. The headline in the *Daily News* reads CONN. GIRL, 15, FOUND SLAIN NEAR PLUSH HOME.

The subtext of these stories is the immemorial fear of trauma in Eden. Violence is for the ghetto, along with drugs, alcoholism, and broken homes. Nobody stops to consider that Greenwich is burdened by all of these save violence. The town's troubled people are like characters from a John Cheever story: sad, lonely, and wrecked, but not violent.

Now violence has come down in this peaceful place. The incongruity, and the vague biblical overtone, give the story force. From the *Times*: "Access to the winding unlighted streets that loop through the quiet area is limited to two roads, both of which are blocked by guard posts. A small private police force patrols the area regularly at night." Such paragraphs mean to suggest that the violence came not from outside but from inside "one of the nation's richest and safest communities."

From the *New York Post*: " 'Influential people' describes just about everybody in Belle Haven. On the night of her fatal Halloween stroll, Martha was accompanied by a classmate Helen Ix, whose father, Robert, is president of Schweppes, Inc.; Jackie Wetenhall, the daughter of John H. Wetenhall, president of the National Dairy Assn.; and Thomas and Michael Skakel, nephews of Mrs. Robert F. Kennedy, the former Ethel Skakel."

The murder weapon itself is almost comically suited to Greenwich—the first object that would come to the hand of an angry rich person. (In fiction, only a farce could accommodate a detail like this: one of those haunted-mansion spoofs in which the lights go out and somebody turns up dead in the secret bar behind the bookcase.) The tabloid headline writers, predictably, waste little time in dubbing Martha's killing "The Golf Club Murder."

The New York papers question the Greenwich Police Department's ability to handle a crime of such gravity. The implication is that the police can't keep watch over their own yard, which draws a defensive response from Chief Stephen M. Baran.

"We don't rely on anyone," he says proudly, noting Greenwich detectives' recent success in the case of valuable paintings stolen from the residence of famous collector Joseph

Hirshhorn. "We not only apprehended the perpetrator, but recovered the paintings, which are now hanging in the Smithsonian in Washington.

"Some people think we need help every time something more important happens than a cow knocking over a farmer's fence."

The self-reliance is simple arrogance, contends John McCreight. "If I've never solved a homicide, what are the odds I can do it by myself? Zero."

On November 1, Saturday, John Moxley goes to the homecoming football game at Cardinal Stadium. He does not suit up for battle against the Rippowam Warriors of Stamford; he's a spectator, but he feels like part of what's being watched.

"I just had to get out of the house," he recalls. "Just had to get away. Before the game started, they had a moment of silence for Martha. You feel like the eyes of the world are on you. You're the center of attention. You want to get out of that spotlight as quickly as possible. There's tremendous paranoia.

"It's like being the kid that broke something. Everybody looking at you. But it's for nothing that you've done. Something bad has happened, and it's nothing you could have prevented. But you're in the spotlight, and all you want to do is escape."

On Monday, Greenwich High School is abuzz with talk of the murder. News crews show up. They flock into the courtyard outside the long glass entryway and try to interview students, but the students feel invaded and pelt the news people with rocks until they retreat.

Martha's friend Christy Kalan says, "It was like, 'You don't have anything to do with this. Get out of here. She was our student, our friend, go away.' You get less honest as you get older, unfortunately, but kids will say it like they feel it." She considers the moment. "I was young. I thought the news crews being there was rude and unnecessary—but maybe it *was* necessary."

In the classroom, Christy loses her faculty for learning to the shock of Martha's death. The words and numbers on the blackboard mean nothing in these hours; she leans her head on the desk and cries.

Sheila McGuire remembers: "The first day of school after Martha was killed—this was partly my paranoia and partly factual—it was like that lottery commercial where everyone in the arena quiets down and you can hear a pin drop. That's what it was like.

"You walk in and everybody turns and stares at you, and they're very quiet, pointing at you—*That's Sheila, the one who found Martha*—and then in the distance I would see Martha's brother, his blond hair and his pale skin and his red eyes.

"I was almost ashamed to see him, because I had seen the horrific thing that caused the pain in his life, and I didn't want him to ask me what I saw. I don't know if he had questions. He never asked me anything, which I was glad about, because I think I would have just fallen apart.

"Maybe I knew his pain a little more intimately, because there were so many things kept from people that I knew—the condition of her body, how brutally she was murdered. People thought she was hit on the back of the head with a golf club, she fell down on the ground under a pine tree, and was dead. Kind of like if you had fallen and bumped your head and died. Like someone hit her, and hit her a little too hard. But it wasn't that. It was brutal and grotesque and horrific. And I remember thinking, *When will I be able to go to school and not feel like the Girl Who Found Martha? I just want to be Sheila McGuire again*."

Even at school, the reporters vigorously seek her out. One day in creative writing class, Sheila's housemaster comes to retrieve her. An NBC news crew is on campus, searching for her—they're armed with a yearbook photograph, checking it against all the young faces—and Sheila and the housemaster hide in his office. Then Sheila's father comes. "They put a coat over me and whisked me out of the school and shoved me in a car, and I was gone."

Later John Moxley will identify with Sheila's confusion—the sudden ways in which the murder changed her. "I can't imagine someone like Sheila seeing what she saw. You drive down the highway and you see a deer that's been hit by a car. Or a dog. The body's been torn apart. I can't imagine what it would be like to see a person like that. How could it *not* change you?"

But at the time John is changing too. He begins to express his sorrow as anger. "I argued with my parents. Drank more than I should. Got into a couple of fights—just this inner sense of anger. *Why me? Why my family? Why my sister? Why did this have to happen in my world?*

"A lot of the anger was simply because you had no control over it—no control over so much of what was going on. Everything was so tenuous. Held together by shoestrings.

What happened to Martha eroded all the strength from the foundation we had, the foundation you were building your life on. It created insecurities and paranoia: *This didn't happen to their family, they must be better than us.*"

Kid Gloves

THE SCREAMS THAT AWAKENED STEVEN SKAKEL the night Martha Moxley was killed came from outside his window, down in his darkened yard. He tells this to his friend Lucy Tart as they ride the bus to Greenwich Country Day School on the morning of Halloween, four hours before the discovery of Martha's corpse. That night Lucy tells her mother, who tells her friend Joan Rader, who tells the police.

Later the police check the story not with Steven but with his father, Rushton, who promises to question the boy. He does, and now the story changes—there were no screams. Steven "was awakened by the sound of the Moxley girl's laughter as she was leaving the house," Detective Michael Powell reports, "and not by the sound of screams."

In this early and overwhelmingly critical hour of the investigation, nobody wonders why after a night's sleep Steven Skakel would remember, and be moved to mention, the sound of a girl laughing.

Detectives Lunney and Brosko return to the Skakel house on Sunday, two days into the murder investigation. They must see to the matter of the Toney Penna golf club. There's a dawning awareness of the maker's rarity, and it begins to seem likely that the murder weapon will be traced to this wealthy and influential family. Yet there's a reluctance to draw inferences and then take the vigorous steps that such inferences would warrant.

Rush Skakel has returned from his hunting trip. He has a fringe of unruly gray hair and a look of merriment about his eyes. He is suitably shocked by the girl's murder, which occurred catty-corner to his estate, and wants to help in any way he can. The detectives find him jovial and expansive. They seek no search warrant. Rush Skakel signs a "consent to search the premises without a warrant" form and readily gives up the Toney Penna five iron.

The set from which this club is orphaned belonged to his wife, Ann Reynolds Skakel, "who passed away several years ago," the police note, though the actual figure is two. Rush had given the clubs to his daughter, Julie, who last used them during the summer.

The "search of the premises" is perfunctory. Nothing like the Hammond search. No washing machines or drains or trash cans or bedroom drawers are disturbed.

The detectives report: "Julie made a quick search of the house and was unable to locate the set of clubs. Mr. Skakel and Julie advised the investigators that they would make a thorough search of the house in an attempt to locate the golf clubs and advise this department of their findings."

They'll search? Report *their* findings? Lunney and Brosko seem docile in Rushton Skakel's presence. What is it? The Kennedy aura? Gold dust flaking from Rush's hands? Or maybe something older, deeper. These are police largely descended from Irish Catholic workers who escaped farming and mean living across the ocean. People were always running from death and coming to America. Police departments began springing up in East Coast towns around the turn of the century, staffed cheaply by that least offensive class of poor immigrants: the Irish. In Greenwich, police kept order not among the rich folk, who were treated with deference even when they behaved boorishly and were deserving of arrest, but among rabble-rousers from neighboring towns and the Poles and Italians, who were poor and coarse and not to be trusted. The officers' wives often worked as domestics in the fine houses, and there evolved a symbiosis between the Irish and the well-to-do.

The Skakels were both. Deep in the mind of the police, the cog slipped, vigilance stalled. The Skakels were, for the moment, offered every courtesy, and they repaid the police in kind.

"Many a time I walked through the Skakels' kitchen while the Greenwich cops were eating lunch," Peter Coomaraswamy, Michael's friend, tells me. "It was fucking unbelievable."

"We were too nonchalant where the Skakels were concerned," admits Steve Carroll. "No doubt about it."

The next day, Monday, November 3, police ask Dan Connor in for questioning. Thickset, with small eyes and dark-blond hair, and twenty-six years old, he fits Charles Morganti's description of the man he spotted walking in Belle Haven the night of the murder.

Connor in younger days earned a reputation as a crank, but neighbors grew to like him once they got past his thorny exterior. Not everyone liked him, though. A suspicious neighbor whispered to the police that Connor was often seen jogging through Belle Haven at night.

Connor tells Detective Vincent Ambrose that on October 30 he went out to the Field Club for dinner, then to a friend's house in Old Greenwich to watch *The French Connection*.

"Any thoughts on who might have done this?" Ambrose asks.

Imagining his remarks will stay confined to police files, Connor hints at the Skakels. Those kids take pills, he says. If Tommy Skakel had taken pills, he'd be capable of a thing like this. Then he'd throw the golf club handle in the Sound.

Connor eventually became a lawyer in town. He would become a close friend of Wall Street outcast Ivan Boesky and was burned by journalists investigating Boesky. He talks to me only after the intercession of friends. He no longer seems to hold the same view of Tommy Skakel's darker capabilities. Or Michael's. "They were a little rambunctious," he offers. "But I'd be shocked if either of them had anything to do with that murder."

He says the Skakels were a close, outwardly happy family. And unpretentious, considering their wealth. Rush Skakel was part owner of the Atlanta Braves baseball team, Connor says, and would take him down to Shea Stadium when the Braves were in town. "Rush Skakel was a good guy. Gregarious. Friendly. A really good guy. Mrs. Skakel was lower key. The opposite of Rush, but a real sweetheart."

Yes, they had been a very close family. "But the dynamic changed when Ann Skakel died." Rush drank; the kids, some of them, ran wild; and Julie was defeated by being cast in the role of surrogate mother.

Like many Belle Havenites, Connor says, the Skakels were good people who had known much sorrow. Connor had also know the Terriens. Georgeann, the eldest daughter, dated Connor's friend Dean Davis. She was terrific. All the Terrien girls were terrific.

But the Terrien boys: Jimmy was a wise guy and Johnny was crazy. Many years later, at Sursum Corda, Johnny would beat his stepfather badly with a riding crop. "And they weren't as down-to-earth as the Skakels. They acted as though they were really conscious of their wealth."

Honest Abe

THE LEGEND, carved in stone above the Brunswick School's front door, is this: "With all thy getting, get understanding." It is a subtle reminder to the privileged boys who attend this private day school near the center of town. But the following lyric, taken from the school's 1976 yearbook and sung to the tune of "There's Music in the Air," is a better reflection of the student body of those years: "There's B.S. in the air/When Brunswick boys are near/You hear it everywhere. . . ."

All about these boys is light evidence of rebellion. Glassy eyes blinking sluggishly behind pretty, unshorn locks. Ties loosened, collars askew, shirttails flopping down over skinny buttocks.

Brunswick did not provide a rigorous course of study. "To be honest, I was surprised by the anti-intellectualism. I was surprised by the mediocrity," Barbara Train Lawrence tells me. She taught history, sociology, and anthropology at Brunswick from 1971 to 1979, and she played a small but intriguing role in the Moxley case. "Brunswick was a reasonably good second-rate school. The standards weren't anywhere near those of the private schools around Washington, D.C., where I had come from. There was a huge emphasis on sports, partying, and drinking. It was like, 'You can't give us a test on Monday, because we're hung over, and you can't give us a test on Friday, because we're gonna be.' But this was implicitly endorsed, because the parents were doing the same thing. The teachers too."

Lawrence herself comes from a high-powered world. Her father, Desmond FitzGerald, was a socialite and a legendary CIA operative who plotted to assassinate Fidel Castro with exploding seashells and poison cigars; her mother was a beauty queen who later had her own radio show; her sister Frances is the Pulitzer Prize–winning author of *Fire in the Lake: The Vietnamese and the Americans in Vietnam*.

While teaching at Brunswick, she saw ample evidence of wealth's destructive tendencies. Not in all the kids, but in a sad lot of them. "They'd talk about how they didn't want a new Jaguar. They just wanted their dad home. It was really pathetic. There were a lot of dysfunctional families. A lot of kids running through big houses with horrendous furniture and a parent passed out on the couch. These kids were so lonely, so many of them."

Yet there was no means of confronting the issues of the neglected young rich. "There was an underlying fear of the parents on the part of the teachers. And the subtext was 'We don't want any conflict here.'"

The Skakels, she says, were typical of the sadness she describes. "But atypical in that they were at the top of the heap. They had that special aura through their connection to the Kennedys. You could see that they had a certain swagger— but it was all surface. They had that quintessential duality: terrible wounds and loneliness beneath a carapace of invincibility."

Tommy Skakel had told the police that after he said good night to Martha Moxley, he'd gone inside, given his sister's keys to Andrea Shakespeare, and sat a moment with Ken Littleton, watching *The French Connection*. He asked Littleton if he wanted anything from the kitchen. Then, he said, he retreated to his bedroom to work on a report Mrs. Train would be expecting soon. The subject: Abraham Lincoln. He was not out killing Martha Moxley but contemplating the Great Emancipator.

The police checked the story with Barbara Train Lawrence. At the time, she was perplexed by what Tommy had said; she still is. "The thing I never understood—apparently I was his excuse. I was told he said he was doing a paper on Abraham Lincoln for me, and that's why he couldn't have killed the girl. Well, I taught him anthropology. We weren't looking too hard at Abraham Lincoln."

Her lingering impression of Tom Skakel: "He was not a good student. He was a sloppy student who had a kind of sleazy charm." She reconsiders. " 'Sleazy' is not the right word. I'm not sure what the right word is. But he was a lazy, spoiled kid. Just sloppy."

There were other students like Tommy, and despite their faults Barbara Lawrence had a fondness for them. Even the wild ones. Even the ones who did not hold the pursuit of knowledge in high regard. That was most of them. Even the drinkers and the pot smokers.

But her love often stemmed from sympathy. Those children were prisoners of their culture. They knew nothing else. "Your culture forms your way of looking at the world. In Greenwich, the culture was obsessed with material abundance. That's where the value was. Money was what mattered. How much you had, how fast you made it. Some of these kids would try to cover all the pain by telling you their daddy was the bathroom king or whatever. But you saw right through it. For the most part they were wonderful kids who had to deal with this chaos swirling around them. This is just speculative, but you can see how that environment and that pain carried to a wild extreme could end in violent death."

Yet when it happened she tried not to consider it too closely. "I don't admire myself in this particularly. But the whole thing was so awful, and we were all so traumatized. Everybody wanted it not to be real, to go away."

The kids begin whispering, however. They give Tommy Skakel a wide berth and chatter about him when they think he's out of range. One student of those years recalls, "Tommy was a hotheaded kid, a troublemaker. If there was a kid in the class who was in trouble, it was him. I remember him with his disheveled white shirt and long curly hair. And we were all saying, 'Wow. Tommy flipped.' Nobody I knew was all that surprised."

Barbara Train Lawrence remembers that Tommy vanished for a time. To Europe. Was he whisked out of the country to escape his inquisitors? This is an enduring myth of the Moxley case. At some point in the winter of 1975, Tommy did go to Europe, to a funeral in Ireland; he did not suddenly skip the country. What is unknown is whether his stay lengthened because of the simmering impression of his guilt.

In the days following the murder, Tommy is present, but closed, inscrutable. He is aware of the whispers. He's sitting in a bathroom stall one day when he hears kids who know nothing telling how he did it. He is angry and alone. Barbara Lawrence recalls, "It felt really weird to have a kid around who had possibly murdered somebody, whom people were protecting.

"But I do have some empathy for him. I see him as a wounded kid trying with a lot of bravado to get through life. A sad, lost kid, but also one who is volatile and easily provoked."

* * *

Cuff Train, a Brunswick history teacher—Barbara's husband—looks up from his desk one day when he hears a violent toppling of desks and chairs.

"Tommy had completely lost it with some kid. I think he would have killed the kid. Tommy was strangling him, and it was almost impossible to tear him off. There were three of us. I was scared to death that something very painful was about to happen."

Train tells me this from his home in Seal Cove, Maine. Teaching is far behind him now. He's gone into real estate. But twenty-two years later, Tommy Skakel has managed to leave an indelible impression in his memory. Train thinks the incident happened after Martha's murder—he's not certain—but his image of a raging Tommy Skakel is vivid.

"This kid he attacked said something to him. It wasn't much. And Tommy's reaction, it was like dropping an A-bomb on a mouse. The kid just squeaked. Hadn't even roared. And Tommy just erupted." Train thinks a moment. "Tommy was periodically out of control, psychologically. His eyes had a wildness to them."

Tommy was a strange kid in a strange era, going through a strange time in his life. "I felt sorry for the kid. His mother had died. There were three brothers that I dealt with. Rush was the oldest. He seemed to be the most together. When the mother died, the father sort of lost it, and young Rush became the father figure, the paterfamilias to the younger kids. Of course, that was an impossible role."

Train speaks of the broader culture in which a boy like Tommy Skakel could founder. "Drugs? There were horror stories; these kids were into whatever they got their hands on." The money multiplied the problems. "All these damned absentee fathers pouring money into their kids' wallets to make up for their absenteeism. We didn't want our kids growing up in that community."

So the Trains moved to Mount Desert Island in Maine.

Too Much Information

A WEEK PASSES. Fall sunlight strains through tall gray windows at police headquarters. The detectives sit behind their desks, scribbling notes, sipping coffee, making calls. When they go home in the evening they carry in their heads the pieces of the Moxley case, like words to a song they are trying to remember. But none of it comes together. So they chase dead ends.

On November 7, Detective Carroll takes a call from a psychiatrist in New York City. A patient of hers who lives in Belle Haven nurses suspicions about her husband. No telling what he could do. The woman is afraid. The psychiatrist asks Carroll to come to her office in the city.

Carroll goes and listens to the woman's story. Her husband's an alcoholic who cloisters himself in his room for days at a stretch. He has not eaten with the family in five years. Six days after the murder, she presented him with divorce papers, and did so in the presence of her baby-sitter, fearing violence. He owns many golf clubs. He's an economic adviser to the Ford administration.

Carroll has begun to see Belle Haven's gorgeous tapestry unravel under the strain of a murder investigation. He sighs, shakes his head.

The woman's husband spends his days in shorts and a

bathrobe. This is how his wife last saw him on October 30, 1975, before they went to their separate rooms. She heard the banging of pots and pans at 11 P.M. But she didn't see him again until 3:30 A.M., when Mrs. Moxley's phone call roused them from their sleep.

Carroll drives back to Greenwich, picks up Sergeant Vinnie Ambrose, and heads down to Belle Haven to question the woman's husband. The house is an enormous Tudor, and it is a stone's throw from the Moxley estate. It's easy to see how a married couple could live in such a house and rarely see each other.

The detectives word their query with care. They say they're checking with everyone in the neighborhood who plays golf. The man gladly shows them around. They go to the basement. Nothing. They go to his second-floor bedroom. There is a plastic putter. They go to the attic: two bags full of mismatched clubs, none of them Toney Pennas. The man's own Ben Hogans, he says, are housed at the Westchester Country Club.

Carroll reports, "The interview was terminated and it was the feeling of the investigators that Mr. W—— was a rational person."

Carroll follows up with the psychiatrist. She suggests that the investigators might have been led astray. You see, Mr. W—— too is a patient under her care. She believes his psychiatric problem once led to an arrest in Florida.

Carroll doesn't know whether to laugh or to cry as he puts the phone back in its cradle.

These Greenwich neuroses settle in like clouds, fogging and confusing things, sending police off in a hundred wrong directions. Police get a tip that Jim Proctor of Mayo Avenue in Belle Haven despises children. Especially the Skakel children. Police run record checks on Proctor and come up with only a drunken driving arrest in San Francisco in the winter of 1967.

They bring him in for questioning anyway. He tells the police the same story he told them the night he, like Joan Redmond and Jeanne Wold, sent forth the name of William Edward Hammond: On October 30, he was inside all evening with his wife, June, watching television. They retired at midnight, heard nothing, saw nothing. Police escort him to Connecticut State Police headquarters in Bethany for a polygraph test. He passes.

Then there's a twenty-four-year-old who shot a popgun at a young boy, striking his face with a particle of dirt; a report of a violent Belle Havenite named Smith (two neighborhood Smiths prove innocuous); a Belle Haven stockbroker who slapped a boy (when the boy demanded to see his daughter's underwear); a man with Belle Haven relatives who beat two women with a tire iron in 1962 (he'd long since moved to Florida).

Week two of the investigation begins in a cold light rain. The investigative weather is not better. The search for the red car that plowed into a speed fence outside Bob Bjork's house leads state Inspector Jack Solomon and Vinnie Ambrose to the Keefe residence on Field Point Drive, one block south of Walsh Lane.

Mart Keefe, twenty, lives in a white wood-frame cottage behind the main house. Solomon asks her if she's ever been arrested. Yes, she replies. This summer. For breach of the peace and resisting arrest.

Also her roommate, Judy Sakowicz, for drugs. Last December Stamford police caught Sakowicz selling twelve pounds of marijuana. Both women are on probation. *Oh, hell.*

They'd find out soon enough. Mart herself sells marijuana to Belle Haven girls. She names the girls. Martha Moxley is not among them.

No, she did not know the girl personally. Perhaps she'd seen her waiting for the school bus. Blond, cute. And no, Martha was never among the girls who knocked on her cottage door, seeking drugs. Yes, she's certain.

Still, the detectives believe they're onto something big. The drugs are one reason. Another is that Mart and Judy are lesbians. Martha Moxley was an attractive girl. The police weigh these facts together. A third reason: Judy's red Cougar shows fresh damage to the right front fender.

The conjecture quickly falls apart. On Mischief Night, Mart and Judy and four friends had driven up to the Cedarbrook Lounge, a gay bar in Westport, and did not return until about 2 A.M. As for the Cougar: Judy had "trouble judging distances" and steered it into the cottage. It happened just yesterday, November 6. The paint still clings to the cottage wall. Solomon scrapes it off and puts it into a bag, then leaves.

Two days later, Steve Carroll and Michael Powell turn up at the home of William Edward Hammond. The door creaks open.

"Can we come in?"

Hammond appears nervous. "What do you want?"

"We just want to talk."

"I've got nothing to say to you." His attorney's advice.

"Well, have you given any more thought to taking that polygraph?"

"My attorney tells me not to take it."

"Will you at least tell us what your blood type is?"

Hammond hesitates. "A-positive."

Footsteps. A rising voice.

"Edward will *not* take a polygraph test!" Marionna Hammond stands in the doorway. She bids the detectives good day and shuts the door.

As the cops pull away, David Moxley strides across his lawn, arm raised. The detectives pull up into the driveway, and David shows them inside. He and Dorthy have received an odd letter, mailed from midtown Manhattan.

New York, November 6, 1975.

Dear Mr. and Mrs. Moxley

First of all, please accept my deepest and sincere condolences for the violent death of your nice daughter Marta.

I would be very surprised if you are ready to sacrifice your love of your Marta and lose your nice daughter by some demoralized, rotten boys from your vicinity.

It is a shame for the whole Nation and the state police in Greenwich and Connecticut, that they want to cover the violent and cowardly crime of one girl which did not want to sucumb to his sexy offers. It is a national shame how the police tried to cover the crime and what they presented to the press. Who wrote about it in New York Times and the Daily News?? who payed for the informations??

The police should take into custody all the group of boys and girls that were together on that evening ... and in two hours they would find who killed Marta.

The police nor the press has the right to cover the crime even if the killer is the nephew of Mrs. Ethel Kennedy.

Marta certainly was not going home alone from the party. One or more boys certainly accompanied her. Why hasn't the police followed through on this??

If I were in your place, I would sue the state police for 5 mil-

lion dollars for insufficient investigation and being accomplice
to the crime.

With best regards
your Friend.

No doubt the letter is intriguing. It seems to have been
composed by someone whose first language is not English,
who seems to know something about the "demoralized, rotten
boys from your vicinity"—an impression of the Skakels no
news story has yet conveyed—and who seems convinced, a
week into the investigation, of an evolving cover-up.

This notion will gain some currency but has not done so
yet. There's also a coarse quality to the letter. That strange fellow Irving Grossman comes to mind: the man who besieged
the Moxley house with emergency phone calls the day Martha
was found. But wouldn't he have signed his name? The police
can only take possession of the letter and wait. There is no
way to track its source.

Dr. Elliot Gross, the state medical examiner, did not arrive in
Greenwich until Saturday, November 1, the day after Martha
was found. His autopsy lasted six hours. Gross concluded that
Martha was beaten over the head at least a dozen times and
stabbed once through the neck. He listed the cause of death as
a fractured skull and bruises and cuts to the brain. He also determined no rape had occurred, even though Martha's jeans
and panties were pulled down. But investigators agreed on
one thing: Gross's autopsy was no forensic masterpiece. The
medical examiner, according to Steve Carroll, failed to examine Martha's body fully for signs of a sexual assault.

Later Gross proved oddly stubborn about the color autopsy

photos he had taken. "It took us a long time to get him to show them to us," Carroll says. "He treated them like his own personal property that he didn't want to part with." (Gross was later fired as New York City's medical examiner amid allegations of mismanagement. Twenty-two years after his autopsy of Martha Moxley, in 1998, his color photographs were discovered to be missing.)

Meanwhile, as Officer Dan Hickman stands by watching Dr. Gross, he is hit by a strange sensation. "Martha was up on the slab, in a facedown position. The same position we found her in. Then the medical examiner would do another procedure, all the way down to the point where he turned her over. Now I'm looking at her face. *Oh my God! I know who this young lady is!* I kind of drew back.

"We had a case up here that summer. Fellow by the name of Ned Coll. Ned Coll had a group of children who were coming in from Bridgeport. They would come down here and try and get onto Tod's Point."

Tod's Point, also called Greenwich Point, is the biggest of the town's three public beaches; all the beaches are closed to nonresidents. Coll was a political activist, who would bus inner-city children to Greenwich and make a show of getting his poor black kids turned away from the beach of the "Cocktail Republicans."

"That particular day we had some officers out there, and we were gonna stop him from coming onto Tod's Point. That was our assignment. We were sitting just before the gate, parked facing the beach. Martha Moxley walked up to the car and said, 'Oh, you must be police officers.' She came around to my side of the car and started conversing with me. She wanted to know why we were there, and I filled her in. She said, 'Oh, okay,' and then she went on her merry way.

"But I remembered her face. Standing there watching her autopsy, the shock was horrendous. Added to that, we've got a wild murderer running around, a maniac we've got to find. All of that, that it could happen in Greenwich—*wow*."

Chapter Four

A Black Tuesday

HOW WILL I ever get through another Tuesday?

Dorthy Moxley wonders this on Tuesday, November 4, 1975, as she dresses for her daughter's funeral. It seems enough to keep composed. To keep composed requires effort and discipline, the strict cooperation of every cell. What little thing will undo her? A shift in the wind, a change in the light? A memory blowing through her mind?

Martha at Tahoe, out in the snow, with a man she has molded with her small hands: apple eyes, carrot nose, raisin mouth. Pine needle bow tie. Stovepipe hat. The snowman beams his Christmas smile at Martha, whose face is gaily tilted and aglow with winter sun. Tears again. Dorthy must not conjure memories now.

The First Lutheran Church on Field Point Road is a low, angular structure, modern in a fifties sort of way. From there you can look out over central Greenwich and see the silvery band of Long Island Sound ease across the horizon; but these grief-darkened faces, the young ones, glance nervously at their shoes.

Fifteen detectives are sprinkled among the crowd. Captain Keegan conceals himself behind a row of cars, shooting mourners with Super 8 film.

Five hundred mourners crowd the church. Blue-and-yellow stained-glass windows make a kaleidoscope of the sunlight, and the air smells of flowers and cleaning solvent.

It is quiet, save for the moving of bodies and shoes and for breathing that is harried by tears barely held back. Amazingly quiet. David, Dorthy, and John sit in the front pew, stunned, impassive. The *New York Times* will report the next day that they seemed calm.

Nine of Martha's friends sit behind, each clutching a yellow rose. The friends gathered at Helen Ix's house to cobble together a eulogy. Someone has remembered that Martha once said she wanted a cheerful funeral when she died: "I want everyone to be happy and remember all the good times we had."

But everyone knows Martha must have been talking about many years from now, after a full life. The girls cry fitfully during the short ceremony, unable to find the happiness that Martha imagined.

The Reverend Richard Manus reads what the girls have written: "Martha Moxley loved life. Every day was something special. After only a short time here she had more friends than most people have in a lifetime."

Then he turns to the Moxleys and says, "You have experienced something which probably none of us here have experienced and probably never will." He offers his sympathy on behalf of the community of Greenwich, "especially the Christian community." He reads scripture. Saint Paul. "We are afflicted in every way possible but we are not crushed; full of doubts, we never despair. We are persecuted but never abandoned; we are struck down but never destroyed. Continually we carry about in our bodies the dying of Jesus, so that in our bodies the life of Jesus may also be revealed."

There is a stir in the second pew. One of the girls' roses has no petals. It is a headless rose, a naked stem. The girls panic.

"Okay, give it here," Tori Fuchs whispers with authority to the others. "Now each of you give me a petal."

Tori collects the yellow petals and pinches them lightly around the stem. There. A patchwork rose. Nobody will know.

The girls rise and prepare to walk up to Martha's closed mahogany coffin. All eyes are upon them. They will place the roses upon the coffin. As they approach it, Tori loses herself in sorrow and forgets the petals she holds in place with her fingers. Her hand moves. The petals flutter to the floor.

The mourners pour out of the church and into the bracing cold. The news crews from New York with their cameras look like two-headed monsters; the newspaper reporters stand a little off to the side. The camera crews hustle up the drive to the open church door.

Blank-faced men load Martha's remains into a hearse, and her friends burst into tears. Others direct quiet fury at the news crews. Sheila spies them and bristles. "I was standing next to my father. Someone said, 'There's Sheila, there's Sheila McGuire.' My dad grabbed me and I went like this"—she gives the up-yours sign—"and I shouted, 'You want my face? You want my face?' And I gave them the finger and I picked up some rocks and I'm running down the driveway, throwing rocks at the cameras. There was nothing controlled about it. I was just heaving them. I think I broke a lens, because I remember hearing a *ksshhh!*"

Later somebody suggests getting a keg and driving up to the reservoir. The reservoir is a lake in the back country, with a broad glacial stone slanting down into the water. High school kids come here in the summer to drink beer and swim and, sometimes, to run from the police. But now, on the edge of winter, it is a place to put grief in abeyance. They'll go there while the family buries Martha in Putnam Cemetery.

Sheila looks out over the lake. *This is very sick. Getting drunk and partying when she's dead.*

A coterie has broken off and gone to McDonald's. Christy Kalan feels as though she's in a fog, because the pieces of the day don't fit: church, coffin, tears, McDonald's. It has the illogic of a dream.

At the McDonald's she looks around and notices that Tommy Skakel has attached himself to the group. She can't believe it. Even then, before the police have taken a hard look at him, there are whispers. "I remember being really pissed," Christy says. "Like, 'How dare you show up here, even if you didn't do it. You're suspected of doing it, so why don't you just clear out?' It was bizarre."

John Moxley recalls isolated thought fragments about the funeral, floating beyond the range of his emotions.

"I remember the church was full of people. I remember walking into the church. All eyes on you. Then walking out of the church. That was the first time I saw television cameras. *Why in the world are there television cameras here?* Just so odd. *Why would there be television cameras?* I remember getting into a limousine. Looking around, thinking, *Oh, so this is a limousine.* I remember going up to the cemetery."

Up in midcountry Greenwich, on some hills between North

Street and Lake Avenue, lies Putnam Cemetery, one of many places in town named for Israel Putnam, a Revolutionary War general who fled from the onrushing British, on horseback, down a steep granite rock face.

The hearse, its headlights faint in the bright sun, rolls heavily through the iron gates of the cemetery, past a little stone house, around a sharp bend in the road, and slows at the foot of a gentle slope. A hole has been cut out of the earth, and fragile roots spring through the smooth earthen walls. Disconcertingly, the grave lies in the shade of a tall pine.

Everyone gathers round, the family and a small knot of friends. John Moxley feels outside himself as the minister's voice intones the Twenty-third Psalm. He feels risen above the scene, above the mourners and the coffin and the dirt pile and the hole where they are about to lay his sister. "Even though I walk through the shadow of the valley of death, I fear no evil; for thou art with me." Then he feels heavy, brought low by grief. He's split in two.

Dirt spatters upon the coffin.

The disassociated John sees his mother, quietly weeping, his father, bowed and rigid. John is incredulous but calm. *Look at this. Look what's happened to these people.*

After the funeral, the neighbors bear steaming pots of food to the Moxley house. Rush Skakel has ordered a turkey. Nobody has much appetite, but once they start to eat, they are surprised at how good and warm the food makes them feel. It's as though they've all been too sick to take nourishment for many days.

Whatever else this is, it is a two-house affair. The adults are at the Moxleys', and Martha's friends are across the street, at Bob and Cissy Ix's.

Something strikes Christy Kalan as weird. A little off. Why is Mrs. Ix standing next to Rush Skakel the whole time? Isn't it kind of disrespectful to the Moxleys? What if his son really did do it?

But the whispers have not yet reached the Moxleys' ears; or Rush Skakel's. Dorthy crosses Walsh Lane; she will comfort the kids, and they will comfort her.

There's Tommy. She gives the boy a hug. "If only I had walked Martha home, maybe this never would have happened." That's what he told Mrs. Ix. Poor Tommy. All torn up about it.

These days Dorthy Moxley wonders this: on the day of Martha's funeral, did she embrace her killer?

The Murdered Girl

CHRISTY KALAN TAKES OUT the sheaf of letters Martha wrote her and reads them again and again. These letters are full of plans. They have a breathless quality, an energy, a fullness of life, and reading them, it is not possible to believe Martha is the murdered girl now.

> Then he said he likes my eyes (again) and after lunch he took this paper of Carol Sorgenfrei's I had and he said the only way I could get it back is if I kissed him, soooo—

The notes that Martha and Christy sent back and forth—sometimes by mail, more often dropped through a locker slot—are a running report of their lives, one tiny intrigue leaping into the next.

> I just got an E on my Spanish test! I don't know what to even think! An E! My first one ever! Oh Christy, I just can't get over it! I wonder what my mom will say? Now Mr. Moye has seen Jeff kiss me two or three times . . .

Martha came to Greenwich from California in July of 1974 and started the ninth grade at Western Junior High School. Most Belle Haven kids went to the town's private schools—Brunswick, Country Day, Greenwich Academy, the Convent of the Sacred Heart—but Martha and John Moxley chose the public schools. This gave them two wide circles of friends. Martha became so instantly popular at Western that her fellow students voted her "girl with the best personality." She'd been in town less than a year.

She wrote in Christy's Western yearbook:

> Let's see, now . . . remember worm hunting with candles in the rain—trying to get "17" off my roof—getting bombed at my house and sorta at yrbk. picnic—sunbathing at Tod's Point—swimming in the waves—the pervert on the Ave.—skating and freezing our little butts off—our fabulous singing . . .

Martha's long blond hair was parted in the middle and hung lankly down her shoulders, in the fashion of the times. In the mysterious way young women have, she had begun to blossom. She had shed her baby fat in that final summer, and her physique had acquired a sexy maturity that no boy could help noticing. Boys always swirled around her now. Peter Ziluca had bested Grey Weicker, the senator's son, for her attention, a victory Peter relishes to this day.

A teacher back in California had described her entering a room as "like a ray of sunshine." She loved cats. She collected frogs. And she had the sort of small mischievous streak that makes a girl highly desirable company.

> Me, Helen and Marianne Jones went pool hopping at four pools but nine times totally. It's really fun. First we all get in and swim around and then before we leave we do cannonballs.

Sometimes as she wrote letters up in her bedroom she'd listen to the radio—her parents had given her a Sony AM/FM digital clock radio, with which she was immensely pleased—and comment to Christy on the top forty hits.

> 15. "Please Mr. Please," Olivia Newton John—*I hate her!*
> 10. "Someone Saved My Life Tonight," Elton John—*the one and only!*
> 6. "It's Magic," Pilot—*boo hoo, this reminds me of Tahoe. LONG STORY!*
> 2. "Swear to God," Franky Valley [*sic*]—*this is a shock!*

(Martha makes no remark about the Captain and Tennille's "Love Will Keep Us Together," the number one song, which played incessantly that summer.) Mostly in these letters she writes about the drama surrounding boys and girls.

> Boy, will you die! Karen and I met six of the cutest, foxiest, most adorable guys in the world!!!!!!! (Now I'll keep you in suspense!)

The worst thing about reading Martha's letters is watching the dates—a few of them are dated—slide through the summer, knowing what will happen in the fall. She writes on August 16, her fifteenth and final birthday:

> Guess who decided to waste a 10¢ stamp and write you? I know this is QUEER but it's too late to call you and I'm gonna see you tomorrow and since it's my birthday I decided . . . WHAT THE HELL! WHY NOT! Right now I'm listening to Sha-Na-Na. "Tell me where the answer lies . . ."

Martha and Christy would go to Greenwich High School together in the fall. They would always be friends. In the newspapers she's the murdered girl now, and some have begun the ritual slaying of the dead. Frank Kalan, Christy's father, nearly decked a man at a cocktail party who suggested Martha had tempted fate. Holly Fuchs tells me, "There were these rumors that Martha was some sort of floozy. Well let me tell you something. She was innocent. Very innocent." Peter Ziluca says, "You know, I was her boyfriend. Martha was a virgin. And I never tried to change that." So Christy reads these letters and remembers—remembers who Martha Moxley really was.

Tori Fuchs sits in her bedroom and picks up a pen. In a swift movement of the heart, she fills the blank page before her. She's written a poem entitled "Martha," and it begins like this:

> Life changed for me a week ago
> I learned new feelings,
> And increased old ones.
> I didn't think life could go on.
> But I tried and I made it.
> I thought that's the way she would want it. . . .

Holly Fuchs chances upon the poem later and makes sure it is kept in a safe place. One day Tori will want to know how she felt at this time in her life.

> I still smile for her
> And I still love her
> But deep down inside I cry for her.

And she feels that way today—one marriage, two children, and twenty-two years later.

The Boyfriend

THEY ALWAYS LOOK at the boyfriend.

Peter Ziluca knows this, but his mind is elsewhere now. He's back in the summer of that year, inside a windless blue day at the Indian Harbor Yacht Club. A speck on the water blooms into a sailboat—yes, a Sunfish—and two bodies slide about in the well, tacking and trimming, but they can't scare up the flimsiest wind, so they bump along the gentle swells at an agonizing pace.

Peter squints. *Girls. One blond, the other dark.* They have rounded the Belle Haven peninsula and are inching into Greenwich Harbor. *Ooh, good-looking girls at the Belle Haven Club,* Peter thinks as they float within the shadow of the clubhouse that stands tall on the harbor. "Two girls out of nowhere," Peter remembers, "and no frigging wind, and a bunch of hungry guys waiting on the dock."

The girls draw up and step ashore. Martha and Tori.

Peter, with his long light hair and his headband and his

doleful green eyes, cuts a haphazardly dashing figure. But staring at Martha Moxley, he clams up. Not a word rises from his lips. "She was beautiful. You know, this beautiful blond hair, and she came from California. She was exciting and new. And she came from California. I know I keep saying that. It was love at first sight for me." By the end of the summer of 1975, Peter and Martha were dating.

They always look at the boyfriend. There's a nest of electrodes taped to Peter's hand and a man in a dark suit across the table. Peter is worried. His heart pounds. He is worried that his heart beats so fast the graph will throw up huge spikes, each one indicating deception.

"Did you kill Martha Moxley?" the polygraph examiner asks in a level tone.

"No."

What am I? A suspect? I was at home with my mom. She'll back up my story.

The machine believes him. Suddenly it is all over and they pop him in a squad car and deliver him back to Greenwich. He does not know that the cops are subjecting all manner of people to these tests—even the Moxleys.

But Peter does not want to think about polygraph results at a time like this. All he wants to think about is Martha—and the last time he saw her . . .

They are standing in the student center at Greenwich High School, talking about Halloween plans. It is October 30.

The student center was then the biggest room in the state, an acre square, and around the fringes, by the potted trees, were jugglers and unicyclists, skateboarders and skirmishers. In winter there were indoor snowball fights. You'd see snowballs arc through the smoke haze that hung about the ceiling and explode with a boggling snap upon unsuspecting heads.

The bell rings. School is out. Martha has expected to go to Peter's house to cook him dinner, but the thing is, he really can't keep his eyes open. He must sleep. Martha stares up at him.

Peter thinks maybe he's smoked too much pot; all he can think of now is crawling into bed. Tomorrow, on Halloween, they'll see each other; maybe he'll call her later tonight. Martha pouts.

Besides, Peter is grounded. His father found a burned square of tinfoil in a bathroom, with something rolled up inside. "I had to come clean and tell him what it was, but I sure as hell wasn't going to tell where I got it, and I stuck to my guns and got chewed out."

Peter is a child of affluence. These always seem to be the rebellious ones, those who question their good fortune or suffer the benign neglect that rich kids often suffer. He grew up in a house built among the midnight-thick woods of the back country, a house so huge and fortress-like that everybody called it the Castle. His father was a stockbroker. Worked hard. When after a long day he came home to the Castle, he did not want to hear children's noise, and so the children kept a watchful silence in his presence. They were seen, not heard. When Peter was twelve, his parents divorced, and he and his sisters left the Castle and went to live with their mother in a lovely house on Old Church Road.

Peter and Martha part in the student center. Martha falls into step with the crowd pouring through the great room, and Peter starts out into the cold afternoon, walking home.

Peter wakes when the sky goes dark and his mother appears. They eat dinner. Nancy Ziluca reads her son's thoughts, or thinks she reads them. "You can take the car and go down and see Martha tonight. I know you want to."

One problem. Peter has no driver's license. "My parents decided I wasn't going to get my license till I was seventeen, because I got into too much trouble with my friends; too many times did the police show up at my door. But my mom was very free that way. She knew I could drive, she'd driven with me, and she said, 'You can take the car and go down and see Martha tonight.'"

It's dark and cold outside. Peter hears branches tapping at the window.

"For once in my life I was scared. I was like, 'No, I'll stay home and watch *The French Connection*. It'll be fine. I'll see her tomorrow.'"

In the years to come, Peter will marvel at fate's little zigzags. What if he hadn't gotten so high? What if he hadn't been so tired? What if he had driven down to Belle Haven? "I mean, if only I'd gotten in the car that night and illegally driven down to Belle Haven. Maybe Martha wouldn't be dead. Or maybe I'd be dead too."

The phone rings in the house on Old Church Road. Nancy glances at the clock and rises to answer it. Dorthy Moxley. The movie has ended, and Peter is lying in bed, awake. Nancy comes in the room and explains the situation, but Peter is unconcerned. "I seem to remember not really going to sleep that night. I may have gone to sleep, but for some reason it just feels like I didn't go to sleep. My mind must have been going all night, thinking, *Where could she possibly be?* I probably went to sleep thinking there's no problem, she's over at Sheila's house or something like that. It's no big deal.

"In the morning, though, Mrs. Moxley called to say they hadn't found her. And then all the wild stuff started going around. They found her and she was still alive and she was raped. That was the story that was given to my mother. We were like, Oh my God, oh my God. And then another phone call, and she was dead. DOA. Dead on arrival, that's what I heard. Dead on arrival. We were like, What? You've got to be kidding. There's no way. All the denial and everything else."

Peter walks out the front door in a daze and down the driveway and into the street. He has no feeling, and the air seems made of cotton. A car roars around the curve, slams on the brakes, misses Peter by an inch. He floats across the street and sees a friend emerging from the gym at the Greenwich Country Day School. Peter stares at him and says, "Martha's dead."

"Things went wrong for me when my parents got divorced. That was before Martha, obviously, but not that many years before. So I was going through a really rough time in my life. My father's in one house, my mother's in the other. . . . I was wild growing up, just like everybody else. At one point my mother said, 'You go live with your father.' So I lived in the Castle with my father, and suddenly my sisters were not part of my life. My mother packed up her bags and moved to Santa Fe. My sisters were gone. It was almost like another death. My girlfriend leaves me, and then my mother and sisters leave me. There I am, left in Greenwich."

The Green Leaf Dance

WHEN THE LEAVES ARE all down and the days are dark in the afternoon, Greenwich Academy holds its Green Leaf Dance.

Set elegantly on a hill, the Academy is a day school for girls. The daughters of Greenwich's wealthy go there, and often they are beautiful and have ski tans in winter. Sometimes they grow up to be famous, like Glenn Close or Jane Fonda or Ethel Skakel Kennedy.

Many of Martha Moxley's Belle Haven friends go to Greenwich Academy, and Martha herself planned to attend the Green Leaf Dance with Peter Ziluca. But Martha is two weeks dead. The girls huddle and decide that Peter must go to the Green Leaf Dance anyway. He'll take Sheila McGuire.

Sheila is numb and drifting and broken, but she will go. Even she must admit it's strange. Martha's boyfriend and the girl who chanced upon her corpse. "I mean, if you think about it, he's devastated, I'm devastated, but we both needed to break out of all the pressure we were under.

"It was the most bizarre little fantasy night in the middle of hell. Here we are, mourning the loss of our friend, I'm living with this horrible picture in my head, and I'm going out with my murdered friend's boyfriend to a dance."

They will be a foursome: Sheila and Peter, Jackie Wetenhall and Tyler Pierce—all of them friends of Martha's. Before the dance, Jackie takes Sheila to Alexander's in White Plains, and they pick a dress off a rack—a cheap navy-blue polyester affair. Mrs. Wetenhall lends Sheila a white mink jacket to throw over it. They all climb into Tyler's woody—a wood-paneled jalopy—and rattle off to the Belle Haven Club.

Peter and Tyler rummage through the coatroom and emerge with funny old hats that older gentlemen will soon miss. On the boys they look like mobster hats. Sheila, in her cheap dress and her fur, and the others stumble into the dining room—drunk and high already, and the night is young—and they sit down at a big round table with a view to the lonely lights on the Sound.

Tommy Skakel and his date are sitting there too.

"Now at this table is the last person seen with Martha, who is also a suspect, the girl who found her, and her boyfriend. I remember sitting there thinking, *My head's going to explode. It was the most bizarre encounter of my life.*"

Later the foursome go to other parties, losing themselves in the strangeness of the night, losing themselves in one another, until it is time to head home. "We were drunk, drunk, drunk, drunk, drunk. And stoned. We were just so high," Sheila recalls. But they had momentarily won out over grief.

They're chugging up Dearfield Drive, toward the Post Road, when Jackie asks to drive. Sheila imagines, with no apprehension, Tyler's car pitching down a ravine and all of them discovered, dead, covered in blood and white fur. It is almost funny.

"Sure," Tyler says, and pulls the car to the side of the road.

Jackie can't drive stick. They're all laughing as the car starts rolling backward down the hill.

Then a siren. Flashing lights illuminating the trees.

Their mouths make little O's of surprise, but then they start laughing again, because the car is jerking and backing and rolling down the hill, and Jackie can't even pull it over to the roadside, and they laugh a bit harder.

Someone finds the hand brake, and they all lurch forward. Jackie is sleek and blond and impeccably dressed. She says brightly, "Hello, officers!" as they beam a light into the funny old car.

Sheila freezes. Through the chemical haze comes gravity, the whole wild night rendered in newsprint gray. "I'm thinking, *Oh my God, oh my God, this is going to be in the headlines. 'Boyfriend of slain girl, girl who found her, party with suspect.'*"

The police escort them to their cruiser, whisk them down to

the station, where the kids blink in the harsh fluorescent light and wait for their parents to retrieve them from this mess. Perhaps the police understand the oddness of the situation; perhaps it is merely a different age, the last of small-town Greenwich, where what can be handled discreetly is.

Sheila says, "I woke up the next day thinking, *I can't handle this. Everybody's like, 'Nothing happened.'* It was just so strange. I'm not faulting them. We all needed to escape, and this was our escape. But you can't escape, because the next morning you wake up and it's all right there, the next news article is printed, and fortunately we aren't in it."

Sometime during the winter of Martha's death, the Skakels invite the Moxleys up to Windham, a small town in the Catskill Mountains, for a day of skiing. They go, despite the whispers of the Skakels' possible involvement in Martha's death. After all, Rush Skakel has been a good friend, proposing the Moxleys for membership in both the Belle Haven Club and the University Club in New York.

"Initially, I wanted to rule them out," John Moxley says. "I said it couldn't have been anyone there. But I remember my parents didn't really want to go up to Windham, and I was lobbying to stay the whole weekend, have a good time with them and go skiing. After spending the first half day with them, I was like, 'Let's get the hell out of here.'

"I didn't know them before that. I found out that I didn't like them. They were cocky and seemed to feel entitled to different treatment."

*   *   *

Sheila is asleep in her room. The night is dark. The wind bears down on the house, which creaks and groans.

She drifts off each night haunted by visions. Somewhere out there, beneath roots or earth or water, there is a missing piece of a golf club. The police have dived in the Sound, emptied pools and ponds.

It has vanished. But it is out there.

Crash! Glass shatters. A thing thump-thumps onto the floor. Sheila flies from the bed. The missing piece, with a note tied to it: "You're next." Next time the nightmare haunts her, the note reads "Watch your step." The time after that, "I'm watching you."

Sheila opens her eyes. Moonlight shines through the branches of the maples. The house creaks and groans in the wind.

Chapter Five

A Northern Detour

OFF THE GREENWICH COAST, near the mouth of Cos Cob Harbor, lies a small protrusion of rock and scrub called Bluff Island. Bootleggers docked their schooners there during Prohibition and loaded crates of rum and whiskey into launches that drifted ashore silently, in darkness, and landed in coves sheltered by overhanging trees.

On Bluff Island are a few triangular holes drilled into the rock with primitive tools. The sides of the triangles bow out slightly—making a shape that is meaningful to certain archaeologists—and the holes are filled with dirt and weeds. Legend holds that Norse explorers drilled them nearly a thousand years ago. They would moor their boats out away from the mainland to keep from running aground and damaging their hulls. They'd slip iron rods into the holes and tie up to a ring at the top of each rod. This system also allowed for a swift departure should hostile redmen open fire with their flint arrows.

The legend: A thousand years ago, Erik the Red left Norway "because of some killings." Erik sailed to Iceland, married, settled in a temperate valley of the south, and fathered two sons. After more killings—apparently the manner in which Erik mended quarrels—he was branded an outlaw and banished, his enemies giving chase.

He sailed to the frozen wastes of Greenland. Norwegians had sighted this vast pitiless land some eighty years before, but nobody had dared to land until the year 978, and those adventurers sorely regretted it. "A shipload of prospective colonists landed on the bitterly inhospitable east coast and spent an appalling winter snowed up there," Magnus Magnusson and Herman Palsson write in their introduction to the *Vinland Sagas*. "Trouble broke out among the members of the expedition, culminating in murder, after which the survivors returned to Iceland to face a savage vengeance."

Erik the Red came to Greenland three years later, in 981, and he came to stay. Wisely he sailed round the tip of Greenland—Cape Farewell—and put into shore among the sheltering fjords of the west coast.

A year or so after that, a Norwegian merchant who had set out to find his father in Erik's brave new colony overshot Cape Farewell and blew into unknown waters. Bjarni Herjolfsson and his crew spent many days drifting through an impenetrable fog; when it lifted and they saw the sun again, they spied land. They went in close and gazed at the low wooded hills, and then they sailed back out to sea, leaving this new world behind, untouched.

Bjarni told the Greenlanders of the distant lands he had seen, out on the very edge of the sea, and the Greenlanders chided him for his incuriousness: How could he make such discoveries and fail to set foot upon them?

Leif the Lucky, a son of Erik the Red, purchased from Bjarni the ship that had borne him to the unknown lands and, enlisting a crew of thirty-five, set off across the western sea. This was in the year 1001.

They glided into a shallow sound laden with sandbars and ran ashore "at a place where a river flowed out of a lake." Some historians, citing archaeological evidence, believe this to be Follins Pond on Cape Cod, near Yarmouth. Here Leif Eriksson and his crew decided to build houses and spend the winter. The winter proved gentle; there was neither snow nor frost, and the grass scarcely withered. Leif named this good country Vinland—wineland or vineland. Clues in the sagas suggest that Vinland lay between latitudes 50 and 40, or between the Gulf of Saint Lawrence and New Jersey, though the descriptions of sand beaches and wild grapes—and the lenient winter—place it firmly in New England, south of Maine.

During the twentieth century, some archaeologists debunked the legend as outrageous, claiming the Norse left no solid evidence of having set foot on North America. The more heretical archaeologists still believe that the Norse explored not only the East Coast but also the Northwestern Plains, where mooring stones were found over a vast area—all at the same height above the sea. This suggests that as recently as a thousand years ago, the Great Lakes extended across Minnesota and the Dakotas.

Nobody agrees about history.

If the Bluff Island mooring stones are authentic—if Norsemen were the first travelers to touch Greenwich shores—no further evidence was left. Maybe the Norse were ousted by the redmen.

Or maybe Vinland was too far from the known Norse world to attract a sufficient number of colonists.

Whatever case, the weather turned hostile early in the fifteenth century. The seas grew perilous. The last boat from Greenland to Europe was believed to have left the ice-riddled North Atlantic around 1410. Norse who stayed behind in Greenland grew puny from exposure and malnutrition and had to fend off Eskimos who had retreated from the Arctic Circle with the deterioration in the climate. The colony had died off completely by the time Columbus was sluicing through the balmy tropics, acquainting himself with the natives there.

Killings. They sent men away to Iceland (Ingolf Arnarsson, who left Norway after "a killing," was the first settler) and then to Greenland—a westward momentum that probably led to the pre-Columbian discovery of New England, all the way down to Greenwich. The Norse believed in curses and spells, premonitions and hauntings. Their sagas are rife with corpses suddenly sitting up on their biers and telling the fortunes of their loved ones, as a kind of atonement for sins committed in life.

Folk legends around the world tell of the restless dead, of spirits doomed to walk the night like Jacob Marley in his shackles and chains. The living are haunted by the dead—in visions and in memories, in bones and in earth—and there's nothing the living can do about it. Nothing save to placate ghosts that inhabit the air.

To say the Norse in Vinland declined to settle on such fertile ground because of a curse would be a marvelous conceit. And yet, six centuries later, a New England town's earliest history would be darkened by killings, beginning with the murder of that town's first white settler, three hundred thirty-two years before the murder of Martha Moxley.

That man's killer fled his makeshift prison during the night and vanished into the Greenwich woods. Thus did fumbling justice set its precedent; thus did the strange charm protecting murderers first cast its spell.

Wretches and Savages

IN THE SPRING of 1640, a red-bearded rogue named Daniel Patrick hove ashore on the stretch of sand where the people of Greenwich now do their beaching.

The proud and vicious Captain Patrick—so described by colonial statesman John Winthrop—would say that he quit the flock at Watertown, Massachusetts, because of its rigid Puritan code. Had the Watertown goodmen cast a blind eye to lechery, however, perhaps Captain Patrick would have been less inclined to flee.

This is from the written testimony of one Elizabeth Sturgis, who thrice rebuffed the captain's entreaties:

> I was sent to Captain Patrick's to help his wife and having business in the cellar he came down presently after me and took me about the middle and would kiss me and put his hand into my bosom at which I was much amazed. . . . After I being married . . . he was at me to meet him in the evening in the Way and he would further labor to convince me of his love to me but with much ado I got away and presently made my father and all the house acquainted with it and durst not go into the Way that night for fear.

John Winthrop himself informs us: "He had a wife of his own, a good Dutch woman and comely, yet he despised her and followed after other women. And perceiving that he was discovered, and that such evil courses would not be endured here, and being withal of vain and unsettled disposition, he went from us."

And so Captain Patrick settled in the woods among the other savages. Soon after, a second family of Watertown exiles joined the Patricks in their wilderness outpost. Robert Feake, son of a London goldsmith, and his wife, Elizabeth, left the Massachusetts Bay Colony for unknown reasons in the summer of 1640. Those reasons could well have concerned Elizabeth, who possessed a strength and originality of spirit almost unknown to women of that age.

The Feakes sailed southward along the coast until they reached a place just beyond range of Puritan influence. They reached Greenwich. It might have been, in those years when Satan pursued shiploads of Puritans across the ocean and haunted them lustily on their arrival in New England, that Elizabeth's strongheaded ways were taken for devil's work. Indeed, Anya Seton, who reconstructed Elizabeth's scandalous life in her popular 1958 novel, *The Winthrop Woman*, has her hastening out of Watertown under suspicion of witchcraft. Yet there is no surviving record of any such dramatic occurrence.

The goodmen and goodwives of Elizabeth's world may have seen unholy significance in the fate of her husbands. The first, Henry Winthrop, a son of John, drowned in a creek in Salem in 1630, a day or two after completing a perilous Atlantic crossing. Robert Feake suffered the beginnings of a mental collapse in Watertown, which would, in Greenwich, devour the remains of his sanity. The third husband, William

Hallett, had been Elizabeth's partner in adultery while Feake mumbled at shadows.

And so blessed Greenwich was founded by a lecher, a lunatic, and an adulteress.

On July 18, 1640, the Patricks and the Feakes paid the Indians twenty-five coats for land that is now Old Greenwich, the sandy spit that became Greenwich Point being "ye peticaler perchase of Elizabeth Feake." Seton, in grand bodice-ripping style, has Elizabeth sneaking off to the beach for a skinny-dip and the dashing Hallett, returned from the Indies with a swarthy glow, spying from a distance: "she lay there on her green gown, naked, beautiful, and defenseless as a child."

For a while, Greenwich kept up its reputation as a refuge for free spirits. Joyously, the settlement had no church and thus was the only town in New England not arrayed around the rock of religion. This irregular state of affairs may have made Greenwich impervious to witch hunts, which would plague the pious towns of the Connecticut River valley before the decade was over and would strike as close as Fairfield by 1653.

The Massachusetts Bay towns live in our minds as the hub of the witch craze, but Connecticut executed more witches. The Connecticut and New Haven colonies formally outlawed witchcraft in 1642: "If any man or woman be a witch . . . they shall be put to death." The same year, Greenwich's founders placed their freewheeling little village under protection of the Dutch, whose New World venture was not spiritual, but commercial.

Yet danger loomed. The Dutch, who had settled at New Amsterdam, on the southern tip of Manhattan Island, fell into the bad habit of swindling and murdering the local Indians. One particularly vile massacre occurred after these Mohegans had sought their protection from the Mohawks, a powerful tribe moving south from the inland hills to exact "tributes" from lesser tribes.

Feigning hospitality, the Dutch slaughtered the Mohegans. An eyewitness named David de Vries stayed that night at the house of Willem Kieft, the reviled director general of New Netherlands. De Vries's chilling account:

> At midnight I heard loud shrieks, and went out on the parapet of the fort. . . . I saw nothing but the flashing of guns. I heard no more cries of the Indians: they had been butchered in their sleep.
>
> The horrors of this night cause one's flesh to creep. Sucklings were torn from their mothers' breasts, butchered before their parents' eyes, and their mangled limbs thrown quivering into the river or the flames. Babes were hacked to pieces while fastened on their little boards—their primitive cradles! Others were thrown alive into the river, and when their parents instinctively rushed in to save them, the cruel soldiers prevented their landing, and both parents and offspring were sunk into a watery grave. . . . Those who escaped and next morning begged for shelter, were killed in cold blood, or thrown into the river. Some came running to us from the country, having both hands cut off; some lost both legs and arms; some were supporting their entrails with their hands, while some were mangled in other horrid ways, too horrid to be conceived.

The Indians rose up in ferocious solidarity all along the coast. The region had turned into a killing ground. Anne Hutchinson, whom the Bay colonies had banished for heresy, was hacked to death in the wilderness west of the current Greenwich border, along with sixteen of her household. (Some historians put her death in the Greenwich back country, but the raid actually seems to have taken place in neighboring Westchester County.)

The farmers and oystermen of the town recoiled in fright. It was then that Captain Patrick and Elizabeth Feake set sail for New Amsterdam, where they appealed to the Dutch for protection from "these treacherous and villainous Indians, of whom we have seen so many sorrowful examples enough." They signed a paper declaring their submission to Dutch rule. (All of this may have been something of a charade. The Feakes and the Patricks were friendly with the Indians they knew; the Puritans were the threat—not to their lives, but to their lifestyle. After the Indian troubles died down, Greenwich clung to the Dutch as long as they could.)

Whatever his faults, Captain Patrick was a brave and savvy warrior who had been a soldier of the Prince's Guard in Holland and a defender of the fort at Boston. Lately he had distinguished himself in the bloody Pequot War of 1637. Still, Patrick had lived peaceably among these Greenwich Indians. He was nothing like the Dutch, who plied the Indians with firewater and made off with their pelts. It was the greed-driven Dutch, more plentiful in these outlands, that the Indians despised.

One day Captain Patrick and two companions went out walking in the woods in search of game. They came upon the intrepid Indian chief Mayn Mayano. The chief drew his bow, howled out menacingly, and let fly two arrows as he rushed through the trees. The companions fell dead. Captain Patrick lifted his musket and gunned down the chief.

The sachem and the captain had once been something like soul mates, proud warriors squeezed between cultures; now the stage was set for slaughter.

A Wicked Course

TO QUELL the Indians and their righteous blood lust, Willem Kieft sent a detachment of Dutch and English troops to exterminate the Indian population at Greenwich in the winter of 1643.

Landing on the beach at Greenwich Point, the soldiers received directions to the Indian camp, now swollen to nearly a thousand, from Captain Patrick. He sent an Indian guide with them.

Snow clouds lowered to the tops of the trees, and the one hundred twenty men turned aimless circles in the iron-dark woods. Exhausted and freezing, the troops retreated to the coast.

The next day, a Sunday, they went to Patrick's house, where they found the captain entertaining some Indians and "were much trobled." A Dutch soldier cried treachery, accusing Captain Patrick of "leading them amiss the whole night." The famously intolerant captain listened without saying a word; probably he was dumbstruck. A second soldier, Hans Frederick, called him a liar.

This was more than Patrick could brook. He stood up and spat in Frederick's face. Then he turned away. The humiliated soldier cocked his pistol and fired at the back of Patrick's skull, "so that he fell down dead and never spake," wrote John Winthrop, noting with Puritan logic that this violent end, "from the hand where he sought protection," was "the fruit of his wicked course."

Winthrop added a final line: "The murderer escaped out of custody."

*　　*　　*

The Dutch remained bent on the slaughter of the Indians. One day in February of 1644, the English captain John Underhill and Ensign Henry Van Dyck, with one hundred thirty Dutch and English soldiers in three boats, put out from New Amsterdam and sailed up the Sound.

They landed at Greenwich Point in a heavy snowstorm and disembarked on the beach, watching the snow tumble thickly into the small black waves. The attack would have to wait. The snow fell all night and all the next day and into that night. Finally the storm swirled out to sea, and the troops set off in the woods.

They pushed through deep snow until the blue sky dimmed to black and a bright moon rose above the trees. They drew up to the Mianus River and sat down to rest for a couple of hours. At ten o'clock they rose again and sloshed through the shallow black water where the river narrowed. The moon lit the new-fallen snow on the far bank as the troops trudged up through the trees. They stopped on a low ridge, crouched, and gazed at small fires burning in the Indian village.

Then they stole down through the woods, broke in two detachments, and closed around the braves. The Indians drew back to a wooded rise and sent arrows in the air, but musket fire blasted through the trees and left the Indians bleeding in the snow. The troops, with their broadswords drawn, drove the remaining braves back to the village of bark huts, where the Indian women and children huddled.

The braves shot arrows from small eyelets in the huts. Underhill, recalling the method of destruction that he and John Mason had used on the Pequots, ordered the village set afire. The soldiers lit firebrands and hurled them at the huts, which burst into flames, burning alive the inhabitants of the village. "What was most wonderful is that among this vast collection of men, women and children, not one was heard to cry or scream," wrote a Dutch officer who was there.

Daniel Mead, a nineteenth-century Greenwich historian, offers a more imaginative version:

> Roasted and tortured to agony by the fire, [the Indians] darted out here and there from the flames only to be brought to the ground by the unerring aim of the soldiery. . . . Finally their horrid moans and cries were hushed, and the hissing of the boiling pools of blood died away, leaving hundreds of bodies on the blood-stained snow.

Five hundred to a thousand Indians, most of them women and children, perished in the bloodbath; eight are said to have escaped, twelve taken prisoner and later sold as slaves.

Not one soldier was killed, and only fifteen were wounded. Underhill's men spent the night on the plain, sleeping around dozens of bonfires. In the morning they woke to find the corpses strewn about the smoky ruin of the village, and they heaped the bodies into mounds and covered them with ashes and snow and then began a slow march to the settlement on the coast. The next day they sailed back to New Amsterdam, triumphant, and Director General Kieft proclaimed a day of public thanksgiving. He was rid of the Indian scourge at last.

The massacre's presence in historical records is a mere smudge. As Seton wrote in her preface to *The Winthrop Woman*, "I wish to say here that the virtually unknown 'Strickland Plains' massacre of the Siwanoy Indians by white men . . . seems to have been as shameful and devastating as any massacre—on either side—in our entire American history."

In time nature quilted the Indian mounds with dirt and

leaves. Then the mounds were more or less forgotten. Around 1800, Joseph Sackett, who owned a farmstead on Strickland Plains, went out into the fields with a workman to dig holes for storing potatoes through the winter. The workman came upon a heap of disintegrating bones and asked what to do. Sackett replied, "Throw in the potatoes anyway. These are only Injun bones. Injun bones won't hurt 'em."

In the 1850s Daniel Mead, the historian, condemned the carelessness of those who lived and worked on the burial ground. "Not only is the place neglected, but absolutely is being demolished by the penny grinders who want dirt to fill the docks. . . . It should have been fenced long ago, and protected from men who will take dirt from dead men's bones."

Today no expert can point out the precise location of the mounds, but this is perhaps a good thing. Spread across Strickland Plains now is the neighborhood of Cos Cob—one of the most populous in Greenwich.

When the smoke of all the Indian troubles had cleared, Willem Kieft was sent back to Holland in disgrace (he drowned in a shipwreck en route—another providential moment), and the Dutch sent a strict Calvinist, Peter Stuyvesant, in his stead.

Taking stock of the Greenwich situation, Stuyvesant inquired about the Feake-Hallett arrangement. Did they farm together? Live together? *Bed* together? Well, they did all of these, and what's more, she was pregnant with his child.

The townspeople had embraced the industrious Hallett as one of their own—especially since Robert Feake had sailed back to Mother England (where the House of Commons pardoned him for some unstated, and perhaps imagined, crime) and had been incapable of managing his estate anyway.

Stuyvesant was livid. In March of 1648 he sent a boat up the Sound with a decree. "Whereas Elizabeth Feake has for adultery been legally separated from her former husband, Mr. Feake, before our arrival, by the preceding director-general and council, and since that time continued to cohabit and keep company with her cope-mate and adulterer in a carnal manner . . . ," Stuyvesant began, and proceeded to order that Elizabeth's children be put under the care of a curator. The Dutch would permit the Feakes to stay in Greenwich ("though deserving of much severer castigation") so long as Hallett was "banished out of this jurisdiction."

The lovers had no choice. They fled north, into the house of the powerful Winthrops.

But Greenwich kept its sovereign aura in bloom. And also its knack for depravity. Benjamin Trumbull wrote in his 1797 *History of Connecticut*:

> The inhabitants of Greenwich were under little government, and demeaned themselves in a lawless manner. They admitted drunkenness among themselves and the Indians, by reason of which damages were done to themselves and to the towns in the vicinity; and the public peace was disturbed. They received children and servants who fled from the correction of their masters, and unlawfully joined persons in wedlock.

Puritans across the brook, in pious Stamford, brayed and howled. But Greenwich insolently thumbed its nose at the Puritan establishment—long after the lecher was killed, the lunatic swept away by his demons, and the adulteress run out of town.

The insolence was a mistake. When the Dutch position in the New World went on the wane—thanks chiefly to Kieft's costly policies—the goodmen of Stamford could safely tattle to the magistrates in New Haven. Greenwich folk were a bunch of godless reprobates, they crabbed, and where God did not rule, the devil surely did.

The magistrates were aghast. Under threat of force, Greenwichites were commanded to surrender their precious autonomy and "fall in" with Stamford. Some Greenwichites, seeing this as a fate worse than a hundred Sabbaths spent in God's house, advised military action of their own. But the tiny town could have mustered only the saddest of armies, heavier on pitchforks than muskets.

They decided to live.

The Curse Continues

IN NOVEMBER 1899, in a remote wooden stretch of Greenwich back country, Sarah King, a printer's wife, was bludgeoned to death.

Charles Cross, the Kings' servant boy, found the sixty-year-old woman lying in her bed, head crushed and drenched with blood. Cross claimed to have stepped out into the night air and made the discovery upon his return; perhaps, he ventured, Mrs. King had startled a thief who had concealed himself in the house: the upstairs rooms had been ransacked. When the servant saw what had happened, he said, he ran through the night woods to find help.

Cross was seventeen and had come from the New York slums, but he possessed what the newspaper called "a wonderful bearing." He denied any role in the killing, and many were inclined to believe him. A county detective did not. Aside from Sarah, Cross had been the only one home; Freeman King, the printer, spent his workweeks down in the city. How could the boy have completely missed such a great disturbance?

All at once Cross broke down and confessed. As the *Greenwich Graphic* rendered it:

> He told how an uncontrollable passion forced him to take advantage of the woman's loneliness; how he secreted himself in her room and sprang upon her; how she resisted him when he knocked her down with a blow; how he then seized her gray hairs with both hands and beat her head against the floor until the poor old woman sank into insensibility. Then he raised the unconscious form and placed it upon the bed.

The last paragraph of this century-old news story strikes an eerie chord:

> The people of the northern section of our town breathed a sigh of relief when they learned that the murderer was in custody. Our neighbor Stamford seems to have more success in hunting down such assassins than Greenwich.

An awareness of unavenged murder had already begun to form.

Today murder in Greenwich is rare. It was more common before World War II, when the town was struggling against a dramatic change in its nature. Up until the late 1800s, Greenwich was composed almost entirely of farmers, merchants, and oystermen of Dutch and English stock. Around the turn of the century, quite suddenly, there evolved a rigid caste system, with captains of industry on the top rung and the Italian immigrants who built their palaces on the bottom rung—even below the Irish Catholics who staffed the palaces and chauffeured the lords and ladies.

Most local murder cases from that era—at least those reported in the paper—involved temperamental immigrants, like the following, from the May 19, 1906, edition of the *Greenwich Graphic*:

> Because Patrick Finnegan, the foreman for J. T. Weir, objected to having an Italian named Dominic Cammani, dump a load of rock on some water pipes, breaking them, the Italian fired a shot from a revolver, point blank at the heart of his foreman, killing him almost instantly last Wednesday forenoon at about 11 o'clock.

Cammani, revolver in one hand and hat in the other, fled up Riversville Road and was believed to have "laid behind a rock all day." When the medical examiner, Dr. L. P. Jones, arrived at the scene—where a mansion was under construction—he tried to "find out from several Italians what they knew about the trouble, but without avail, for all claimed to have been in a position not to have seen the murder." There is no record of Cammani ever being caught.

The belief that local authorities have never solved a murder is technically untrue. Several killers confessed, as Charles Cross did; in other cases the identity of the murderer was self-evident. Almost every homicide requiring real sleuthing, however, did indeed end in mystery. Like the George Lockwood matter. In the 1870s Greenwich oystermen were a prosperous lot, selling their harvests to the finest New York restaurants. But thieves also worked the oyster beds. George

Lockwood was a strapping man with a big brown mustache who lived alone on a little island in Cos Cob Harbor. The oystermen hired him to scout their beds under cover of darkness.

At dusk on November 18, 1874, Lockwood pushed off in his round-bottom boat into a cold, wind-lashed Sound. Night settled on him as he rowed along the coastline. Then he went missing. The timing hinted at malice: five days after his disappearance, Lockwood was supposed to have testified in court against some alleged oyster thieves, but the proceeding had to be adjourned when he failed to show.

On the sixth day, John Merritt went out oystering. On his way back into port, he decided to check some fish traps he had set in Indian Harbor. As Merritt drifted into shore, he saw a body lying on a mudflat. He went in close and inspected it. There was a deep gash beneath the left ear, which had severed an artery. The skin on the face and scalp seemed to have been scalded off. But undertaker Jonas Meade recognized the clothing and also the deep cleft in the chin: they belonged to George Lockwood.

Lockwood's boat was found adrift in the Sound off the coast of Northport, Long Island, and Lockwood's father towed her back to Greenwich. There was no indication of an on-board struggle; not the slightest clue ever came to light.

In May 1889 an old post office clerk in the back country, Shadrack Close, was murdered as he closed up shop for the night. His wife woke early the next morning and in her nightgown walked the few feet to the post office. She found her husband sprawled on the front porch, his head badly beaten. An iron fence rail, bloodied at the tip, lay at Close's side.

Since the crime occurred at a post office—federal property—the Pinkerton detectives were called in, but they turned up no suspects; even the motive seemed cloudy. Ten dollars was discovered missing from the cash drawer. Missing too was a business ledger. But Close's wallet was untouched. Here again was a murder by a head wound—a weird continuum that started with Daniel Patrick in 1643 and ran through Martha Moxley in 1975.

In September of 1931 a Greenwich inventor named Ben Collings, along with his wife and young daughter, was spending the night aboard his forty-foot cruiser, *Penguin*. Collings anchored off Price's Point, near Northport, Long Island, and then Lillian Collings put the girl to bed. The Collingses chatted for a while in the salt breeze, and then Lillian too retired belowdecks.

At about 10:30 P.M. she heard the muffled voices of two other men. She caught snippets of conversation: "We have a wounded man in our canoe . . . we have to get him to a hospital in West Norwalk. . . ." She heard her husband decline to take up anchor: *Penguin* had no running lights and could not be navigated at night. The voices grew heated. "I'll shoot you . . . ," somebody said. Then came the sound of scuffling and breaking glass and a thump on the deck. "Don't tie him too tight. . . ."

Then a splash.

The cabin locked from the outside, and Lillian had no key. She listened helplessly as the strangers bound her husband and tossed him into the Sound. Then the cabin door opened, and two figures in the dark guided Lillian—without the girl—to the canoe. There was no sign of a wounded man. The men paddled into Oyster Bay and dumped Lillian in a motorboat called *Bo Peep*. She fainted in the boat and did not wake until daylight. The killers had cut *Penguin*'s anchor, and later the bewildered little girl was found aboard the wandering yacht.

Seven days after the attack, Ben Collings's body washed

ashore below the mansions of Cold Spring Harbor. His skull was badly broken—the coroner counted eight distinct wounds—and his arms and legs had deep bruises from the binding cord. Investigators found a shattered milk bottle aboard *Penguin*. There was blood on the glass fragments.

The story lingered for two weeks on the front page of the *New York Times*. Thirty-five New York City detectives were put on the case, and they combed the shore for fifty miles in search of clues. Briefly Lillian Collings herself fell under suspicion, but the widow's account held under rigorous questioning. And the detectives found evidence to corroborate her story—the canoe and some bloody clothes—but they never found the killers.

Before the Moxley case, there had been one other known instance of murder in Belle Haven. It happened in the spring of 1931—same year as the Collings murder—at the residence of Edwin H. Baker on Broad Road, one block east of Walsh Lane.

Otto and Lucie Vogel, a domestic couple who lived on the third floor of the brick Georgian mansion, were beaten to death with a furnace stoker and then set afire. FOUND MURDERED IN BELLE HAVEN HOME, read the headline across the June 2 edition of the *Graphic*. "Chauffeur and Maid Found with Bashed in Skulls."

Edwin Baker was a produce broker whose fortune had gone down in the crash of 1929. He and his wife were spending the long Memorial Day weekend with friends at the Montclair Country Club in New Jersey. The Vogels were alone on May 31. The following afternoon Edward Snell and Chester Lynch were repairing an awning when they noticed wisps of smoke rising from the Bakers' attic window. Firemen found the bodies—each struck multiple times—partially burned beneath a feather mattress. The killer had probably hoped to burn down the house, but feathers do not burn well, and the fire smoldered and then expired. Sometime in the early-morning hours of June 1, a person unknown stole up the stairs with a three-foot furnace stoker. "The heads of the Vogels were horribly mangled," the *Graphic* noted.

Police found the stoker between the bodies. Suede gloves and a pair of bloody shoes lay nearby. Hours later, Baker's missing Cadillac turned up on 136th Street in Harlem.

Greenwich Police Chief Patrick Flanagan quickly seized on Henri Paul Richards, a volatile Frenchman who lived with his wife in Bayonne, New Jersey. Richards had recently worked as the Bakers' chauffeur. Edwin Baker told Chief Flanagan that Richards had a bad temper and was prone to making "scenes." Then one day Richards quit, boasting that he would sail home to France to receive the medal of the Legion of Honor for his valor in the Great War. But he never went; his wife had refused to leave America. By the time Richards asked for his old job back, Baker had already given it to Otto Vogel.

The police developed a weak case. Richards had lied to them about spending the day of the murders in Newark, at the house of his sister. And employees at the Pickwick Theatre in Greenwich swore they had spotted him at that night's show—*Dishonored*, starring Marlene Dietrich—which the Vogels had also gone to see. But there was nothing more. Not even a fingerprint on the Cadillac. The day after Governor Wilbur Cross refused to sign extradition papers, Richards and his wife boarded a boat for France.

* * *

The murder of Grover Hart, in the summer of 1949, was the last Greenwich murder mystery before the Moxley case. Early on the morning of July 23, a "scar-faced ex-convict" named Frank Smith broke into the Indian Harbor Yacht Club and shot the night watchman dead.

Grover Hart had assumed the watchman job just three days earlier. A stumpy, solid man of sixty-eight, he had spent most of his working life at the American Felt Company, on the Byram River, and as a chauffeur for millionaire Dan Topping, an owner of the New York Yankees. Now in semiretirement, Hart had agreed to work at Indian Harbor until the regular night watchman recovered from an illness.

Just after 2 A.M., Hart heard a ruckus coming from the dining room. He walked up a flight of stairs, into the kitchen, and through a set of swinging doors.

"Who's there?" he called, and spied a crouching man, his face obscured by a colored handkerchief.

Hart did not see the burglar's Colt .22. Smith cursed and fired five shots; three of them hit Hart, in the shoulder, arm, and kidney. Smith ran off with his loot—trinkets from the lost-and-found box—and jumped into a waiting Cadillac.

Hart lay on his back, propped against the doors. His moaning awoke the club's assistant manager, who scrambled to his aid. Hart was able to tell police what had transpired and give a description of the "fresh, shaggy-haired man" who shot him. A dozen blood transfusions and forty hours later, Hart died.

The twenty-five-year-old Smith, who lived in the nearby town of Norwalk, was racing through a three-week crime spree. The week before, he'd broken into another club in Greenwich, Innis Arden, and stolen a box of cigars. The week before that, he'd held up a car full of party guests on their way to opera singer Marian Anderson's house in Danbury. Now police hoped to catch him in what they called "a nationwide dragnet."

Smith abandoned his stolen Cadillac in Brewster, New York, and began roaming the rural towns north of Greenwich. He kept to the woods. Four days after the shooting, he broke into the empty home of Ernest Krehbiel, in Wilton, Connecticut, forty minutes away from Greenwich. Instead of striking and fleeing, Smith collapsed in bed, Krehbiel's shotgun at his side, and let himself fall into a heavy sleep. He awoke next morning to the sound of the Krehbiel family car crunching up the gravel driveway.

As the Krehbiels bumped through the back door with their suitcases, Smith darted out the front. Ernest Krehbiel immediately dialed the police. Just after midnight, state police were rattling along Reservoir Road, a dirt lane that cut through the woods. They careened around a curve, to find the startled Smith gawking into their headlights.

Smith made no attempt to flee. He was carrying a kitchen pot in his hand and a packet of hair dye in his pocket. He'd planned to turn his blond hair red, then black. Smith was convicted of murder and sentenced to die in the electric chair. In 1954, after numerous stays, his sentence was commuted to life in prison.

But the Greenwich Curse was Smith's good fortune. In May of 1967, shortly after being transferred to the minimum security prison farm at Enfield, Smith drove a work truck out of the prison yard and sputtered off into the Connecticut countryside. He was last seen in Bridgeport, parking a stolen car behind a funeral parlor. Dressed in prison duds, he emerged from the car, walked away, and was never seen again.

Chapter Six

A Funeral

IN SEPTEMBER of 1966 my father drove me downtown to see a funeral at Saint Mary's Church. Black limousines hummed down Greenwich Avenue and parked three deep in front of the great stone church. There was no sound, save the scraping of fine leather shoes against the broad stone steps leading into St. Mary's.

The man in the casket—what remained of him—was George Skakel, Jr., Rushton's and Ethel Kennedy's older brother. He had been killed in a plane crash in Idaho. The tiny Cessna he and his party of elk hunters had boarded careened into a canyon wall, then fell like a tapped-off cigarette ash to the floor of Crooked Creek Canyon.

My father wrote his observations of the funeral in a column for *Greenwich Time*:

One man nudged a friend and nodded toward the street, where Ted Kennedy was getting out of a limousine with his wife. "There's Teddy," someone said, and no one spoke during the time it took Ted Kennedy to walk slowly across the street and up the steps, without using a cane. [Kennedy had survived a plane crash two years before. He had broken his back.]

Other cars came around the corner of Lewis Street and pulled up in front of the rectory. "There he is," a tall man said with finality. And there he was—Robert Kennedy, looking tan and fit, but perhaps older and tireder than one might have expected. He was an honorary pall-bearer and he wore gray gloves like the others. He took his place in line. A woman reached out and placed her hand on his back. He didn't move. She turned to her companion with a delighted smile and looked at her hand. Twenty feet away, another woman softly said, "Isn't that awful?" A few moments later two men came and stood behind Kennedy.

Later, as they all came out of the church, a man pointed to the Kennedy brothers and said to a boy with him, "There goes a future president." He did not say which one he meant.

Neither the man—my father—nor the boy—me—nor anybody else in attendance that day could have foretold the tragic events to come. Nobody could have foretold, either, that a curly-haired little boy among the mourners—a nephew of both Bobby Kennedy and the deceased—would be hounded all his adult life on the suspicion of murder.

As for the deceased, George Skakel, Jr.—he was a devil. A darkly handsome man with broad shoulders and a high, strong forehead, he had lived an unruly but very full forty-four years. He was an adventurer, a prankster, an adulterer, a charming rogue, a madman in headlong pursuit of death.

Once, he drove a motor scooter up the grand stairway of the

Hotel Plaza Athénée in Paris, clad only in underwear. Another time, he toppled from a tower of chairs while showing friends how to mount an elephant, and broke his leg badly. After a day of hunting wild horses in Utah, he got his calf sliced open when tossing knives with a Ute Indian. In Aspen, he drove his car up a sidewalk and then, defying a policeman who tried to arrest him, said, "Somebody better be ready to die."

He pawed and kissed the actress Kim Novak at John F. Kennedy's inaugural festivities, drawing the ire of Bobby Kennedy, soon to be attorney general. But George would not be told what to do. Least of all by the Kennedys. His sister Ethel had married Bobby in 1950. But even so.

The mourners who knew George best believed that his character was his fate. They had imagined, some of them, that he might die recklessly. It is impossible to know what instructions he may have given his pilot that day in Idaho. But Jerry Oppenheimer, who wrote a detailed history of the Skakel family, called *The Other Mrs. Kennedy*, quoted one of the elk hunters who watched George go down. Skakel, the hunter maintained, wore "that terrible grin he'd get on his face when he was looking down the muzzle of a police revolver."

George may have entertained death by living so high. But there was also the matter of the family curse.

The Skakel fortune had started in the Midwest. With two friends, George Skakel, Sr., had founded the Great Lakes Coal & Coke Company in 1919. He moved the family east in the 1930s, and they alighted in Greenwich in 1934.

The town was close enough to New York City to see the grand spires shimmering in the smog—Skakel had installed Great Lakes Coal & Coke in the most visible of them, the Empire State Building—but far enough away to feel removed to the country and its life-giving air. A critical third element, no state income tax, made the town an ideal habitat for rich folk.

The Great Depression quietly ravaged Greenwich. Club memberships sagged, great estates were put up for sale, the servants who staffed them dispersed, and the era of East Coast palace building came to an abrupt end.

But airplane builders flourished. Lindbergh and Earhart had lodged flight firmly in the public mind, and now the common people of the United States themselves stood on the brink of flight. Companies that supplied aluminum to aircraft manufacturers—chiefly Alcoa and Reynolds Aluminum—battled hard for dominance of the flight industry.

A short man with a thickening middle and little formal education, George Skakel, Sr., was a hustler and a visionary. Business, not family, was his life's passion. Even the hunting and golf outings—ostensibly his recreation—were designed to woo clients, as were the endless parties that filled the cavernous rooms of his Greenwich mansion with drink-sodden laughter.

His success was built upon piles of dusty coke. Coke is a solid by-product of gasoline refinement, and in the twenties and thirties, big oil companies stockpiled it in heaping gray yards, and when the yards filled they dumped it in rivers. It was worthless. An annoyance. George Skakel took the coke off their hands and paid them for it besides. Then he secured a loan from Continental Bank of Chicago to build a refinery. He distilled the dirty stuff into clean carbon, an element that is critical to the manufacture of . . . aluminum.

Coke worthless? It was gold. And George Skakel possessed a monopoly. As the country slid deep into the maw of the Great Depression, he found he was a millionaire.

A Dutch Protestant, George had married a fanatical

Catholic who insisted that her children be raised in the One True Church. Big Ann, as she was called, had a library full of religious artifacts and rare books and manuscripts, including those of a young Trappist monk named Thomas Merton. The Skakels were benefactors of Our Lady of Gethsemane Abbey in Kentucky, where Merton lived and worked. Later, through the influence of friends, Big Ann became Merton's secretary. This meant she hired girls to type clean copies of Merton's manuscripts, and kept the priceless originals.

The Greenwich mansion in which she stored them sat in a clearing in the woods off Lake Avenue, in the back country. Even today, after a resurgence in the building of great houses, the Skakel place seems monstrously, incomprehensibly huge. But the design is beautiful. It is a sort of English manor house, with vast lawns and gardens spilling down across the land. George Skakel bought the estate in 1934 from the widow of Zalmon Gilbert Simmons, builder of the Simmons mattress fortune, for one hundred thousand dollars.

"Rambleside" was the lawless preserve of the seven Skakel children. Of the boys, Jimmy and George were the wild ones—reckless, gun-loving lads who shot up statues, street-lamps, and mailboxes with high-powered rifles. Once, in a motel in Moab, Utah, George aimed a pistol at Jimmy, squeezed the trigger, and grazed his stomach. Rushton, the younger brother, was sweet and good, but also scrawny, homely, and rather simple—"a bumbling idiot, but a nice man," one of his Belle Haven neighbors would tell me.

Ethel was like Jimmy and George. She was fun and she was wild. She sped cars down the Merritt Parkway at night with no headlights shining, she galloped her horse across the black marble floor of the great house. The other sisters, Georgeann, Pat, and Little Ann, had a fragility, a wounded quality, that is another expression of neglect. Their parents often were away for months at a time, and when they were home they existed behind a membrane of drink.

The Skakels had everything, but what they had most was trouble. Some said they were touched by evil; others ascribed their bad luck to the alcohol that ran in their blood, to congenital recklessness, or to karmic payback for lives corruptly lived. Maybe the so-called Skakel curse was all these things, and maybe it was none of them. But there can be little doubt of the curse itself.

It all began in the 1950s, soon after the coupling of the Skakels with another cursed but far more famous family, the Kennedys of Massachusetts.

The Kennedys and the Skakels were large, wealthy clans, the wealth self-made, reared in the Irish Catholic tradition. Pious family matriarchs had brought forth wild and competitive offspring, sent them to strict private schools, and then the hard-charging patriarchs sought to raise them high—the boys anyway.

There the likeness ends. The Kennedys were liberal Democrats, the Skakels conservative Republicans; the Kennedys were frugal as *Mayflower* Protestants, the Skakels generous but showy. While the Kennedys found acceptance in Irish Catholic Boston, the Skakels butted their heads against a social glass ceiling down in green Episcopalia. The Kennedys were public and press-hungry, the Skakels intensely private. George Skakel, Sr., would say, "You can't quote silence," a strategy that serves the family well to this day; indeed, only when they veered from it did trouble come.

The two families nurtured a chemical disdain for each other. George junior was the first to encounter a Kennedy—Bobby— at Portsmouth Priory, a prep school in Rhode Island. "A real little dick" is how George described him, according to Oppenheimer's *The Other Mrs. Kennedy*. After his sister had married him, he was "that little bastard" or "that little prick."

The antipathy seemed motivated by competition, especially as the young Skakels and the young Kennedys began traveling the same rarefied circuit. Once, while sailing in a regatta off Martha's Vineyard, George and John F. Kennedy battled over how to trim a sail. "Look, Jack, are you going to keep screaming at me how to trim this sail when I know damned well better than you how it ought to be trimmed?" Kennedy, glaring, replied, "Shut the hell up and do as you're told."

A Skakel didn't take that from a Kennedy. George gave Jack the finger and abandoned ship.

Once, a CIA agent in Cuba borrowed Jim Skakel's forty-two-foot Chris-Craft *Virginia* to ferry Americans off the island as the Bay of Pigs invasion drew near. Jim never got it back. Bobby Kennedy later told his sister-in-law Georgeann Terrien, "The Bay of Pigs was worth it just to nail one of your brothers."

While the Skakel and Kennedy males went at one another, the girls made friends. Ethel and Jean Kennedy—the mother of William Kennedy Smith, who would play a cameo role in the Moxley case—met in the fall of 1945 at Manhattanville College. By that time, Georgeann Skakel and Eunice Kennedy had become friends, and Pat Kennedy and Pat Skakel had been roommates at the Convent of the Sacred Heart, Maplehurst, in New York City; and then the Skakel boys started dating Kennedy girls, and Skakel girls started dating Kennedy boys.

Odds favored a union.

The marriage of Ethel Skakel to Robert Francis Kennedy took place on June 17, 1950, at Saint Mary's Church in Greenwich, the same church where my father and I stood on that somber occasion sixteen years later. The linking of "two large fortunes," as the *Boston Globe* put it, rang in the decade on a promising note. But marrying a Kennedy was like marrying misfortune; as the years rolled on, several in the wedding party would die suddenly and violently. In 1955 the bride's parents, George and Big Ann, were killed when their private plane blew up over Oklahoma. Everyone knows what happened to the best man in Dallas in 1963 and the groom in Los Angeles in 1968; and in between, crazy George had gone. (Two Kennedy air disasters had eerily presaged the Skakel tragedies. Joe Kennedy, Jr.'s experimental navy plane exploded in midair over England in 1944. Joe's younger sister Kathleen Kennedy Hartington went down in a fog outside Lyons, France, in 1948.)

George's death did not signify a break in the awful skein. Two months after Idaho, his eldest daughter, Kick, accidentally killed a neighborhood girl whom she had taken for a joyride. Shortly after that, George's son Mark took a match to a glass salt shaker he'd filled with gunpowder and blew himself up, but lived.

On Mark's return from the hospital, Pat Skakel, George's widow, threw a small party at her handsome brick mansion on Vineyard Lane. At one point she got up from the table and disappeared down the hall. She never came back. She had choked to death on a shish kebab. She was thirty-nine.

Then Ted Kennedy drove off a tiny wooden bridge on Chappaquiddick Island in the summer of 1969, leaving twenty-eight-year-old Mary Jo Kopechne to drown in a tidal pool. Ted had been an usher at Ethel and Bobby's wedding. The curse went on and on, leaping like a live wire between the two families.

The Rushton Skakels had suffered less ill fortune. Rush and his wife, Ann, had settled in Belle Haven in the 1950s, in a white brick house flanked by silver birches. Rushton himself had never spoiled for trouble, the way his brothers had; he was a good man living a clean life. In 1965 his son Tommy had tumbled out of a limousine while wrestling with his sister, Julie, in the back seat. He cracked his skull on the pavement. He recovered, except for the seizures and the paroxysms of rage that seemed to date from the injury.

That, really, had been the worst of it. Then Ann, in her early thirties, had been diagnosed with cancer. A vivacious woman and an excellent athlete, she fought the cancer for many years; there were times when she seemed to have beaten it. By 1973, however, she was confined to Greenwich Hospital, refusing to let her children see her ravaged shell.

Rush would visit her every day. I'd heard that Ann went blind toward the end, and that Rush would bring roses every day for her to smell. On his way home he would stop at a friend's place for martinis, which gave him comfort. He became desperately alcoholic. One morning he walked out to where his boys were waiting for the school bus and told them that their mother had died. Then the boys went off to school.

In those years, the Skakels still had some refracted glow from those fallen gods the Kennedys. There was a density, an aura, a charm. Today when Greenwich people think of the Skakels, they no longer think of the family's horrendous luck. They think of a man who might have got away with murder, and a family determined that this should be so.

Heartland Folk

DORTHY'S MEMORIES ARE full of longing. These memories seem ancient now, driven deep beneath the weighted sorrow of her later years.

There was a tiny wood-frame house in Michigan. Two acres of land at 942 Willard Road in the town of Rochester, a few miles north of Detroit. The house was set back from the street, behind an orchard. There was a swing roping down from a bough full of apples. A small vineyard in the side yard, with two rows of grapevines. Even now she can almost smell the sweet grapes she cradled in her small arms, and the memories flow and flow.

"My dad planted all kinds of fruit trees. Every kind of fruit you can think of that would grow in Michigan. Peaches, plums, apples, pears. We had strawberries and raspberries and blueberries. Oh, how he loved to garden! He planted potatoes, corn, beans. I mean, we had everything. My mother would can all summer long and make jams and jellies, and my father would garden, and I had a wonderful, wonderful childhood."

John William Jolgren, Dorthy's father, was a tool-and-die man in the Detroit tool rooms. He worked for the Dodge brothers, and for the naval ordnance plant during World War II. He was Finnish. He had emigrated from Finland with his parents around the turn of the century and settled in Champion, a little town on Michigan's upper peninsula, where iron ore and copper were mined.

Emma Ingeborg Lundwal's parents, Dorthy's maternal grandparents, crossed over from Sweden. Emma's father was a mechanic at a mine near the town of Iron River, just north of the Brule River on the Michigan-Wisconsin border.

Emma Lundwal was heading back to Iron River when she stopped off in Detroit to meet a girlfriend. John Jolgren was the friend's brother, and he went along with his sister to the train station to pick up the girl. Perhaps he was curious. John and Emma married a week later.

Their first child was stillborn. The second was a boy they called Buck. Five years later, in 1932, came Dorthy. The four of them moved up to Rochester when Buck was nine and Dorthy was four. The Jolgrens were poor, but they lacked nothing that they needed and they were happy.

The house on Willard Road had no bathroom. You had to go out the back door and trek down a path to an outhouse. Jolgren kept adding to the house, first a bathroom, then a garage, then other rooms, and the house kept getting bigger and bigger. Emma Jolgren was feisty and vigorous and ruthlessly clean. Though ulcers and kidney stones plagued her, they did not slow her down very much.

"Our house was probably the cleanest house in the neighborhood. Everything was immaculate. And my mother had all these double-ruffle curtains at all the windows. They were all ruffly and always clean. She was always taking down the curtains, and they were always white."

John Jolgren was an easygoing fellow who told lively stories and made things with his hands. He made Dorthy a pair of skis, and Dorthy would put them on and glide down East Hill after a good snow. The winters were cold. Dorthy can remember her father carrying her all the way home from Butts' Pond one afternoon because she had frozen like stone and could not move.

Dorthy had to walk a mile along a gravel road to school. The children were always careful to keep to the roadside because of the gravel trucks rumbling by. One day when Dorthy was in the second grade, her best friend, Diane Blackett, was run down and killed by a truck.

"I was walking behind her. I must have been about twenty feet back. We knew something had happened, but I blanked it from my mind. I remember she was walking in front of me and then something happened. I don't remember anything after that."

It was Dorthy's first encounter with death, and the last bad thing she would have to blank from her mind for a very long time.

In high school Dorthy was a cheerleader for the Rochester Falcons. She led a frenetic social life, as she always would do, and was voted the most popular girl in her class. Buck was president of his high school class, but then the war came and he went off to join the navy. His mother delivered his graduation speech while he was off at sea.

Time passed quickly. Dorthy attended Michigan State in East Lansing. There were casual encounters that turned out to be life-altering. In her senior year, Michigan State played in the Rose Bowl in Pasadena, California. One of Dorthy's sorority sisters went out west to watch the game. When she came back she said, "That's where we're going. We're going to California."

Dorthy and three others got teaching jobs in Long Beach. Dorthy taught the fifth grade at Patrick Henry Elementary School. Nearby there was a naval base. One night Dorthy and her friends went out for a drink to El Sombrero, and they met a young naval officer named David Moxley, a Kansas boy, son of the assistant postmaster of Atchison.

"One of my friends had the biggest crush on David, just thought he was the greatest. And I wasn't very impressed at all. I guess because he didn't impress me it was very easy for me to talk to him, and my friend who liked him couldn't talk to him at all."

The friend asked Dorthy to please talk to David for her, to find out this and that, and Dorthy said sure. They talked so much that they fell in love. They met in October; got engaged on New Year's Eve; and married that March in the chapel at Terminal Island, on Los Angeles Harbor. The year was 1956. "I always said the greatest gift David ever gave me was marrying Dorthy," said David's sister, Mary Jo Rahatz.

The Moxleys went back to Kansas. While David earned his MBA at the University of Kansas at Lawrence, Dorthy taught school. They rented a tiny apartment and had no money. Dorthy's meager salary and David's GI Bill kept them going while they laid the foundation for their life together.

"It was hot, hot, hot in the summer and cold, cold, cold in the winter, and we had all these cockroaches or water bugs or something in our apartment. I worked hard to get rid of them. And David worked so hard and studied so hard, and it was the beginning of never seeing David. He was always busy working. But he was an honors student all the way through graduate school and he passed the CPA test without any experience."

David got his degree in 1958. When the summer came and the Kansas heat simmered on the endless fields that rolled away from Lawrence, they went back west. Touche, Ross & Company, an international consulting and accounting firm, offered David a job in San Francisco. Dorthy was five months pregnant with John. They were thrilled to be heading back to California.

The years passed. John was born in October of 1958, Martha in August of 1960. The Moxleys bought a house in

1962 up in the Berkeley Hills, north of Oakland. They were still poor but things looked bright.

Baby Martha would stay up all night and sleep during the day. John the reverse. That way Dorthy got to spend time with both of them. The children grew a little older, and Martha took ballet and piano and violin. John took trumpet and played every sport under the California sun. John fell out of a tree once and broke his arm. Martha went into the hospital with a high fever. Nothing serious. It was a life without trouble.

David was never home. That was the worst part. He put in long hours in the Oakland offices of the Kaiser conglomerate, one of Touche, Ross's biggest accounts. David was raised with a strong work ethic. He had temporarily suspended this ethic in college—as though he needed a long, last good time before embarking on a brutally disciplined professional life. "David was smart as a whip," John McCreight recalls. "He worked very hard doing hard things. He was tenacious, honest, and creative. I had boundless trust in him. If David said he wanted to go down a certain road, I'd go a long way down that road with him."

All these qualities advanced him quickly. And finally David was afforded the chance to go east to join the business aristocracy. He would manage the firm's New York office, if his family supported the move. At the dinner table one night, he asked, "How would everybody feel about moving to New York?" He searched their faces for signs of distress, but John and Martha greeted the prospect with undiluted joy.

And so the Moxleys came east in the summer of 1974.

Chapter Seven

Looking for Lies

OF THE DOZEN persons whom police will ask to sit for the lie detector, Tommy Skakel is first.

Jim Lunney and Ted Brosko—the detectives who spotted the six iron's sister club in the Skakel house five hours after the body's discovery but did nothing about it for two days—appear at the Skakels' doorstep on the evening of November 3. Will Tommy take the test? Rush Skakel agrees without hesitation, and then Tommy himself agrees; perhaps he believes he has no choice.

The four of them ride an hour over dark hills to the Connecticut State Police Polygraph Unit in Bethany. The detectives and the polygraph examiner lead Tommy to a small bare room with a table and two chairs and a one-way window. The examiner sits the boy down and reviews aloud the questions he'll ask, including this one: "Did you kill Martha Moxley?"

Then he fits a blood pressure cuff around Tommy's arm; rubber tubing around his chest; and a couple of electrodes to the fingers of his left hand. Wires lead from the apparatuses to a silver box studded with switches and dials; there are also the five needles, which graph changes in respiration, pulse, blood pressure, and galvanic skin reflex—or sweating.

As Tommy sits there, everyone notices how tired he looks. He seems to have gone without sleep. He answers no to the four questions that pertain to the death of Martha Moxley, but the examiner does not interpret his answers as truthful. Neither does he believe them clearly to be lies.

The examiner runs him through the test two more times. His ruling: "Inconclusive."

"He was too washed out, like a wet rag," Keegan, the captain of detectives, will later tell *Greenwich Time*. Tommy got up early that morning and has eaten no dinner. The test is administered at midnight. Complicating the matter is Tommy's epilepsy—a disturbance in the brain's chemistry—for which he takes the anticonvulsant Dilantin.

That Tommy does not pass the polygraph test seems to tally with the murder weapon's source—the Skakel house—and the fact that Tommy is the last known person to have seen Martha Moxley alive. But police seem unwilling to believe that a nephew of Bobby Kennedy holds the answer to their question; or perhaps it's that they're sold for the moment on William Edward Hammond.

Men have tried to detect lies since ancient times. The Chinese, knowing that one physiological indication of deception is a dry mouth, made suspects chew uncooked rice; difficulty spitting it out signified a liar.

The first lie-detecting machine, invented in 1895, gauged changes in pulse rate and blood pressure. In 1921 John Larsen improved upon the original with a machine that measured respiration too and recorded the bodily changes on a graph.

Polygraphs do not reveal absolutely whether one is lying; rather, they measure the involuntary physical responses that could indicate lies. Some people are constitutionally bad at taking polygraph tests, their fears and nervousness registering harshly at the key questions. Those with heart or respiratory ailments, chronic pain, and mental illness may also have trouble with polygraphs.

Law enforcement officials are sharply split on the polygraph's accuracy. In the 1920s and 1930s the machine was viewed as a modern wonder, as infallible as the pope. Bruno Hauptmann, convicted kidnapper and killer of the Lindbergh baby, flunked his polygraph, accelerating public blood lust.

Other cases quickly checkered the machine's reputation. A polygraph test "convicted" an innocent man and "exonerated" the killer in a 1928 murder-kidnapping case in Florida, prompting FBI director J. Edgar Hoover's order to "throw that box into Biscayne Bay." The FBI criminal lab did not open its Polygraph Unit until 1978, three years after the murder of Martha Moxley.

The accuracy of polygraph tests depends heavily on the examiner, who must be skilled in the art of interpretation—like a tarot card reader. Not only must the examiner be able to recognize what the graph is telling him; he must read body language and know when the person being tested is trying to beat the machine. Does he breathe heavily or tense his muscles on the control questions and relax on the key questions? Does he have a secret means of inflicting pain—say, a tack in his shoe? Pain can even out the graph. So can certain drugs. Only an expert can distinguish a truth-telling graph from a drug-flattened one.

Carl Wold III is next to take the polygraph. A twenty-three-year-old who went out walking the night Martha was killed, he had "pestered" her for a date six days earlier, at the Moxleys' cocktail party. He passes.

Of the half-dozen youths who were with Martha thirty minutes before her murder, only Tommy and his brother John are tested. Tommy returns to Bethany on November 9, and this time he beats the machine. It is unknown why straight-arrow John is selected to take the test and not his brother Michael. Perhaps police have confused the two.

Michael is the Skakel who knew Martha best. He is also the wildest of the bunch, a scattered, mischievous boy of fifteen. He teases dogs, slings mud at houses, destroys tree forts. Once, he rode his skateboard drunk on vodka and broke his arm. He has rakish charm. He is funny and lively—not explosive the way Tommy is, but not stable, either.

John passes the test. Michael, who will become a suspect as the years wear on, never submits to the polygraph. During this small window of Skakel cooperation, he is never asked.

But others, further from Mischief Night's ground zero, are asked: Franz Josef Wittine, the Skakel handyman, who lives in the basement; Judy Sakowicz and Mart Keefe, the small-time drug dealers; and Peter Ziluca, Martha's boyfriend.

And, after some coaxing, William Edward Hammond. Hammond and his lawyer, Augustus Kelley, agreed on three conditions: the findings will be inadmissible in court; the police will "get off his back and stop harassing him" if he passes; and the police will work through Kelley should leads implicating Hammond develop. Steve Carroll and Joe McGlynn pick him up early on the morning of November 14 and drive him to Bethany. His answers constitute no pattern. The graph dances erratically, and the examiner offers no opinion.

Could it be the Antabuse Hammond takes to keep himself away from alcohol? "This circumstance may account for the erratic nature of his responses," the examiner notes, though Hammond's family doctor tells the detectives that Antabuse has no effect on the nervous system.

On the way back to Greenwich, Hammond tells the detectives about mysterious phone calls to his home. Three of them. The voice of a teenage girl telling Marionna Hammond: "I saw Martha with Edward." Nothing more.

Hammond returns to Bethany one week later. This time he passes the test, and police interest in him fades rapidly.

The investigation has splintered into a series of thin, hopeless leads.

Detective Michael Powell tracks down the wife of a Bronx man arrested in Belle Haven four years earlier. He exposed himself to a woman who lived on Otter Rock Drive.

Powell finds the wife in a Laundromat on 184th Street. She says her husband spent the evening of October 30 at her parents' house, also in the Bronx, with their two children; he was home watching television by ten o'clock, when she returned from a class at the School of Visual Arts in Manhattan.

Next they talk to the husband, who is thirty-one and works in a factory in Brooklyn. He hasn't set foot in Connecticut since he was released from Fairfield Hills psychiatric hospital early in 1973. His story matches his wife's. Another day wasted, and the investigation moves farther and farther from Belle Haven.

A cop from New Rochelle calls to tell Greenwich police of "a known sexual deviate in that jurisdiction." His name is Steele. He's a stocky guy with blond hair, who tries to lure young girls into his 1971 Plymouth. And another thing—he always keeps a couple of golf clubs in his car.

The detectives can't find Steele anywhere. Finally they catch up with him through a detective in Greenburg, New York. Steele tells the detective, Carmine Tierella, that he was home with his wife on October 30.

Tierella wants to know about his golf clubs.

They're Wilsons. He keeps them at Wykagyl Country Club in New Rochelle.

Back in Greenwich, police follow sinister clues. The night of the murder, a teenager named James Frattalone had stopped at a red light on the Post Road, when a heavyset man with red hair and bad skin slipped into his car. The man said, "I didn't mean to do it. You like me, don't you?"

Alarmed, Frattalone drove with him a half mile to the My Way Bar, a little dive in the blue-collar section of Greenwich called Chickahominy. The man kept wandering around the bar asking the patrons if they liked him, and Frattalone was relieved to see him leave with someone else.

Later, police have Frattalone view a fellow named Bill Gallagher. He's twenty-five and lives in Port Chester, New York. Frattalone says he isn't the man who slipped into his car on October 30. But afterward, Frattalone calls Steve Carroll to say he did not tell the truth; he was afraid of getting hurt.

Gallagher tells Lunney and Carroll he has no recollection of the events of October 30. He has no memory of the My Way Bar. Lunney and Carroll are suspicious: no memory, none at all? Gallagher says his days slip away from him, one flowing into the next, none quite remembered. That's how it is when you're an alcoholic.

The detectives sigh. *An alcoholic. Another one. Might as well round up the whole damned town.*

Three weeks into their investigation, Greenwich police receive a Teletype from the Maryland State Police. They'd stopped a thirty-year-old New Jersey man for speeding and the man got so angry that he charged at them. His name was Compton. He was red-haired and solidly built, and the troopers threw him to the pavement and searched his car. They found a bloody coaxial cable and some freshly washed towels. They carted him off to jail, and when another prisoner asked him what he was in for, he said he was a killer. He knew nothing about any blood on the cable, and the police files made no mention of its having been tested. Compton hadn't been in Connecticut, he said; he was playing cards with friends the night before Halloween. "He is definitely a person who gets annoyed easily, and makes remarks when angered," a Middletown detective tells Detective Powell in a letter. But Compton has agreed to go to Greenwich for questioning—if the police pay his expenses.

The police abandon Compton and go down other roads. They check out all bloodstained clothing brought to local cleaners. There's a man who beat a nurse with a fungo bat at a VA hospital in upstate New York. A man named Pennock calls police with a tip, but it turns out that Pennock himself, a Stanford graduate who lives on Park Avenue in New York, is a "neurotic" who's been in and out of psychiatric hospitals for eight years.

A nineteen-year-old deaf-mute from New Rochelle, Darryl Anthony Brooks, is next to turn detectives' heads. He was arrested in January 1974 for murdering someone with a golf club. His case was dismissed in June. An official of the Westchester County Jail tells Vinnie Ambrose the victim was a young girl, but like so much information that swirls up from the depths of the Moxley investigation, this is wrong. The person whom Brooks was charged with killing was a middle-aged black man.

Still, what can the police do? When confronted with such facts, they must follow up. Draining energy from the center.

By late November, though, the police have caught up with much of the rest of Greenwich. They begin, finally, to take a hard look at Tommy Skakel.

Building a Case

THE CASE IS already sliding away, and the turf over Martha's grave has not yet fused with the surrounding grass.

Technically, Tommy Skakel was a suspect from the first day; but only in December do police seriously confront the possibility of his guilt. They begin to watch for telling details.

Captain Keegan makes Lunney and Carroll the lead investigators in the Moxley case. They are regarded as talented detectives, but homicide investigation is an art unto itself and requires much experience. Lunney and Carroll have none.

They spend the middle of December requestioning the kids who were with Martha in her last moments. Tommy Skakel appears at the detective bureau on December 13 and reiterates his story: He chatted with Martha out in the driveway and said good night and went inside. And it was his brother Michael who liked Martha, not him—though this does not explain why it was Tommy who tried to feel her up.

The detectives notice that Tommy talks without emotion. There's an intense stillness about him. His eyes are wide but vacant. But he is well mannered and cooperative. "Tom Skakel was also asked if he would allow investigators to take several strands of hair from his head. He readily agreed," Lunney reports.

Lunney snips off a lock, and now police possess samples of both Tommy's and Edward Hammond's hair. This was in the days before DNA testing, and the detectives could not have known how much more valuable a hair attached to its follicle would be. But Tommy's hair matters little. He was with Martha the night she was killed, and it is not unreasonable to expect that a hair or two of his shoulder-length mop could wind up on her clothes.

The detectives are quietly confused. The Skakels eagerly help the police in every detail. Tommy's story—with the curious exception of the Abe Lincoln report—continues to stand, and it's not as though he's a clever boy. "The reason the Skakels couldn't have killed the girl is that they're too stupid to get away with it," Joan Redmond will tell me. "Especially Tommy and Michael. They just weren't very smart."

Smart or slow, Tommy has a fierce temper. This is no secret. Even Rush Skakel says so. There have been times, he volunteers, when he literally had to sit on the kid to calm him down. There's a rumor that Tommy busted a statue up at the Whitby School as his mother's health failed. Whitby, the first Montessori school in the United States, was founded with Skakel money; before the school was built out on Lake Avenue, classes met at Sursum Corda, the Terrien estate. Tommy and Michael had learning disabilities and foundered amid the loose structure Whitby gave to learning, just as they would founder amid the loose structure of their family life. Ann Skakel had grown disenchanted with the school. She put the boys in Brunswick and Julie in the Convent of the Sacred Heart, a Catholic school located on what was once an estate in the back country.

Lunney and Carroll know the general fact of Tommy's temper but lack anecdotal evidence. They don't know how he nearly strangled a fellow student during study hall. How in moments of rage he'll rip doors straight off their hinges (as his sister tells a friend, who later tells me). The most disturbing incidence of violence is told by a neighborhood boy about Michael: he liked to corner squirrels and chipmunks and beat them dead with a golf club, the boy says. He also liked to entice birds with food and then blow them away with a gun. He kept the dead birds in a burlap bag.

In the 1970s the matrices of violence were only dimly understood. Since then, FBI psychological profilers have come to recognize animal beating and fire starting, especially in concert with bed wetting past early childhood, as dire precursors to murdering humans. Physicians, most of them, know of the Jekyll and Hyde nature of alcoholics, and even of the violence that sometimes attends their male offspring. "Alcoholism in parents, crime in children," goes the clinicians' axiom. There is also an awareness of the connection between head trauma and violence. Police traced Tommy's mercurial aspect to the accident in 1965—the one in which he fell out of a moving car and badly cracked his head. He began to suffer seizures, and that is why his neurologist prescribed the Dilantin.

In the 1980s the body of evidence tying head injuries to violence grew dramatically. A 1986 study of forty-two murderers found an uncommonly high incidence of head injuries and epileptic symptoms. One such symptom—spells of amnesia—turned up in twenty-three of the murderers. Nine of these claimed they couldn't recall committing murder.

Meanwhile, the search for the missing piece of the murder weapon continues. Broken golf clubs start turning up all over, dozens of them. A builder finds one in a sewer grate on Milbank Avenue. A cop from Queens stumbles across a grip and shaft, but it's a McGregor. Someone from Darien finds an old shaft with a cardboard handle lying by the Post Road. A security man at Northeastern University, in Boston, commandeers a headless club from a couple of students at a beer party and mails it to Greenwich. A Bridgeport man finds a twenty-eight-inch shaft on the grounds of Saint Mark's Lutheran Church. A nursery school kid finds a rusty shaft, twenty-three inches long, on a playground in Greenwich. Detective Pendergast drives over to Stamford to investigate a report of a broken golf club at a house on Iroquois Road. It turns out to be a two-foot-long shoehorn.

The young son of a Greenwich police officer finds a broken club in some leaves near the dump; a playmate tells him, Maybe that's the club that killed Martha Moxley, "but the boy tossed the shaft into the woods." Then there's a shaft somebody used for a stoker at an incinerator. Then a broken ski pole.

But the shaft that went through Martha's neck never turns up. Not even at the muddy bottom of Long Island Sound. Police look there, after a fashion. They have a man about Tommy Skakel's size hurl a shaft into the water, and then they send divers down in that vicinity.

One day late in the fall, when the colors of nature dim to monochromatic silvers and grays, Lunney and Carroll pay a visit to the Brunswick School.

They find Ken Littleton out on the football field. Littleton used to be a talented football player; it is even said he was drafted by the Chicago Bears. Now as assistant coach of the

Brunswick Bruins, Littleton instructs his young charges in the finer points of gridiron destruction. He's teaching them a little maneuver called the "forearm shiver."

Littleton frowns as he watches Carroll and Lunney head across the grass to the sideline. "He started swearing and cursing and all this," Carroll recalls. "He shouts, 'I'm not going to help you build a case against Tommy Skakel!' And we looked at him in surprise: 'Oh, really? What made you think we wanted you to do that?' "

Privately Carroll begins to wonder about Littleton. There is something phony in this display. Something overly dramatic. It makes Carroll wonder what Littleton is up to: is he trying to lead police to the Skakels with his pretense of protecting them—thus leading them away from *himself*? Or is he simply reacting to the swell of rumor around Tommy Skakel?

The detectives get nowhere and walk off the field. But there are bad days ahead for Ken Littleton. Even now he walks toward the mouth of his own personal hell.

Case Closed

THE YEAR ENDS. Martha is, of course, the only murder victim in Greenwich for 1975, and only the third in town since World War II. But in the national tapestry she's a statistic, one in 21,310—a quarter of them women—an average year for murder in these United States.

There is one odd thing: 1975 turns out to be a banner year for bludgeonings. There are 1,001 such murders recorded, the first time bludgeon killings cross that numerical threshold and the last time they'll do so for another five years.

Talk of the murder settles to a whisper. Police have questioned more than two hundred residents but learned little of value. The people of the town grow quietly restless and lose faith in the police; some feel certain that police failings are intentional, and this wounds men like Lunney and Keegan and Carroll.

"There were a lot of people who thought that we weren't going to pursue it because the Skakels had money," Carroll says. "That wasn't true. Not true at all." He gives a short, mirthless laugh. "When Jimmy Lunney and I would go into a local diner or restaurant, somebody would always say, 'This meal is on Carroll and Lunney!' Like we were being taken care of."

He understands how the impression was born. Much is clear now that wasn't then. "I didn't think any of us were *intimidated* by the Skakels. But I think we were just too casual about it. Much too casual. Lunney and I went down on any number of occasions and actually had coffee with Rushton. Telling him we'd like to look for this or that. And he'd say, 'Oh, go ahead. Help yourselves.' And we would. We'd go through the house by ourselves."

Two days before Christmas, the *New York Times* publishes a lengthy story on the case, headlined FRIENDS AND A FUND RECALL THE MURDERED GIRL IN GREENWICH. The story tells how Martha's friends do not talk about the murder anymore but instead remember the good times they had when she was alive. They honor her through the Martha Moxley Scholarship Fund, which has grown to $11,400.

The *Times* story mentions a subject *Greenwich Time* has been too timid to broach: the "ill-concealed impatience by some in the community against the Police Department." The *Times* reporter, James Feron, asks Chief Stephen M. Baran about rumors of his "protecting the influential." He denies it heatedly. " 'You can be certain that we would act if we had any evidence linking a person to the crime,' he said. 'We certainly do not have evidence at this time to substantiate any arrest.' "

By January, however, the rumoring begins to darken heavily over Tommy Skakel. Carroll and Lunney, their scant leads exhausted, have turned to amassing background information on the Skakels. It is this approach that at once parts the waters and freezes them over.

On January 16, 1976, Rushton Skakel gives his written permission, on town stationery, for the release of all records—medical, psychological, school—pertaining to his son Thomas.

Carroll and Lunney send letters to school psychologists; to the deceased Ann Skakel's obstetrician; to her children's pediatrician; to Greenwich Hospital's records department; to Norman Pedersen, headmaster of the Brunswick School; and to Paul Czaja, headmaster of the Whitby School. They call a man who runs a remedial reading school in Mount Kisco, New York, which Tommy attended from 1968 to 1970, and the neurologist who treated him after his head injury in 1965.

And then they wait. On January 20, Christopher Roosevelt, a lawyer for the Whitby School, sounds the first jarring note. He'll talk to Rush and Tommy personally before releasing any records. And then, according to police reports:

Mr. Roosevelt became highly agitated by the investigators' request and interpreted [it] to be something akin to an actual arrest, and his attitude was such that the youth had already been arrested. He further related that if this happened, Thomas would be defended by a battery of lawyers who would claim that Thomas was temporarily insane.

It all breaks on January 22. The morning starts a little oddly: Julie Skakel comes to see the detectives, worried about the nuns. She's aware the detectives are doing background checks, she tells them, and goes on to say that she has no rapport with the nuns up at Sacred Heart and is worried about comments they might make about her.

The detectives shake their heads. The Skakels seem utterly unaware that one of their own is under suspicion of murder. Even Rush is curiously blasé: doesn't he understand the implications of the record checks? The questions about Tommy? All he does is wave his hand in the air, saying, "Do whatever you need to do! Be my guest!"

Carroll goes up to the Whitby School. Unknown to him, Paul Czaja is meeting at that very moment with Rush Skakel. Carroll waits. He makes small talk with Chris Roosevelt, who, curiously, is also there. When Czaja emerges he fixes hotly on Carroll and screams, "Get out!" Carroll tries to speak. "Get out!" Czaja orders. Carroll tries again. "Get out, get out, get out!" the headmaster shouts all the way down the hall at the detective's back. Carroll walks out into the winter glare.

At 1:20 P.M. Rush Skakel appears at the police headquarters complaint desk and drops off a letter addressed to Chief Baran. It reads:

Dear Sir:

This is to inform you that I, Rushton W. Skakel hereby withdraw the "Authorization to Release Medical and School

Records" concerning my son Thomas Skakel, executed January 16, 1976. This withdrawal shall take immediate effect.

From police headquarters Rush Skakel and James Donovan, a lawyer for Great Lakes Carbon, of which Skakel is now chairman, drive to the Ix house on Walsh Lane.

Cissy Ix shows them to the study and goes to fix refreshments ("and we know what refreshments are," Carroll later tells me with a wink). A strange feeling comes over Rush Skakel. He lifts his hand to his chest and holds it there. There is pain. It worsens. Cissy Ix calls for help. Belle Haven police officer Al Robbins rushes in and fits an oxygen mask over the ailing man's pallid face. Greenwich patrolmen Bill Carroll (no relation to Steve) and Michael McDermott speed down to the Ix house in a police ambulance. They get there fifteen minutes after Skakel dropped off his letter at headquarters. Skakel complains to them of chest pains, brought on, apparently, by bad news he has just received. The patrolmen lay him on a stretcher and hurry off to Greenwich Hospital.

That afternoon Lunney and Carroll go down to the Ix house to see if they can make sense of the curious incident. Cissy Ix says she doesn't know what the "bad news" is. She does know that Rush Skakel met with Messrs. Czaja and Roosevelt and seemed upset afterward.

Lunney and Carroll visit Skakel in the hospital. His ailment seems to be not a heart attack but a reaction to great stress. There's a priest, Father Mark Connolly, outside the room. But he does not signify imminent death. He's one of those celebrity priests who conduct Mass on television, and his presence here signifies the influence of wealth.

Rush Skakel has been sedated, but the attending physician lets the detectives in for a brief conversation. So what was the bad news? they ask him. Rush Skakel will say only that for his son's protection he's hired a criminal lawyer, Emanuel Margolis, who works out of Stamford.

Lunney and Carroll are left to assume that Rush Skakel finally understands that Tommy is a suspect in the murder of Martha Moxley. His failure to have recognized this before now seems stunning. He must truly be an idiot if Czaja and Roosevelt had to spell it out for him.

But Rush has been blind the way Greenwich police have been blind: there could be no killer in this family, this exalted clan; one would be mad to think so. When Rush let the detectives run loose in his house, he was simply showing them respect.

"I'll tell you something up front," Steve Carroll says. "There was one point in time, months after this happened, that we all met up in the prosecutor's office. Don Browne—he's still the prosecutor, by the way—me, Jim Lunney, Tommy Keegan, and Jack Solomon, a state cop.

"We were discussing the case—what we had, what we didn't have. Over and over and over. And I said to Don Browne, 'Why can you not convene a grand jury—have them bring in a true bill or not a true bill?' " A "true bill" is the grand jury's finding of grounds for arrest. Tommy Skakel is the person under discussion.

"Browne says to me, 'Don't tell me how to run my business!' And then he turns to Keegan and says, 'I don't want him up here anymore!' "

In 1991, fifteen years later, Carroll sees something puzzling in the newspaper: Don Browne saying it's too late to convene an investigative grand jury. Carroll holds the paper in his hands and thinks, *Sure it is*—now.

As for the detectives: the Skakels' sudden rebuff hints at the presence of secrets. Of something important just learned. Now the police have lost access, but they have their break. One could not have happened without the other.

Emanuel Margolis is a tough little man with a soldier's puffed-up bearing. He counsels the Skakels to have nothing more to do with the police; the police will have to reckon with him now.

Meanwhile, Detective Steve Carroll receives word from Dr. Donald P. Kenefick, who profiled the Boston strangler, that the murderer of Martha Moxley is probably a teenage white male with an explosive temper, an athletic boy, a boy who may have hang-ups with girls, a boy who may be impotent. He says the killer was not in his right mind. He was killing meaninglessly, like stepping on a bug, and he has probably blocked it all out.

"You mean he can't remember doing it?" Carroll asks.

"It's a possibility."

A disturbing one. It explains why the killer could pass a lie detector test and remain convinced of his innocence. "You know these stories that come up from these psychiatric people," Carroll tells me with a dismissive wave. "I find it difficult to believe—very difficult—that he couldn't remember a thing like that."

Kenefick says a battery of tests is needed to explore the further reaches of Tommy Skakel's psyche. A month earlier Rush would have consented. Now police scramble to set up meetings. On February 18, Keegan, Lunney, and Carroll meet first with Father Thomas Guinan of Saint Michael's Church in Greenwich and then with Father Connolly.

Keegan tells them, without quite accusing Tommy, how urgent these psychological tests are. The police want to sit down with Rush Skakel. They want to say, "Look here, Rush. These tests could clear this whole thing up."

Father Guinan, flat and remote, is not so sure. "These tests," he murmurs. "I don't think they would be good for the boy."

Connolly tells the detectives he'll see what he can do.

"What we wanted to do because of this situation indicating that Tommy blocked it out"—Carroll and Keegan and Lunney already begin to assume Tommy is the killer—"we wanted to do sleep deprivation tests, Sodium Pentothal [truth serum], all kinds of tests. We asked Mr. Skakel to come in and discuss it. So he came in, and along with him was Father Guinan—now Monsignor Guinan—and another priest, named Connolly, who used to do the Mass on Channel Thirteen. The Skakels were big benefactors of the Church."

On February 25 the priests, Rush Skakel, and Manny Margolis sit around a table in the police library, on the second floor of headquarters, and listen as Keegan tries to convince them of the need, the *urgent* need, for an extensive examination.

Margolis says nothing. Nobody has accused Tommy Skakel of murder, but it is clear enough what the detectives' suspicions are. Finally Margolis says the police will have his answer in short order.

On March 4 there's a memorial Mass for Ann Skakel at Saint Mary's Church on Greenwich Avenue. It has been nearly three years since she died, and in that interval the family has gone to pieces, like an old house without the center beam. They are chaotic and wrecked and sad. It seems metaphorically apt that Tommy—at home in bed with the flu—should miss this healing ritual, this chance to come to terms with the sorrow in his life.

The day of Ann Skakel's memorial Mass is also the day Manny Margolis carves a moat around the Skakels. They are visible but untouchable now, unless the police want to arrest someone. The police will glare across the moat, but they will never touch Tommy Skakel again, though not for lack of trying.

Even after Manny Margolis shut the door on the police, Carroll and Lunney managed to find Tommy Skakel "on the street."

"I wouldn't say we shadowed him," Carroll says. "Just whenever we had the opportunity—even after we were told to get lost—if we saw him on the street we would go after him. Not chase him down. But we would make sure we talked to him: 'Hey, Tommy! Can we talk to you a minute? Let us buy you a beer!'

"There were several times prior to Margolis getting involved where Tommy did accommodate us. But we were never able to get anything."

Nothing but an impression.

"His demeanor was like he was in a trance. Almost like he was on drugs. And when you were talking to him you were talking right through him. We'd say, 'You know, Tom, when you were talking to Martha after Geoff and Helen left, you were trying to feel her up and she fell down.'

" 'Oh, no, Martha never fell down. No, no.' "

They'd chat a little longer, and then the cops would come back to Martha falling. On the side of her face, by her left eye, a long indentation had been made; perhaps with a golf club shaft, perhaps by her falling on the iron ribbon that lined the Skakel driveway.

" 'When Martha fell down, did she hit her head?'

" 'No, no, no, no. Martha never fell down.' "
Carroll grins. "He would get pretty adamant about that."

An Old Drunk

FRANCIS WALSH is one of many intriguing minor characters in this story. In 1975 he's sixty-four, out of work, and a heavy drinker. He lives above Mickey's Restaurant, a smoky, bustling dive near the bottom of Greenwich Avenue. He's been mouthing off to Mickey Briggs—owner of the bar and the building—about something he overheard a couple of days before Halloween, and when Mickey Briggs hears it he calls the police.

Detective Joe McGlynn corners Walsh, and the old man tells him the story. He was sitting at the bar, just inside the front door, when three young men came up to him. He thought they might want to bum a drink off an old man. One of the young men appeared to be eighteen or nineteen, fairly tall, with medium-length brown hair; the other two did not look old enough to be served. All of them drank beer. The younger two called the older one "Skakel."

"Skakel" told Walsh that he was going to kill a girl in Belle Haven with a golf club.

Walsh stared at "Skakel," and one of the others said, "That Skakel is crazy."

"Skakel" showed Walsh the head of a golf club—it was a cheap-looking iron with a circle engraved on the back of the head. Walsh did not see the brand name.

The desire to kill the girl, Walsh thought he heard, had something to do with getting even with the girl's brother.

(When police check with John Moxley, he says he never had a run-in with one of the Skakels; he barely even knew them.) Then the old man moved a couple of barstools down, "because that kind of talk disagreed with him."

A couple of days later, Walsh switched on the radio and heard the news. He thought, *That kid was really serious,* but he did not go to the police. Friends told him that if he did go, he would never live to testify. The Kennedys would kill him. So he did not go.

Walsh tells Detective McGlynn his story on February 4, just after all the heavy weather descends on the Skakels. The police believe Walsh may be the circumstantial witness who will deliver them from their paralysis. But McGlynn notices that Walsh is "semi-intoxicated" during questioning. Perhaps he will not make a credible witness after all, if it ever comes to that.

McGlynn tries to check out the story. The bartender at Mickey's has a vague recollection of Walsh's chatting with three young men; and the bartender across the street, at the Greenwich Restaurant—it seems Walsh knows quite a few bartenders—remembers Walsh telling him he knew the kid who killed the Belle Haven girl, but he paid little attention to the old man. Walsh's son listened to his father's story too but gave it no heed. Still, nobody knows Walsh to spin wild tales, even in the haze of the Irish flu.

McGlynn questions Walsh again the following day. The story frays: now Walsh believes the three young men did not show him the head of a golf club; this image seems to have come from another place and time, perhaps from friends who carry golf club heads for protection from muggers.

Walsh is confused but insists the kernel of his story is true. He is certain about the part that counts. A few days later, when

Lunney and Carroll get hold of him, Walsh says with conviction that the youths never showed him the head of a golf club, but this admission only serves to cancel out his reliability as a witness.

Lunney and Carroll ask Walsh to submit to a polygraph examination; this, the detectives say, will determine the veracity of his story.

The detectives figure Walsh for a lonely old man who needs attention and made an outrageous utterance to get it; sadly, no one listened to him, and the poor devil dove back into the bottle.

On February 17 Walsh consents to the polygraph—and passes.

Chapter Eight

A Thousand Pieces

BY EARLY 1976 the people of Greenwich do not talk so much about the murder anymore. An assumption has grown, as intractable as a need, that Tommy Skakel killed Martha Moxley, but around this assumption there is more heat than light.

The new year begins as strangely as the old one ended. On January 3 another fifteen-year-old girl who lives on Walsh Lane, Margaret Moore, goes to baby-sit at the house of Dr. James Spencer on Field Point Road.

Dr. Spencer and his wife get back at about midnight, and then the doctor drives Margaret home. When he returns, the phone rings and a voice whispers into his ear, "You're next." He cannot tell whether the voice belongs to a man or a woman; again it whispers, "You're next," and then the line goes dead.

At first Dr. Spencer does not think much about it. Then he realizes with a jolt that the call might have been meant for Margaret. As he considers this, it occurs to him also how much the girl resembles, in a general way, Martha Moxley.

Steve Carroll goes to Margaret's parents and explains the situation, and the Moores are greatly alarmed. Two days later, there is a midnight call to the Moore house. The caller does not speak. But the whisperer is never heard from again.

By February the police feel as though they had begun to put the puzzle together, only to watch it shatter into a thousand pieces at their feet.

By now John McCreight is deeply involved in the case. "Early on, the police had confirmed my fears of that first night, that they were completely out of their depth," he says. "And their challenge was exacerbated by the sophistication of the people they were dealing with. A lot of sophisticated people live in Belle Haven and in the town—smart, well-informed people, and the police were outgunned. Way, way, outgunned."

McCreight arranges for the Greenwich detectives to pay a visit to some experts. So on February 4 Lunney and Carroll go down to La Guardia Airport to catch a plane for Detroit. They meet with seven experts of the Detroit police department's homicide squad. Detroit Homicide investigates eight to nine hundred murders a year. Surely they'll come up with something of value here. For six hours Lunney and Carroll brief them on the case; show them slides and photographs; explain the topography; point out who lives where.

Later the Greenwich detectives report with apparent relief: "After reviewing the case numerous times it was determined that the investigators had, in fact, conducted a proper investigation leading to a possible suspect."

Martha Moxley, aged fourteen, six months before her murder. This was the photo used for the posthumous portrait done by Frank Kalan. (COURTESY DORTHY MOXLEY)

*Martha and her father,
David Moxley, summer
of 1961.* (COURTESY
DORTHY MOXLEY)

Martha in third grade.
(COURTESY DORTHY
MOXLEY)

Martha at Lake Tahoe in the winter of 1969. (COURTESY DORTHY MOXLEY)

Martha and her father, 1974. (COURTESY DORTHY MOXLEY)

Martha (in camel hair coat) during a field trip to New York in 1974. (COURTESY DORTHY MOXLEY)

Martha and friends at Lake Tahoe in June 1975, just before her fifteenth birthday.
(COURTESY DORTHY MOXLEY)

The Moxleys (John, Dorthy, Martha, David) at Lake Tahoe in June 1975.
(COURTESY DORTHY MOXLEY)

Greenwich Avenue, downtown Greenwich.

The Moxley home on Walsh Lane, showing the circular driveway, as it looks today.

The Skakel home, seen from the road, as it looks today.

One of the Belle Haven police booths.

The back of the Skakel house, showing the path Martha would have taken on her way home on October 30, 1975.

Michael Skakel, third from right, top row, shown with teammates from Brunswick School's ninth-grade soccer team, 1975. (COURTESY GREENWICH LIBRARY)

Ken Littleton, standing at left, in a photograph of Brunswick School's junior varsity basketball team, 1975. (COURTESY GREENWICH LIBRARY)

Tommy Skakel, second from left, top row, with Brunswick School's varsity soccer team, 1975.
(COURTESY GREENWICH LIBRARY)

Eleventh-grade photo of Tommy Skakel, Brunswick School, 1976. (COURTESY GREENWICH LIBRARY)

Early photo of Dominick Dunne with his daughter Dominique, murdered on Halloween, seven years after Martha's death.
(COURTESY DOMINICK DUNNE)

A new house under construction in Belle Haven, near Long Island Sound. The house is to have a twenty-seven-car garage. Note sign on right.

Martha Moxley's grave.
(PHOTO COURTESY EVELYN WHITBURN/GREENWICH MAGAZINE)

Detroit Homicide, meanwhile, theorizes that the murderer lives in the neighborhood and knew his victim; that he's a troubled young man with an explosive temper; that he will "definitely perform the act again," for such behavior is deeply inscribed.

Lunney and Carroll return to Greenwich, their intuitions confirmed by the world's leading murder experts—and with the bonus of their compliments on a job well done.

But it all leads nowhere, and the police, the Moxleys, and the Skakels are stuck in latitudes of time. Dorthy Moxley cries much of the day, and her son can only avert his eyes as he walks past her on his way to his room. David Moxley disappears in his work, and sometimes he disappears with John McCreight, to hash over the vexing details of his daughter's case. He does not talk about the case at home, despite his wife's intense desire to do so; perhaps talking about it would cast him into the emotional morass he seeks to avoid through constant recitation of the facts. So Dorthy goes on crying and crying, alone.

Rush Skakel is hospitalized for alcoholism in February. Tommy gets the flu in March and misses a couple of weeks of school. Toward the end of the month the Skakels leave town, and the detectives who are conducting surveillance keep driving past the darkened house on Otter Rock Drive.

On March 7, four months after the murder of Martha Moxley, Carroll and Lunney go back to the Brunswick School. This time they will talk not to Littleton but to the friends of Tommy Skakel.

The detectives find out he doesn't seem to have any close friends. "It appeared that all his friends are relatives," Lunney reports. "The consensus of opinion of the students interviewed is that Thomas Skakel is a strange kid and that he is obviously aware of the wealth of his family."

Two days later, Franz Wittine, the Skakel handyman, appears at the detective bureau for one last interview. Retired now, he has moved to upstate New York. When in Rush Skakel's employ, he was represented, along with the rest of the nonfamilial household—Ken Littleton; the cook, Ethel Jones; and Nanny Sweeney—by Manny Margolis. Carroll and Lunney believe that now Wittine might feel free to speak his mind.

They're right. There is one bothersome impression, a gut feeling, and he lets go of it: "He felt that everyone in the household had been treating Michael [Skakel] as if he knew something. He further related that the brothers and sister in the family were being exceptionally nice to Michael since the incident of Oct. 30, 1975."

Tommy may be the most tightly coiled of the Skakel boys—there is an inward tension to him, a strangeness about his eyes—but Michael is the most obviously unhinged. It will be Michael, not Tommy, who in the coming months unspools like a ball of yarn.

Rushton Skakel, heeding the advice of Father Connolly, has Tommy submit to a battery of psychiatric tests. Tommy tells Cissy Ix he's surprised that his father thinks he's capable of murder, but he'll go ahead with the tests.

On March 24 Rush calls Cissy, greatly relieved. The tests show Tommy was not involved in killing Martha Moxley. Next time Cissy sees Tommy, she notices needle marks all up and down his arm—from the tests. The precise nature of the tests is unknown, beyond Sodium Pentothal and a monitoring of Tommy's brain waves.

"Why are you people so set on Rush's boys?" she asks Carroll and Lunney. "What about Ken Littleton? Why haven't you checked on him?" Cissy Ix is the first to suspect Ken Littleton. She's been watching him—he walks out to the gazebo in the nude, right past the startled old Nanny Sweeney. They've found "girlie" magazines in his room. He's a bust as a tutor: "Michael had all F's on his last report card, and Tommy's was almost as bad."

Cissy Ix is also troubled by a recent report in the Associated Press in which state's attorney Donald Browne claimed a certain family "is clearly impeding" the investigation. Everyone takes for granted who that family is. Why isn't Rush more upset? He just seems glad Tommy's been "cleared." He seems to think it's over with. Cissy calls her sister, a lawyer in Boston. Tommy passed this test: should they furnish the results to the police? No, the sister-lawyer counsels. Then the press will get hold of it, and the headlines will say Tommy's undergoing psychiatric treatment.

And so the impeding goes on.

Rush appears on Sunday, March 28—at the Moxleys' front door. He sits down with David and Dorthy and reports some good news. The Moxleys regard him with a not unfriendly midwestern reserve. Against the advice of his attorney, Skakel says, he has submitted his son Tommy to a battery of psychiatric tests. The Moxleys are skeptical. Tests? What tests? The conclusion, Rush says, is that the boy could not have killed their daughter. David shows him to the door. Outside, the efforts of spring are beginning to show: the soft greening earth;

the rebirth of leaves; the stubborn patches of snow shrinking into black mounds on the roadside.

Martha is still dead. There is no relief for the Moxleys.

Gerald Hale, commander of the Detroit police department's Major Crimes Unit, and Inspector John Lock fly into New York on the last day of March and book a room at a run-down motel on Greenwich Harbor called the Showboat Motor Inn. Curiously, in 1975, Greenwich lacks a good hotel.

The murder case is five months old, an age at which most such cases are given up for dead. Hale and Lock have gamely agreed to turn over old stones. Commander Hale is cool and analytical, and with his business suit and salt-and-pepper hair, looks like a typical Belle Haven executive. He ascertains what the Greenwich detectives have long known: nobody in Belle Haven other than the Skakels owns Toney Penna golf clubs.

Hale also questions people who have been questioned several times before. Among them are Helen Ix and Geoffrey Byrne, the last known persons, besides Tommy Skakel, to have seen Martha Moxley alive.

Hale confirms what could be a crucial detail. On the night of the murder, Tommy and Martha were not merely chatting but also playing rough with each other. He writes in his report summary: "This, after careful questioning, consisted of Martha pushing Thomas and Thomas pushing Martha. At one point, Thomas pushed Martha down and either fell or got down on her. This point is not clear as it happened partly out of view of Helen and Geoff behind a brick wall."

Following his visit, Commander Hale no longer speaks of the Greenwich detectives in congratulatory tones. He tells the reporter Len Levitt, who wrote exhaustively about the Moxley case for *Greenwich Time,* "There should have been a thorough, formal search of the house. If Rushton Skakel was as cooperative as the Greenwich police say, why not go and do it immediately? Then, if he refused, they could have asked for a search warrant. Because when it came to the Skakels, the Greenwich police were treading lightly."

Hale recommends in his report that police seek a warrant to search the house of Rushton Skakel—even after all this time. Somewhere there are bloody clothes and the missing handle of a golf club, and the Skakel house, Hale believes, is the best place to start looking.

So, six months after the murder, police apply to Donald Browne for a search warrant. He rejects the application.

On the morning of Friday, May 3, Tommy Skakel checks himself into Greenwich Hospital and is treated for "hemorrhagic castritis." The condition is not as bad as the name suggests— it means bleeding from the stomach or the intestines. You get hemorrhagic castritis when you drink too much or take too much drugs or aspirin. Tommy checked himself out of the hospital late on Saturday night. Jim Lunney notes in his report: "Investigators were not able to determine what caused the problem with Thomas Skakel."

When one scrutinizes the course of events, overlaying them like the acetate pages of a human anatomy textbook, one begins to see how Tommy Skakel could have arrived at a murderous moment. It's a continuum, deep history to immediate history: the head injury; the emergence of a volatile temper; the death of his mother and the alcoholism of his father and the consequent rudderless adolescence; the trouble with schoolwork; the sense of entitlement that he perhaps believed compensated for the absences in his life; the advances to Martha, which she rejects with her hand; the "playful" aggression that follows moments later.

Considered alone, these things are close to meaningless. When they're taken together, a portrait begins to emerge. Still, something is missing: the piece that bridges Tommy's history to what happened behind the brick wall where he and Martha pushed each other. What is missing is the burning fuse, the underlying immediacy, that might have readied Tommy for detonation.

I will soon discover what that missing piece could be.

Tommy's Bad Day

CUFF TRAIN, the former Brunswick School teacher, puts me onto a fellow named George Boynton. Boynton was a history teacher and a soccer coach at Brunswick, who had a connection with the Skakels. Cuff Train doesn't tell me more than that.

When I call to explain my business to Boynton, he sounds wary. He says, "There was one pivotal event in this whole story," then pauses. He seems to be testing me.

"The death of Mrs. Skakel?"

"Without a doubt, without a doubt," he agrees quickly. "Ann Skakel was easily the most impressive woman I have ever met. Easily. Call it what you will. A commanding presence. Charisma. When she walked into a room, you just kept your mouth shut and paid attention."

Boynton tells me the family unraveled when she died. Per-

haps everything *really* would have gone to hell had it not been
for the cook. "Ethel Jones kept that family together."

Rushton Skakel, meanwhile, abdicated the responsibilities
of fatherhood. "He was not able to cope," says Boynton. "He
was despondent and very sorrowful. Neighborhood people
came over to help him out." He was sweet and kind when they
visited. He seemed to rise out of his sorrow while they were
there, but then he would fall right back in. "It wasn't as
though you wait your eighteen months and then you're over
it. Mrs. Skakel was the sort of woman you never get over.
That's why Littleton was there."

And the children, in their grief? "The Skakels were great
benefactors of the Church, and there were always Catholic
priests around. They painted the Catholic patina on the
wounds, and on the surface it held fast."

How does Boynton know all this? He was the 1974-model
Ken Littleton. He did not live in the Skakel house, as Little-
ton did, but he would come over in the evenings to be with
Julie and the boys, and then stand over Tommy and Michael
while they did their homework. Not the others. Rush junior,
John, and Julie were focused on their work.

But Tommy and Michael "were bouncing off the walls."
They could not concentrate. They had fallen badly behind in
their schoolwork. Tommy would constantly offer Boynton
food and drink. "He had that game down nicely. Every two
minutes he'd come and talk to me."

Boynton and the kids all ate together in the dining room.
Rushton Skakel would retire to the back room and flick on the
TV. Ethel Jones served him his dinner there.

"When I came to say hello he had a glass of wine in his
hand, and when I went to say good night he had a glass of

wine in his hand. He just had no fire in him. He was having a very rough time. I think he was blown away."

Boynton never had Tommy or Michael Skakel in class, but he taught them how to play soccer. Michael had natural gifts but no discipline. He was easily distracted. He was bent on making trouble, "tripping guys, hitting guys." Boynton guessed that it was Michael who was most severely damaged by the death of his mother.

Tommy was possibly the most talented athlete of the Skakel boys. He was strong and determined. He took obvious pleasure in thrashing about the field. Playing soccer gave him confidence and an identity of his own.

"And then one day I asked him to leave the team."

Tommy simply decided not to show for a game. If you have ever played competitive sports, you know this is a cardinal sin. You have to show; if you don't, you are wasting the coach's time and failing your teammates.

Boynton had been forced to take from Tommy the thing he did best. "He wanted to play," he says, "but unfortunately, only when it was convenient for him."

Tommy was contrite. He went to Boynton and pleaded to be let back on the team. Boynton stared at him levelly and said, "Tell you what. If the kids say you're back on the team, you're back. Come see me at the end of practice, and I'll tell you what's going to happen."

On the field, Boynton gathered his charges and asked them what he should do about Tommy Skakel. "They said, 'Mr. Boynton, no way. We don't want him back.'"

Then Boynton had to deliver to Tommy the news that his peers had rejected him. He was very, very upset, Boynton tells me. "When he walked away, he was in tears."

The date was October 30, 1975. Tommy Skakel would encounter yet more rejection that night, from the pretty blonde who lived across the street.

When I talk to Boynton he expresses strong opinions on the subject of Ken Littleton. "I told Frank Garr, 'You guys ruined a life.' He got a little huffy about that. But Littleton had no money. He wasn't some rich guy with lawyers. The cops see this great big guy and they go, 'Who the hell is this?' Then they barge into the classroom, no appointment, nothing. Try to break him down. Hell, he was a good guy. I told Garr, 'Ken Littleton didn't do it. If he did it, I did it.' "

The Tutor Cracks

IN THE SUMMER of 1976, some burglaries on the island of Nantucket confound the investigation into the murder of Martha Moxley.

Nantucket is an old whaling island twenty miles off Cape Cod, now a summer destination for the wealthy and the beautiful. Half of Greenwich pours onto Nantucket in July and August, and this fact plays a part in what will happen there that year.

The thief is Kenneth Littleton. Nantucket police arrest him when he tries to sell some things he has stolen to a fence who turns out to be a police informant. There were four burglaries and several petty thefts. Police charge Littleton with grand larceny.

What does it signify when a respected schoolteacher becomes a thief? What is the psychology? Littleton has stolen a curious assortment of items—a sundial, a lawn jockey, some scrimshaw. Also a painting and a lamp and a credit card plate.

None of what he has taken is very valuable, but there are so many things that their cumulative worth is estimated at four thousand dollars.

The items he does not try to sell he buries in the front yard of the house he is renting. Later, when detectives in Greenwich get wind of the arrest, it is the burying that captivates them. What else has he put in the ground, and where? Is the murder weapon among his buried loot? And has he buried with it an outrageous memory—one he cannot reconcile with his greater self?

Brunswick parents who summer in Nantucket read of Littleton's antics in the *Nantucket Inquirer & Mirror*. They are not amused. They go home at the end of the summer and complain to Brunswick headmaster Norman Pedersen, and with regret Pedersen fires the teacher. This is when police learn of the thefts in Nantucket, and at once they put aside their certain conclusion.

"Those incidents in Nantucket cried out for attention," Captain Tom Keegan will tell *Greenwich Time*. On October 18, 1976, Littleton sits for the polygraph machine. The examiner runs through the questions three times. Littleton fails badly—the only person of a dozen to do so. The machine indicates Littleton lied when he said he did not kill Martha Moxley; lied when he said he did not hit her with a golf club; and lied also when he said he didn't know who did.

Littleton tries to explain: his father has lost his job and he himself has started drinking heavily. And when he drinks he steals things—from lawns, shops, boats at anchor. The arrest for crimes he is guilty of are somehow feeding into the machine—that's what it is.

Littleton agrees to take the test again, on another day, and to let police administer Sodium Pentothal. But lawyers gum it all up: John Meerbergen, Littleton's attorney, and later Greenwich's town attorney, counsels his client against taking the tests. Perhaps if Littleton had gone against Meerbergen's advice he would not have sunk so deep into the mire; perhaps he would not still be a suspect today.

In late November, Lunney and Carroll go on a journey north. The detectives hop aboard the ferry at Woods Hole, Massachusetts, and head out into Nantucket Bay. The water is cold and gray and desolate now, and so is the island, though the hardy souls who winter there believe Nantucket is loveliest at this time of year.

Ken Littleton spent his summer here working as a bouncer at Preston's Airport Lounge, a rock'n'roll club three miles out of town. After work, Littleton would go drinking at the Chicken Box or the Mad Hatter, and then, under the power of alcohol, he would filch lawn jockeys and sundials, whatever caught his fancy, on the way home.

In Nantucket, the two detectives learn that between the summer of 1975 and that of 1976—since Martha's murder—a new Ken Littleton has emerged, one who is as loud and obnoxious as the old Ken Littleton was quiet and studious.

Jimmy Manchester is Preston's proprietor. Manchester hired Littleton as a bouncer both summers, and he tells the detectives that Littleton "had made a complete turn-around and was drinking heavily" and "not doing his job." He also had taken to wearing a white three-piece suit, with a shark's tooth dangling from a chain around his neck, and "was playing up to any and all women that he saw."

I catch up to Manchester in January of 1998. Preston's burned to the ground in the spring of 1979, he tells me. These days he's doing small contracting jobs around the island. He remembers Littleton as the quintessential Charles Atlas weakling—"the skinny guy who got sand kicked in his face and then pumped himself up with weights." Particularly, he remembers Littleton's voice on those seventies summer nights calling, "It's hot and it's humid—get down and get dirty!"

The scuttlebutt among the workers at Preston's, according to Manchester, was that Littleton was suffering a crisis of sexual identity. "That's the indication I got from our workers—that he was going through some sort of personal change and didn't know whether he was gay or straight."

Lunney and Carroll go to see a woman I'll call Katie Fielding ("I don't want to have Kenny Littleton showing up on my doorstep. I'm serious. I'm not afraid of anybody, but because he's a disturbed person, I don't want him tracking me down"). Fielding, who worked with Littleton at Preston's, has also noticed the change in Littleton. Last summer, she tells them, he dressed in khakis and a polo short. This summer it was the Great White Suit. She also says that while he worked the door he would flex his muscles, cadge drinks from the waitresses, try to get drunk on the job, and hug the girls at random. Once, she remembers, a couple of girls dumped a stein of beer on his head.

Katie tended bar in Nantucket for twenty years. Today she owns a school and runs a gallery, and the bar days seem as though they were someone else's life, but she still remembers Ken Littleton. She had not thought of him for many years when she saw his name in *People* magazine. It was May of 1996. The magazine had published a summary of recent events in the Moxley investigation, and now she read that Littleton—"the tutor"—had become a suspect after the incidents in Nantucket. Her first reaction was, "What the hell could he be tutoring anybody in?"

"But he was a weird guy. One summer he was a very circumspect college-type guy, and the next year he came back and now was a macho asshole."

I tell Katie that today Littleton suffers greatly from mental illness—manic depression is what I've heard—and that he is nervous and paranoid and easily driven back to drink. But not violent.

"Oh, I think he could be very violent," Katie counters. "That's where you're totally wrong. At least that's my impression."

It's also the impression of Linda Cahoon, whom Littleton decked that summer on the dance floor of the Chicken Box. Cahoon is Nantucket's dog officer—a tough, sturdily built woman. She worked the door at Preston's one summer accompanied by her pet tarantula. "We've been friends since I was thirteen," Katie Fielding tells me. "She has a history of being—how do I say?—not being told what to do. Kind of a tough chick."

In July of 1976 she was dancing at the Chicken Box and accidentally bumped Littleton's girlfriend. Cahoon quickly apologized, but Littleton struck her face with the back of his hand and sent her sprawling to the floor. Soon after this happened, Cahoon ran into Littleton downtown and he said he was sorry. But he added, "You really shouldn't fool with my woman."

Today Linda Cahoon lives on a houseboat behind the Angler's Club. She paints an unforgettable picture of Ken Littleton as he was in the summer of 1976.

"He wore a white vest, jacket, and pants, and white shiny shoes. He seemed to be very enamored with himself. He was a pretty bulky guy, but I never saw him lift a weight. I don't know if it was steroids or what. He was always preening himself on the beach. Nobadeer Beach, which you can't get to these days because of all the new houses. He would put all this oil on himself and do these weird poses. Bodybuilding poses. He would stick his leg up in the air and rub the oil around. Like he was in his own world."

"Did people stare?"

"I don't know how you couldn't! He would stick his leg out, arch it back. He was so obnoxious. He really grated on your nerves. He walked down the street like, 'I'm cool, I'm beautiful,' right there in your face. He was so obnoxious about it. He'd stop and flex in the shop windows and fix his hair— oh, he was always combing his hair! He had that little greasy black comb in his pocket."

"Was there a point at which Littleton stopped appearing on Nantucket?"

"Right after those detectives came. Was it fall? I remember leaves were all over the ground. The detectives had guns strapped to their ankles. I'd never seen that before. They came because he stole a whole bunch of stuff. He stole all this bizarre shit that people wouldn't normally steal, and he buried it. He buried a statue in his front yard."

"What about the time he smacked you?"

"Well, he backhanded me and I went down. But I got even. Whether it was right then or at a later date I can't recall, but I took a swipe at him."

I remark that the Moxley story is chock-full of oddballs.

"By Jesus," she says, "you're talking to another one."

Eventually the detectives conclude that there is not much beneath the surface of Littleton's waywardness. "I don't think most of these were done maliciously," Carroll says about his petty thievery. "This is why we kind of ruled him out. It would usually happen after he'd been drinking. He'd get off work and stop and have a few beers, which is normal for a young guy. And then walking home—Nantucket is not all that big, and he didn't live far outside the town—he'd pick these things up walking by somebody's house. He was getting his jollies. Getting a rush. And then, burying them, he was eluding the police."

Nonetheless, on their way home, Lunney and Carroll stop in Belmont, Massachusetts, to visit Ann and Wayne Littleton. The detectives ask about their son's history, and the Littletons are guarded. Ken has never said much about the Moxley murder—only that he had been at the Skakels' that night and the police had questioned him.

The Littletons do not seem to know much about their son's recent life. It is the detectives who tell them of the failed polygraph. Carroll reports: "Mrs. Littleton was still under the impression that her son was working at the Brunswick School and would be getting out of school for Thanksgiving vacation."

Littleton was living then in a house on Sherwood Place in Greenwich, a stone's throw from the Brunswick athletic fields. For a while, he had no work. Rush Skakel had fired him from his tutoring chores, for no clear reason. "I never understood why he turned against me," Littleton later tells *Greenwich Time.* "I think he wanted to separate himself and his family from me when the police began pressuring me."

Then parents and police squeeze him out of his Brunswick job. On Sherwood Place, Littleton has a roommate named Patrick Sikorski, who teaches at Saint Luke's School in New Canaan; Littleton gets part-time work there, teaching math and English to high school seniors, in the winter of 1976. But the police come calling, and headmaster Richard Whitcomb, though he regards Littleton as an excellent teacher, can't chance having a murderer among his boys and is forced to let him go.

"Jimmy Lunney and I were responsible for him losing I think three jobs," Steve Carroll says. "Not that we meant it that way."

Early in 1977 Littleton, his teaching prospects shattered, returns to Nantucket to answer his burglary and larceny charges, and a deal is struck: Littleton will be sentenced to seven to ten years in Walpole Prison, but the sentence will be suspended. He will serve no jail time. The court gives him five years probation. Finally, a break. One curious thing, though: Littleton would have got a far better deal had he agreed to return to Connecticut and submit to a truth-serum interview. He adamantly refuses.

Littleton gets work as a commodities trader, but there's a nervousness, a touchiness, that has crept into his character and deepens with the passage of time. The detectives in Greenwich keep up with him through his probation officer, John Quinn, who describes Littleton as cooperative but distant.

Quinn gets Littleton on the phone while he has Jim Lunney and Tom Keegan in his office in Cambridge, and Littleton demands to speak to them. "I never want to see you fucking guys again!" he tells them. "I'll talk to you on the phone, but you fucking cocksuckers aren't going to bother me anymore—stay out of my life and leave me alone." Then he hangs up the phone.

In March 1978 detectives receive word that the commodities firm for which Littleton is working, Lloyd Carr of Boston, has gone bankrupt and is under federal investigation for fraud. Littleton's out of work, living with his parents in

Belmont, and looking for a new job. He seems to have no friends.

He bounces around from job to job. Finally he is reduced to working on a loading dock. Beginning in 1981, Littleton stops reporting to his probation officer, and in the spring of 1982, Massachusetts state court orders his arrest. But he is nowhere to be found.

Wayne Littleton tells Jim Lunney that, yes, he's spoken to his son but does not know where he is or how Lunney can contact him. Eventually Lunney learns that Littleton has wandered down the East Coast, met a girl in Florida, and gone back with her to Canada.

Later Lunney hears that Littleton has been released from probation, after paying $658.20 in restitution for the things he has stolen. He is a free man but a haunted one. Ultimately he loses himself in Australia, which is about as far away as one can get from Greenwich, Connecticut.

Exposure

ONE SUMMER EVENING in 1977, Sheila leaves the Best Wurst— a downmarket German restaurant that existed briefly on Greenwich Avenue—where she works. She is walking on Field Point Road, less than a mile from home. The faintly striped lawns of old estates sweep down to her feet.

A silver Chevy Vega hatchback pulls up beside her. "There was this icky-looking man inside. Like a little urchin. He was saying things like, 'Nice day for a walk.' And I'm like, *O-o-kay, I'm not stopping for anything.*"

A red backpack is slung across her shoulder. "You going

hiking?" the man asks her. Sheila throws him a sidelong glance and a non sequitur. "That's okay. See you later. Bye."

Another car drives up. The Vega moves on. *Good. He's gone.* But the silver car circles around again. *God. I've got a problem here.* The man leans over and leers.

"Want a ride?"

"No, thanks. Don't need one."

"Oh, you like to walk, you like to hike?"

He's adjusting something below her line of sight, moving his hand around.

Sheila maps out in her head where she must go. She considers making a break for it, but if she speeds up a driveway and nobody is home, she's a goner—he'll have her all to himself on a deserted lawn. The lights of the great houses have not yet come on, so Sheila cannot see whether bodies move about inside. She imagines herself trapped, cornered, banging on the door of an empty house.

Sheila comes to the Sweeney home, which always bursts with children and classical music. The Sweeneys are saintly folk with a vast adopted brood. Sheila considers, reconsiders: no, she can't lead this creep to a house full of children.

"So then I scooted up the hill, and he seemed to be gone. But he came back. I'd reached a point where there wasn't much grass on the roadside, a place where bushes and tiger lilies grow, and he kept trying to get my attention. But I wouldn't look at him or talk to him. I ignored him.

"My heart was beating fast, and I'm thinking, *Is this the guy who killed Martha? I'll bet it is. This is exactly how it happened. He stopped to figure out where she lived, he went and got her on Mischief Night. And now he's gonna get me. This is the guy that's tormenting me in my nightmares, and maybe it wasn't a blue car I saw on Walsh Lane. Maybe it was a silver car. Maybe it was his car.* I'm thinking all those things, and I'm trying not to panic."

Yet her eyes record the scene: his car, the things inside it, the license plate, the clothes he's wearing, the features of his face. She walks down the road pounding these details into her memory, saying them over and over again like a mantra.

The Belle Haven guard booth is near. She tries to make out a form in the window. *Shit! It's empty. This is my day. This is the day I'm going to die.* Brazenly he halts by the booth, opens the door, gets out, and exposes himself.

A car rumbles near. "It was Mrs. Rader, my guardian angel. She drives right up, and I jump in the car and say, 'Take off! Take off!' And she goes, 'Are you okay?' And I just say, 'Take off!' As we drive down Field Point Road, I tell her about this guy and what he did. She says, 'Don't tell anything more. Go over all your information. Call the police.' I gave them the information and they went out and found him. He admitted exposing himself. He was from Flushing, New York—the famous Flasher from Flushing.

"The police came to my job the next day with a photo lineup, and I had to pick him out. And I had to go down to the police station. I was going through all this stuff, and I remember thinking, *A year and a half ago I was here for Martha's case, and I don't think any of them even know who I am.*"

Michael's Demons

UP IN WINDHAM, New York, in March of 1978, Michael Skakel goes berserk. He's driving along a mountain road at 3:45 A.M.

when he sees lights flashing up ahead. There's been a car accident, and some cops are piecing together how it happened.

One cop steps into the road and signals for Michael to stop. Michael tries to run him down. Then he speeds up the dark road, and the cops give chase. Michael comes to rest against a telephone pole, unharmed.

He's charged with speeding, unlicensed operation, failure to comply with an officer's order, and driving while intoxicated. In court he pleads guilty to all but the drunken driving.

Later that afternoon, a plane lands at a local airport. Michael is handcuffed, and two attendants and a doctor wrestle him aboard. Then the plane whisks him off to a hospital in Poland Springs, Maine. It's called Elan. Windham police chief James Scarey tells Jim Lunney that lately Michael "has been causing numerous problems for his family."

At seventeen, Michael has become an alcoholic. Keegan and Lunney want to know what's behind it, but quickly a Skakel family lawyer, Tom Sheridan, steps in. Don't bother Michael, he says. He's making progress and doesn't want a relapse.

By November Michael's still in Maine, reportedly at a strict school for problem children. On November 15 police learn that he's run away. There's momentary concern, but it seems he's only gone to Boston and New York and then returned to Maine with Rush junior.

A couple of weeks later, Michael escapes again, and two weeks after that, he's still at large. Then Rush returns the young man again to the place he hates. Later the rumor surfaces that Michael's been taking regular beatings at the hands of the staff. A boy who needs love—beaten, estranged, alone.

Psychic Images

MARINUS DYKSHOORN IS a small, stout man dressed in a dark suit, his graying professorial frizz pushed back off his broad forehead. He struts into the Greenwich Police Department's Detective Bureau on August 31, 1978, and places his hand on the right shoulder of Howard Reynolds, the new captain of detectives.

"So, how's the shoulder?" Dykshoorn asks him in Dutch-accented English.

"What do you mean?"

"You broke it in the surf at Fire Island."

Indeed Reynolds had, and so the captain murmurs: "I know you're clairvoyant now."

Fifty years before, as a child of five, Dykshoorn stood one day at the window of his house in a small Dutch village. Snow fell thickly outside, and in the falling snow an image materialized before his uncomprehending eyes. *A man entering a barn with a length of rope and slinging it over a beam. Hanging himself.* Then the vision disintegrated in the weather, leaving the boy confused. What had he seen? What was its source?

Dykshoorn told his father about the man in the barn, and the father became upset. What sort of five-year-old dreamed up such psychotic fantasies? Two weeks later, on the outskirts of town, a suicide by hanging occurred—in a barn, rope slung over a beam.

As Dykshoorn grew up, the strange gift threatened to drive him mad. His personal relationships were bombarded by psychic impressions; he knew the fortunes of his friends, their worries, their secrets, their sins. He could hear conversations taking place in private, could foretell illness and death. The burden of his gift pressed him hard. Then he learned a simple little trick to shut off the pain it brought him. When he wanted to evoke his clairvoyance, he would hold a loop of piano wire in his hands, and the wire would work like a dowser's fork, moving of its own volition as visions flooded forth.

So the psychic with the piano wire went about Europe in the company of police detectives. He found himself able to reenter the emotional intensity of an act, taking on the properties of both victim and killer. Once he assumed a murderer's limp and grimace, another time he made the gurgling sound of a man immersed in water. Easiest for Dykshoorn to "see" was the sort of murder that police found hardest to solve—spontaneous outbursts of brutality, like the one that killed Martha Moxley. It was the emotion that drew Dykshoorn in, as though such murders created a kind of force field that only he could detect.

Reynolds hears about Dykshoorn—now living in New York—through a hypnotist who had helped solve a rape case in Greenwich. Without briefing Dykshoorn, Jim Lunney and Joe McGlynn take him down to the Moxley estate. Dykshoorn immediately knows that a girl was killed there with a golf club, and he shows the detectives exactly where it happened.

The wire spinning furiously in his hands, Dykshoorn heads away from the Moxley house southward, toward Long Island Sound; he believes he is tracing the killer's path. The path takes them to a large white brick house with a lawn sweeping down to the water. The house belongs to the piano-comedian Victor Borge. When Dykshoorn reaches the water's edge he points to a breakwater and tells the detectives that the missing piece of the murder weapon is down there, under the rocks.

The detectives are confused—until they learn, later, that this part of Victor Borge's breakwater was built after the murder.

Afterward Lunney and McGlynn take Dykshoorn to lunch at the Showboat, just across the harbor from Belle Haven. To get to the dining room, one has to walk down a long corridor with photographs of celebrities on the wall. There are several photographs of John F. Kennedy, who took many trips aboard a presidential yacht, no longer in use, docked in the harbor outside the dining room windows. Dykshoorn stops before a picture of Kennedy and begins to tremble; Lunney and McGlynn watch this reaction with quiet alarm. I must leave, I must go home, Dykshoorn tells the detectives. He is "shaking visibly," says Reynolds, who tells me this story in 1998.

Reynolds telephones McGlynn at his home in South Carolina all these years later and McGlynn confirms Reynolds's memory of the incident. But for me, McGlynn will neither confirm nor deny it. All he says is this: "Not everything in those [police] reports makes it to you writers." Lunney and McGlynn's entry for the Dykshoorn incident is all of two lines long, and includes nothing of the above story.

Dykshoorn is an old man now, living with his wife, Cora, in the Bronx. I reach him there by phone. His reaction when I mention the Moxley case is strong—he will not talk about it. But he asks me, "Do you know the girl's family? I am glad I do not. The pain . . ." He is not talking about their pain so much as his peculiar ability to make it his own.

He begins to speak of the day he visited the murder scene. "A car came with a light on top. We had to stop." He says no more. He will not elaborate. To keep the conversation alive, I ask him whether he went to a restaurant after viewing the murder scene.

"Do not answer that!"

It is Cora's voice. She has been listening in.

"I cannot talk about it," Dykshoorn says wearily, and our conversation comes to an end.

There have been at least three psychics who worked on the Moxley case. One was a woman who, in October 1978, claimed to police that for three years she'd been having a dream about the murder; the woman's name, and the substance of her dream, is excised from the police reports that were eventually made public. Then there was "Psychic Sue," whom Dorthy Moxley met while on vacation in Hot Springs, Arkansas, in July 1981. "Something's not right with one of your children," she told Dorthy. Dorthy Moxley is not especially keen on the pronouncements of psychics, but neither is she closed to them. Psychic Sue kept telling Dorthy things that only a psychic (or a resourceful con artist) could know.

Psychic Sue came to Greenwich on September 27, 1981. Jim Lunney took her to Belle Haven. Whatever Psychic Sue had to say about the case, it must have been intriguing: her impressions take up nearly twelve full pages of the police reports, all of which are blacked out—by far the longest redaction in the nearly five hundred pages of reportage. I wanted to find out where Psychic Sue is today. "She's dead," Dorthy Moxley tells me. "Her house burned down—with her in it."

Chapter Nine

A Decade of Silence

YEARS PASS. The flow of events moves along rapidly and leaves the Moxley murder far behind. Yet the case retains a subliminal presence. Even for Rush Skakel. "Well, of course you know he was a roaring alcoholic," one of his neighbors tells me. "He might have stopped drinking by this point. But do you know what he *did* do? He walked all through Belle Haven carrying a golf club in his hand. A golf club! So finally somebody called Anna Mae, his new wife, and said, 'Anna Mae? You've got to do something about Rush walking around with that golf club.' And Anna Mae said, 'Why?' And this somebody just went, 'Oh my *gawd*!'"

Geoffrey Byrne died mysteriously on December 27, 1980, one month shy of his seventeenth birthday. The boy had been only eleven the night of Martha Moxley's murder—the night he believed himself chased home through the woods. I had been told he was never quite the same after that. He turned distracted and skittish. But he found solace in drinking and drugs, and it is widely believed that he died of an overdose.

He did not. An autopsy showed he was clean at the time of his death. Arthur Byrne, Geoffrey's father, is a kindly, soft-spoken man who maintains a house in Belle Haven but lives mostly in Florida.

Geoffrey died asleep in his water bed on the third floor of the Byrne mansion. He appeared to have suffocated; Geoffrey had a serious sinus problem. Was his death accidental? Arthur Byrne says, "I've always been under the impression that he willed himself to die.

"Now, how much of his memory of what transpired in 1975 contributed to his . . . feelings of despair, shall we say? He never said what he thought. He never gave me an opinion, or the police an opinion, of what he thought had happened."

A *Greenwich Time* reporter called Geoffrey Byrne two months before he died, on the occasion of a story marking the Moxley case's fifth year. "He didn't do it," Geoffrey said of Tommy Skakel. "I know he didn't do it. He's not the sort of person who could have done such a thing."

Though the Moxley police reportage dribbles on into 1982—the last entry concerns *Greenwich Time*'s efforts to gain access to the reports—Geoffrey's death seemed to mark a symbolic end to the matter.

The town had other concerns now. One of the great calamities in Greenwich history struck on a balmy moonlit night in June 1983. Werner Albrecht saw it happen. He was on his boat in Mianus Harbor, at 1:30 A.M., when he heard a sound like a bass drum. He pressed his face to a porthole and saw a pair of headlights cascade off a highway bridge in the distance. And then another pair of headlights. And another. Albrecht left his boat and hustled up the shoreline to where Interstate 95 crossed the Mianus River. What he saw made him shake his head and blink his eyes.

A hundred-foot span had dropped out of the Mianus River Bridge, precipitating four vehicles and six passengers into the dark water seventy-five feet below. Three people died: two men in a BMW that landed in a deep part of the river at high tide, and a man named Bracy, who had been hauling a truckful of meat up from Louisiana. Hunks of beef and ham floated on the water. As police dived for bodies, they reached down not knowing whether they were pulling up the dead or a side of beef.

There had been warning signs, but those who noticed them did not know what they signified. First came a high-pitched keening, the sound of straining metal, and then the starlings that had roosted under the bridge all flew away. And so, in the early-morning hours of June 28, the eastbound half of the bridge, built in 1959, gave way under the tonnage of Bracy's meat truck—though the actual cause of the collapse seems to have been a combination of poor design and poorer maintenance and inspection.

News media from all over descended on Greenwich as never before. The word "infrastructure" entered common usage. America's roadways were decaying, politicians began telling us, and presidential candidate Gary Hart (pre–Donna Rice) astutely held a press conference using the crippled bridge as his backdrop.

Meanwhile, one of America's busiest arteries was choked off at Greenwich. Rumbling, snorting tractor trailers were routed through the narrow streets of Cos Cob, clogging the Post Road and infuriating the merchants. Their businesses suffered badly as the world that had whirred quietly past on

the interstate now jerked through Greenwich, expelling nox-
ious fumes. It was too much work to drive to the store.

When First Selectman Rebecca Breed went to the bridge
one day to try to calm the residents of Cos Cob, who were sick
of the noise and the fumes, some in the crowd picked up hand-
fuls of gravel, and the police had to whisk the town leader
away. Breed, an attractive woman with a blond bouffant and a
brisk manner, later learned that threats had been made against
her life. She'd been called Hitler. Politically the bridge presented her with an impossible situation—the outside world
had breached the town, and the town needed a scapegoat.

One day the following summer, a boy walked out of his
house in the working-class neighborhood of Glenville with a
fishing pole in his hand. Matthew Margolies, thirteen, was
last seen walking along the Byram River on August 31, 1984,
at about 5 P.M. He did not return for dinner. He did not return
the next day.

Matthew was a skillful fisherman and a strong swimmer,
and it seemed unlikely that he had drowned in the river.
Friends speculated that the boy had gone into hiding; he had
been grieving over the recent death of his grandfather, the
man who taught him the art of fishing.

But even as the friends voiced their theory, they knew it
sounded wrong. A sweet-natured boy, Matthew was not given
to dramatic adolescent displays. Police and neighbors began
scouring the riverbanks on the night he failed to return. The
search resumed early the next day: men in scuba gear dived
the river; a helicopter cut the air overhead. On Sunday—the
third day—police called the FBI. Monday went by. Tuesday
went by. There was hard rain and intense heat, and soon the
feeling crept in that something evil might have occurred.

On Wednesday afternoon a volunteer searcher named Fred Lambert climbed a thickly wooded ridge opposite the river and stumbled upon a pair of black-and-white checkered sneakers. They were the kind Matthew Margolies had been wearing. Lambert brought one sneaker down and showed it to the police. A couple of youth officers quickly went back up the ridge with Lambert, and after a few minutes of kicking around in the brush they made a horrible discovery: the decomposing body of what looked like a teenage boy buried hastily beneath some rocks and leaves. The cops summoned help, and then they stood in the woods and cried.

It had been nearly nine years since the murder of Martha Moxley. And here was another slain child. He had the same initials. You might have taken it for a reminder or a haunting.

Matthew Margolies had been stabbed many times and also asphyxiated. The murderer appeared to have had a sexually motivated torment in mind and taken it way too far—farther than he had planned. The boy's white gym shorts were stripped off, but as with Martha, the medical examiner found no solid evidence of sexual assault. The next day police found the murder weapon amid the leaves: a ten-inch kitchen knife with a wooden handle. Tom Keegan, now chief of police, announced, "There's a killer on the loose," and the village of Glenville closed in upon itself.

Of all the villages that constitute Greenwich, Glenville is among the most tightly knit. The community grew up around a felt mill and a textile mill, both on the Byram River. Immigrants, chiefly Poles, worked in these mills and settled in the river valley. After the murder, Dan Warzoha, a town engineer who has lived his whole life in Glenville, told me: "Glenville is unique. It's one of the few communities in town that's still a neighborhood. It hasn't yet become a transient community where people live awhile and then move away. You find families who have lived there generation after generation after generation. There is a distinct closeness. But obviously, all of that has been changed forever."

Sometime before World War I, people began calling Glenville "Happy Valley," but the term fell gradually into disuse. These days they called it simply the Valley. The textile mill is long gone, the felt mill turned into an upscale commercial center, and now a murderer had threatened the closeness that remained. The people of the Valley watched and waited in fear. The playing fields emptied out toward evening, and Vinny Ferraro, who owned the pizzeria across the street, stared wanly out his shop window. Alton Fox, the school crossing guard, stood with his arms at his sides. Two boys delivered the paper instead of one. The fear seemed purer and deeper than the fear that had hit Belle Haven after Martha Moxley was killed.

The Greenwich police were bent on solving this one. For years, criticism over their handling of the Moxley case had rankled them, and so for Matthew Margolies they would be absurdly rigorous. "We're going to break this thing, whether it's tomorrow, a week from now, or a year from now," said William C. Andersen, the police captain who headed the investigation.

The police never did. Too much had gone against them. Matthew had been dead five days before his body was found. The rain had washed down the ridge and destroyed the crime scene. The heat and insects had ruined the corpse quickly, further complicating the matter. And here in Glenville, just as in Belle Haven years earlier, certain residents shut their doors on the police as they hunted for clues to the killing.

This time there was almost nothing bad you could say

about the police, however determined you were. You could not accuse them of bowing to the influence of the wealthy. You could not accuse them of slipshod work. You could not accuse them of taking lightly the report of a missing boy. The police questioned more than a thousand people, generated a stack of police reportage that dwarfed that of the Moxley case, resorted to psychics (as they did in the Moxley case), and hired crime experts from far afield.

John Douglas, the FBI's psychological profiling guru, judged Matthew's killer to be a white male who lived nearby; who knew Matthew and also knew that he fished almost daily along the river; and who felt remorse for what he had done. The police narrowed the field to five suspects, some of whom were known sex offenders. But there was nothing to link any of them to the crime, though some felt certain that a young Glenville man who lives there to this day was the killer. Without evidence the police had no case.

When all the leads dried up, Greenwich police hired a retired New York City homicide detective, now a consultant to police departments, to critique their investigation. "The homicide of Matthew Margolies was a lust murder," wrote the detective, Vernon J. Geberth. "Lust murders are extremely difficult cases to solve. They are sex-related homicides in which the motive is in the mind of the killer. They are committed by persons who may act on the spur of the moment, but the act has been premeditated in their obsessive fantasies." Geberth had quibbles—no unsolved case could be perfect—but on the whole he pronounced the investigation "professional and exhaustive."

The police did not give up. They are still working the case. One fairly recent strategy was to get hold of some Defense Department satellite images, which can be manipulated to show a thing as small as a license plate. It was hoped the images would actually show Matthew Margolies together with his killer, but as it turned out, the satellite was not trained on quite the right region.

The Greenwich Curse had manifested itself again. But unlike Martha Moxley, nobody talks about Matthew Margolies from Glenville anymore.

In the 1980s Greenwich began to experience a great change. New wealth poured in—boisterous young New York wealth and shimmery international wealth—and the town shook off its Waspy cobwebs.

The people with new money built tall stone walls around their estates. They bought mansions only to tear them down and build bigger ones, many crammed onto lots where grand manor houses once lorded over hills and hollows. A tempestuous young millionaire named Peter Brant bought the fifteen-hundred-acre Rosenstiel estate and transformed it into the *new* most exclusive part of town. The land is extraordinarily beautiful; light seems to shine strangely there, as if from the pages of a picture book.

Brant kept the old estate name—Conyers Farm. Eighty years before, Edmund C. Converse (of which "Conyers" is the Old English spelling), a founder of U.S. Steel and Bankers Trust of New York, assembled the farm. In the early years of the century it had been the glory of the back country, a world unto itself. Converse raised poultry, cows, and pigs, produced milk, butter, and eggs; above a blue lake stretched apple, pear, and peach orchards. On the topland, towering over a reflecting pool and an English garden, was a great stone manor house with an ornately gabled roof. Ivan Lendl bought the decrepit Conyers Manor in 1983, but arsonists torched it two years later.

The centerpiece of Conyers Farm today is a polo field, where in summer the best in the world—the cream of Argentina and Mexico—play matches that are sometimes attended by British royalty. New York glitterati emerge from the gray city to the green countryside; Bianca Jagger, Andy Warhol, George Plimpton, and Jerzy Kosinski were some I recognized. And all over the back country you began to see gorgeous young people with long, sun-lightened hair, enthroned in marvelous sports cars.

As Greenwich's stock rose sharply in the 1980s, what had grown old was new again. And, inevitably, the celebrities flocked.

Diana Ross moved onto the old Reynolds estate in Belle Haven. Harry and Leona Helmsley bought the Topping estate on the crest of Round Hill. The Trumps, Donald and Ivana, spent weekends in a great white house on Long Island Sound. Frank and Kathie Lee Gifford moved to an old farmhouse in the back country. Ron Howard was the first of the new Hollywood stars to settle in Greenwich. Tennis stars Lendl and Mats Wilander bought houses in town, and two years in a row they drove from Greenwich to Flushing to battle each other in the men's final of the United States Open.

These new celebrities joined a distinguished constellation: abstract expressionist painter Robert Motherwell; actor George C. Scott; art collector Joseph Hirshhorn; Pulitzer Prize–winning writer Barbara Tuchman; musical comedian Victor Borge; baseball Hall of Famers Tom Seaver and Ralph Kiner; Nobel Peace Prize winner Elie Wiesel; and movie producer Joseph E. Levine. There were also homegrown stars: figure skater Dorothy Hamill won Olympic Gold in 1976; San

Francisco 49er Steve Young was in the process of becoming the best quarterback in pro football; and a girl that Young had dated in high school, Christie Fichtner, was crowned Miss USA of 1986.

In 1988 another homegrown eminence, George Bush, was elected president of the United States. Sometimes the roads from Westchester County Airport would be blocked off and you would catch a glimpse of the presidential motorcade humming noiselessly to the house of the president's mother.

For Greenwich's marquee millionaires, the decade soured toward the end. The Trumps divorced. Leona Helmsley was convicted of tax fraud. And so was Peter Brant, the king of the back country, whom some had come to call "Donald Trump with taste."

Meanwhile, there were two more killings. On December 1, 1985, Kurt Peterson walked into his mother's back country house and shot her dead with a .22 caliber pistol. Later he appeared behind police headquarters and told an officer that he wanted to turn himself in. It was a very sad case. "We grew up together in a house of poisonous hatred," Peterson's sister wrote the presiding judge. "Not for one second was I surprised that someone died in the house with a gun."

Janet Peterson, the mother, had wanted to die. Once, in Canada, she tried to commit suicide, but Kurt had saved her. Now the good son was simply satisfying his mother's deepest wish. It was like something out of a bad Tennessee Williams play. The prosecutor, Bruce Hudock, called the case "a Greenwich gothic horror," and nobody objected when Peterson was sentenced to only seven years in prison.

More troubling was the case of Mary Capozza, a mother of two who was in the process of a divorce. She vanished in 1987 on a date Greenwichites knew well—October 30. Her body turned up a month later in a duffel bag in the Kensico Reservoir, across the New York State line. No one was ever charged with her murder.

Family Secret

I'D KNOWN Mary Heaney for a couple of years before she startled me with her Skakel story. It was undramatic but also unforgettable. Later, when I found myself neck-deep in the Moxley case, I phoned her: Would she tell me the story again, for the record?

Sure she would, she answered, so long as I didn't use her real name. She didn't need the Skakels hounding her. But she did tell the police, so if a Skakel ever comes to trial . . . She'd rather not think about it.

I take a seat at a Starbucks and wait for her. Mary breezes through the door. Coffee addicts peer over the rims of their cups. She has luminous skin and a pillowy voice. An Irish Catholic heritage. She has almost everything a Skakel might covet.

David Skakel went out with her first, in the summer of 1986. This was when the Moxley case was sleeping, when months went by without a haunting in the news or in the air. David was the youngest of the Skakels, nine at the time of the Moxley murder and twenty the summer he dated Mary Heaney. He drove an old woody and played Bob Marley ceaselessly.

When they were getting to know each other, Mary asked him what he did for work.

"I have Jesus' job," he said.

"Oh, you're a shepherd?"

He frowned. "A carpenter."

One night David took her out to Nino's, a restaurant in the fashionably leafy town of Bedford, New York, just north of Greenwich. It was a double date; the other young man was a relative of Richard Nixon's. Or so he said.

"They really rolled out the red carpet," Mary recalls.

Maybe Nino's treated everyone that way, I suggest.

"Oh, they knew. David was part of the Kennedy clan, without a doubt. And part of me liked that. It was nice, I'm not going to lie. But I liked the special treatment, not David."

Afterward they drove back down to Greenwich and went to Portofino. It was the hot local bar for a couple of years in the eighties. Mary found herself talking about how well she gets along with her mother. She asked innocently, What about you, do you get along with your mother? This was his stepmother, Anna Mae Skakel. Rush married her in 1983.

"He said, 'I don't want to talk about my mother! I hate my mother!' He had this look of utter and pure hatred on his face. It was like this monster had come out, this nut, this demon. For six seconds it was really scary. I knew right then I didn't want anything to do with him."

David took her home to the street where she lived. It was a modest street, but Mary's was a beautiful old house. "I think he thought I didn't come from the proper social stratum when he saw my mother lived here and not on Round Hill Road. It's like that Kennedy idea—always marry up."

Still, he kissed her good night. Marrying was one thing, kissing another.

"I couldn't wait to get in the door. It was a really long night. Have you ever heard the term 'energy vampire'? Well, he was one."

David called a few more times, but Mary put him off. She

thought him strange. He was well mannered, but nothing shone out of him; there seemed to be a void, a lack, a space he filled with studied eccentricity. "He thrived on being weird. He'd ask me to play scuba ticktacktoe in his pool. Stuff like that. He reveled in being unusual, quirky, offbeat."

The summer of 1986 wound down. Mary went with some friends to Portofino one night. They ran into David's brother Steven, then twenty-three. It was Steven who was jarred awake by screams, or laughter, on the night of the Moxley murder.

"Oh! Mary!" he said jovially. "You went out with my brother. He told me all about you. You guys went out to dinner, right?" He grinned. "Why don't *we* go out to dinner?"

She laughed him off.

"The Mug and Ale, then."

"Oh, all right."

The Mug and Ale was a sweaty dive in Rye, New York, fifteen minutes away. The bars in New York stayed open later than those in Connecticut, and on weekend midnights there was a steady flow of weaving taillights down the Post Road and across the border to Port Chester and Rye.

On the way, Mary got pulled over for running a stop sign. She was drunk, but the cop let her go. "This family really *is* charmed," she told herself.

When they got to the Mug it was late and Mary was tired. They did not go in. They stood out in the parking lot and talked as the late trains from the city rumbled down the tracks. Steven was leaning against his blue Volvo station wagon when the words floated out of her mouth.

"I said, 'You know, your family is so interesting. Remember that situation? Did your brother really kill that girl?' " She did not specify the brother, but she meant Tommy. "His face got very somber and sad. Then he looked at me and nodded slowly. He didn't say a word."

"Bummer," Mary said to him.

"Yeah, it sucked."

Back at Starbucks, Mary gazes out the window and says, "I think he was amazed that I had the brass to ask. He seemed to be turning it over in his mind, like it was a silent thing he didn't talk about but wrestled with in his psyche.

"I tried to change the subject, to seem as though I wasn't shocked. I turned the conversation toward lighter things, like his jacket."

But the thing lingered.

"He seemed so ashamed and so affected by it. From that day on, there was no doubt in my mind that Tommy was guilty."

Mary wanted to be gone. "I gotta go," she said to Steven.

He said, "Let's have dinner. My father belongs to this private club in New York. It's really wonderful."

Mary sips her coffee, rolls her eyes. "I just wanted to exit as gracefully as possible."

She encountered the Skakels over the years. The following winter she saw them bowling at Greenwich Lanes, which has since been turned into a fashionable shopping center. "Whenever I see them, they give me a big kiss and a hug. Once you're accepted by one member of the family, you're accepted by all of them."

Tommy was there.

"He had white skin and dark hair—that black Irish look. He said, 'Oh, I've heard about you.' He was very gracious, very pleasant. Even sweet. He made an effort to be polite and friendly. But at that point I knew what had happened."

Mary ponders the manifold victims of the Moxley murder,

among them the Skakel family. "It must be sad for them. Wherever they go, they're the Skakels. They can't get away from themselves."

The Moxleys moved away from Greenwich in 1977, first to New York City, then to Annapolis, where David and Dorthy would spend time powering around the Chesapeake Bay on their forty-two-foot cruiser.

He was restless in retirement. He joined Bob Dole's presidential campaign in 1988—they were both Kansas boys—but when Dole withdrew, David found himself restless again. Finally he spoke publicly about his daughter's murder. "In hindsight, I would have pushed back," he told Len Levitt of *Greenwich Time.* "In hindsight I would have gotten aggressive as hell. Within twenty-four hours I would have brought in outside detectives. I would have brought in outside attorneys. I would have offered a reward. There'd have been an uproar, I'll tell you that."

David Moxley went back to work: a new direction for him—managing a firm of powerhouse New York lawyers, Lord Day & Lord, Barrett Smith. The Moxleys put the Annapolis house on the market. On the Sunday before Thanksgiving, Dorthy took David to the train station. She would join him in New York the day before Thanksgiving, after she got some busywork cleared away—paying bills, seeing to the realtors, giving their two cats a little attention.

"I was going to stay and get things done and drive up on Wednesday. And that's what I did. Now, I hadn't talked to David after he left. I thought it was funny that I hadn't heard from him, but I thought, well, he's just busy. He was having a wonderful time getting into this law firm. Running the board meetings, taking charge." Dorthy laughs at the memory of David back in his element. "Oh, he was enjoying himself.

"So I drove up on Wednesday—we were subletting this little studio apartment—and I got there at about two-thirty in the afternoon. I unlocked the door and walked in and David was in bed. He never did things like that. He was a workaholic, he never got sick, and if he didn't feel well he still went to work.

"And I looked at him and said, 'David, you're home! My God, you look terrible.' Then I thought, *Oh my God*. And I realized he was dead. I called 911, and I called John, who lived up on Eighty-fifth Street, and then I just sat down and waited for someone to come."

David Moxley had died in his sleep of a coronary arrest. He was fifty-seven years old.

His sister, Mary Jo Rahatz, tells me, "You never did know what David was thinking. He was a very private person. I understand it because I'm the same way. He didn't express his feelings—I don't think to anyone. I'm sure you know I think he was a victim the same as Martha. He just did not talk about it. Wasn't his nature. If only he could have blown off steam, gone to somebody."

Dorthy casts back to Thanksgiving the year after Martha died. "We were having Thanksgiving dinner at the University Club, the three of us, in New York. And it was terrible because I was trying to get John and David to just say *something*. Neither one of them would. It was just in the last five years before David died that he could talk about Martha at all. I always thought that in some way, keeping it all bottled up could have had an effect on his general health—and that's why at fifty-seven he was gone."

* * *

After Martha's murder, people had serious concerns about John Moxley—they thought he might never quite recover. "I just muddled through," he says. "I was on autopilot for several years. I went to Choate for a year after high school. I didn't apply to any colleges. I asked my dad if I could go into the military—kind of half-assed. If he'd said yes, I don't know if I actually would have done it. But he said no.

"Choate gave me a convenient stopping point for a year. To try to mature, heal up a little bit. Then I went to Ohio Wesleyan. I never talked about Martha. In college, a couple of people said they'd been someplace and it had come up. Or they'd call and tell me how it frustrated them, what people would say. I'd just say, 'Yeah, okay, fine. Did you go to the Yankee game yesterday?'"

Avoiding the subject of Martha's murder kept John from building close ties. There was an unbridgeable distance around him. Finally he met Cara, who challenged the distance. He married her. "She's not the kind of person who can let something just sit. She's the kind of person who'll hash it out until it's exhausted, one way or another. She's been a tremendous help in getting me to exorcise some of my demons."

The death of John's father also helped him to break down the distance. "My father was a smart guy. He got things done, he made things happen, and it was easy to let everything fall into his lap. And I didn't have to deal with it. And my father and I would keep things in. He asked me one time if I wanted to have a father-son talk. I thought he wanted to talk about sex. I was thirteen at the time, or twelve. Then he said, 'We can have a father-son talk about the facts of life, or you can wash the car.' I said, 'I'll wash the car.' And he said, 'That's fine.'

"But my mom would go through things backwards and forwards. To see my mother cry as she had cried, to see such emotional venting so many times, was really, really painful. And my father and I would just, like, shut it off. But I knew he would handle the investigation, he would bring all the resources that we as a family could possibly marshal. So I could just isolate myself and not have to worry about that stuff.

"But when he died, I had to step up to the plate. I couldn't allow my mom to do everything on her own. It wasn't until about 1990 that I was able to look fully at the situation. I'll tell you the worst part. I was watching a television program one night, and I found out that my sister had been stabbed through the neck. I remember this wave went through my body. I had never known that. For a long time I thought it had been, for lack of a better expression, a clean kill."

Chapter Ten

New Owner

SNOW TUMBLES from a heavy green sky. Belle Haven rises above the black water, its icebound mansions like ghostly etchings from a Victorian picture book. Nestled deep in the peninsula, among tall pines, is a faded Spanish villa. The old house glowers behind a tangle of shrubs, its arched windows spilling red light onto the snow. An actor named Jon Lee lives there now. The wooden door swings open, and Lee stands framed in the storm light, a stout Asian American with steel-gray hair down to his shoulders.

He beckons me in.

"No, the brokers never mentioned it to us," he says. "It wasn't to their advantage, you see." Lee's cool baritone might have fallen from a cloud. His was actually the voice of a TV creature called Swamp Thing. "When I told friends which house we had bought, they said, 'Ooh, the *Moxley* house.'

Like it was the Bates Motel. I said, 'What do you mean, the *Moxley* house? They only owned it for a couple of years.' Then they explained all the details."

He gazes out a picture window to a formal garden. A tiny red bird stands motionless in a fountain quilted with snow. "Tell me," Lee asks, "have the Greenwich police *ever* solved a murder?"

Technically, yes. The last man convicted of murder in Greenwich had driven his convertible Buick from the crime scene, a fine contemporary house whose owner now sagged in his swimming pool, to police headquarters, where the killer unspooled an astonishing confession. If you call that solving a murder, why, yes, the police had done it. But perhaps the dismal police record owes little to incompetence. Since the town's murderous beginnings, I mention to Lee, killers have amassed a quiet history of getting away with it.

Lee steers me into a wood-paneled library. I see the window seat where Dorthy Moxley fell asleep as she awaited her daughter's return that late-October night many years before. "The girl's portrait hung right above your head," says Lee. A local artist named Frank Kalan—the father of Martha's friend Christy—painted it after the murder, from a small color photograph of Martha Moxley holding an armful of schoolbooks. Lee saw the portrait briefly, while touring the house with a broker, and learned later that the wholesome blonde on the wall was the girl murdered on his lawn.

"Anyway," Lee continues, "if you want to attack somebody, you dump the body in Greenwich."

Lee tells me how he and his wife came to buy the Moxley house. From the green hills of the back country to the craggy waterfront, Jon and Joan Lee had scoured Greenwich for the perfect home. Their broker told them of a delightful prospect on Walsh Lane—a Spanish house with twenty-four rooms and a wine cellar.

"A Spanish house?" Lee said without enthusiasm. "I'm not interested in a Spanish house in Greenwich." Such a house seemed to him a silly conceit, like an English Tudor baking beneath the hard blue skies of Arizona. Lee did not go to Walsh Lane.

And so a local builder decided to buy the Spanish house, with the vain expectation of splitting the two-acre lot in half, constructing a second house, and selling both. When that plan went afoul of the zoning hawks, a young New York couple settled on the Spanish house. Not long after Lee heard this, the house appeared to him in a dream. Then he learned that the couple's mortgage bid had collapsed.

"Normally I wouldn't take a look at a Spanish house," Lee says, "but too many things drew me to it." When he at last beheld the house, it did not strike him as very Spanish. Perhaps Moorish. Built around the turn of the century, it had presided alone over Walsh Lane for many years and now seemed a smoldering uncle amid its polished heirs. Jon and Joan bought the house for $290,000—a steal in Greenwich, even for 1977. It was before closing on the deal that the Lees learned they were buying, too, a fragment of Greenwich history. One that his neighbors did not care to remember.

Lee had questions about the Moxley case but hesitated to put them to his new neighbors. Here he was, an actor, and an Asian one at that, among all these silver-haired business titans. One wrong move could land him outside decorum's capricious circle. "Friendly? These people, they're *civil*," Lee says evenly. "And they're gracious when they meet you and say hello. But no, I can't use the word 'friendly.' After all these years, I've only been on the inside of three homes on

Walsh Lane. And they've all been on the inside of this one." Lee slips his hair into a knot. "You never can tell whether you're being discriminated against. How does that old saying go? Oh yes. 'The kike is the Jew who just left the room.'"

Lee had been told that Joseph E. Levine, the legendary film producer, was denied membership in the Belle Haven Club for being a Jew. Of course, Lee's sources added, the club let him entertain there, so long as he attracted such illustrious houseguests as Kirk Douglas and Sophia Loren. (In fact, after much friction, Levine was allowed to join.) Some griped when Diana Ross bought the dank old Reynolds estate, but it was true, by 1979, that the grumblers composed a declining minority. Bigotry seldom disturbed Greenwich's languid facade. It ulcerated deep in the town's boggy soul and now and then oozed up like a gas bubble. After a friend proposed Lee for membership in the Greenwich Country Club, a gentleman of consequence let slip, "You know, Jon, we're trying to get another Oriental in the club." Lee quietly withdrew his name.

Only one neighbor welcomed Jon and Joan to Belle Haven. He ambled up the lawn in wrinkled tennis whites, hefting a drink in one hand. "Rush Skakel," he announced cheerfully. "Anything I can do, you just let me know." Lee recalls the ruddy-faced widower's abundant use of the word "super"— everything was "super"—a mood that may have overtaken him in the afterglow of the Moxleys' departure.

Lee often wonders where his neighbors stand on the matter of Tommy Skakel. His own impression is that Tommy possessed too light a frame to have carried out such nasty work. "Several people told me they thought only somebody much bigger could have done the damage that was done to that girl," Lee notes. And, of course, common folk were all too ready to scald the rich. "It goes with the territory when you have a name like that. Nobody named Schwartz would have got so much attention."

Still, Lee was curious: few in Belle Haven found the business of this unsolved murder terribly pressing; it seemed to irritate them like a cloud of gnats at cocktail hour. "They're dragging *that* up again," someone might venture. Or, to Lee, "Did you see your house in the *National Enquirer*?" But no hard line of inquiry emerged from the peninsula. The collision of Belle Haven's obliviousness with the sporadic hammering of reporters gave Martha Moxley a negative presence, a presence like antimatter. "She's like the nineteenth-century pregnant girl," Lee observes. "Where did she go? She went *away*. No special place. Just *away*.

"I don't think this attitude had anything to do with the Moxleys personally. I think it had to do with somebody invading their neighbors' privacy. An acre here should come guaranteed with a certain amount of privacy." He points to the window. "Don't forget—there's an armed guard on the corner. You wouldn't need that unless you feared for your safety or you wanted to exclude people. In this case it's to exclude people. I can guarantee it.

"The bottom line is values," Lee says, turning from the window. "Real estate values. But it's never talked about." Lee looks like a warlord risen out of feudal Japan. But he was born in the Bronx, of Korean and Irish blood. Living now in one of America's grandest neighborhoods and bearing a visage far more exotic than the usual, he might have invented for himself a delectable past. He chuckles and says he knows people in town bent on such Gatsbian deceptions. "A lot of people in the community have to assume an identity that other people want them to assume. They don't like common folk. If a guy lives in a twelve-million-dollar mansion, they find it hard to accept if he says, 'Two days ago I only had twelve dollars in my pocket.' People have to establish things and put up pictures. It's not unusual in this community to go out to antiques shops and pick up daguerreotypes and tintypes from families that were not theirs. And just scatter them around the house, for ancestral worship. I went to the home of a Jewish friend recently and sat down in the living room. There was a picture of some straight-arrow Mormon on the wall. And on the table, next to a little pair of antique glasses, lay a Bible, a great big family Bible, with pictures and inscriptions dating from Boston, 1848. 'Wait a minute,' I said. 'I thought you came from Minsk, in 1913.' The fellow shrugged. 'Well,' he said, 'my decorator felt the book would look good on that table.' "

I go out into the storm, glancing back once, to see Lee's door thud shut and his shadow slide into the dark of the Moxley house. The Lees have divorced since moving here, so perhaps the house holds its own private misery for them. Now Lee wants to sell it. I trudge across the yard and stand under a streetlamp, trying to conjure the fury of that Halloween Eve. The willow tree under which Martha was attacked is gone. Later I phone Lee and ask what happened to it. "Seven or eight years ago, there was a storm. The crash woke me out of a sound sleep. When I looked out the window, I saw that the tree had toppled over—the roots had come out of the ground."

Revisitation

STEVE CARROLL'S VOICE is hushed, nervous. He has not been back here for two decades. Across the street a disembodied hand draws a curtain open; no face appears. We've come to Jon Lee's house—Martha Moxley's house—and we are tramping through the scene of the kill.

Carroll is a handsome man, with a rugged tan face and thick white hair. But his senses seem out of tune. His eyes dart over the lawn, up to the house, out to the quiet lane where no cars pass.

"This is a little weird," Carroll murmurs. "I can picture that day. A whole bunch of us standing around here with our thumb up our ass, really, not being able to do anything. We called in the state police crime unit, and they didn't get here till late. This was all lit up. It was ridiculous."

He waves his arm before the house, shakes his head.

"Hindsight is always twenty-twenty. If it were to happen today, you'd hope somebody in the department would have enough sense to say, Okay, this is where the body is. *Schwipp!* Rope all this off. And put people at each point. Nobody walking around squashing things."

He puts his hands on his hips, squints. "Something's different."

"Right. Mr. Lee put in a new driveway. A more direct approach to the house."

The old driveway still exists, a crumbling gray path that angles out to Walsh Lane.

"Oh. Okay, okay, yeah. That's where I got confused. Now I got it. The house is up here, and the kitchen is on this side, is it not?"

"Right."

Carroll starts moving with confidence about the lawn as the memories stream back.

"Now, these trees, of course, were here."

The front lawn is painted with the blue shadows of big

trees, but sunlight comes in where the willow was. That patch of lawn is bright.

"She's running home, right?" Carroll commences his scenario. He glances across to the Skakel house and sweeps his arm to indicate the path Martha must have traveled home. "This was all covered with leaves, because it was November, almost, and it had been cold, so it was all covered with leaves. Now, the body was found over there"—he points to a towering pine—"and then we kind of pieced it all together."

We walk to the front of the house, just short of the front door. "We found the head of the club over here, on this part of the lawn, about fifty feet from the house."

I recall a newspaper photograph from the time of the murder. Somebody had driven a wooden stake into the ground. "Did that mark the place where the club head was found?"

"Probably. You had to mark it because everything was covered with leaves."

We take a few steps toward the street. Carroll stops, pats the air with his right hand.

"She's hit here. I might be off by a few feet, but not much. She's hit here and knocked unconscious or semiconscious. Now Mrs. Hammond, who lives here"—he points next door, to the simple white colonial amid some evergreens at the end of Walsh Lane—"is coming down the street. So he panics. He grabs her by the feet and drags her, facedown." We're standing on the old abandoned asphalt. "Her face is bouncing across the driveway. There are pine needles in her skin, and her face is bloody, her nose, her chin—all bloody."

We cross the driveway and stand on the thick green grass of the side yard. I look up at the master bedroom and imagine how threatening the sight of Mrs. Moxley moving behind those windows would be to a man in the midst of a murder.

"He drags her across, and somewhere in here, this is where we feel her jeans and her panties were pulled down below her knees, but she's not responding, she's not responding. So then he takes the club and just beats the shit out of her, all around the head.

"And somewhere in here he stands on the club and breaks it. Then we find the two pieces. . . . Let's see—the head ends up there, by the front of the house. The handle is missing, and the eight-to-ten-inch piece, that's what he stabbed her through the neck with."

"Not the handle piece?"

"Not the handle piece. The handle piece is never recovered."

Something makes no sense.

"Okay," I say, "but you can tell from examining the middle piece that it had done the stabbing?"

"Well, yeah. We found it in a pool of blood right here."

We stare at our feet.

"It was all smeared, like somebody had run his hand up and down it. And covered in blood, as if you'd stuck a knife in a piece of steak and pulled it out. Very, very bloody."

"No fingerprints?"

"Nothing. Her hair—she had long blond hair—was pulled through the wound, so that her hair was coming out the right side of her neck. Of course, we didn't know she'd been stabbed. They discovered she'd been stabbed when they were cleaning her up for the autopsy." Carroll viewed the wound in an eight-by-ten-inch color photo. "The wound was obvious. Couldn't miss it. There was two, three inches of hair coming out the right side of her neck."

Carroll walks past a ponderosa pine, then comes to a second one, farther back on the property. "We came upon the body way back here, beneath this tree. But there was a path. A bloody path. Traces of blood all through here." He stares down at the spot where Martha's body lay all night and into the next afternoon. "Her hair was all over. But you could make out her features, her nose and ears. Her face was not touched. I saw a picture that was taken when she was lying on the slab. Her face is just fine. Except her chin and nose and forehead are all scratched. It's her head that was beaten in."

"Was the killer facing her?"

"No way," Carroll says. "Not unless the club had some kind of wild curve in it."

"Was Martha way under the tree, out of sight?"

"No. Just under one of the boughs."

The wind gusts through the trees, which sound as full and loud as ocean surf.

"There were bruises. . . ."

"Right. Her pelvis and her groin. It appeared that somebody forced—" He stops, reconsiders. "But you see, she never had her skivvies completely off, so her legs never really came apart. He pulled her jeans and panties down . . . seems he was trying to force her open."

We leave the place where Martha was found and amble toward the street. Carroll halts momentarily and stares at what used to be the Hammond house. "Okay, now, here's the situation. She's here, right?" He points to the big pine, then to the Hammond house. "That's his bedroom window."

From Edward Hammond's window it appears there's a clear view to the pine. Martha's body would have been easy to see; had Hammond looked out his window, it seems as though he could not have failed to miss it.

"Joe McGlynn and I first talked to him. We didn't have to get any search warrant. Probably today you'd have to. But in this particular case, we were just interviewing people. If we'd taped anything, then we'd have had to get a warrant, so we could present it in court. Otherwise they'd throw it out."

Hammond consented to the detectives' search. He did not act like a guilty man. But he managed to be his own worst enemy.

"So here he is, in his room, and she's being beaten right over here. And we say, 'Didn't you hear anything?'"

He claimed he didn't. And in retrospect, Carroll believes there was no screaming. Not from Martha anyway. If anyone was screaming, it was the killer, he says, and his screams would have been carried off in the wind. But if there was no screaming? "The only thing Hammond would hear is somebody being beaten like a pumpkin with a golf club. And it was cold. The windows were shut. But you know, that's one hundred feet—one hundred feet from where she was beaten."

We're out on Walsh Lane, following the path Dorthy Moxley took to the Skakels' on the dawn of Halloween, 1975.

We're facing the Skakel house. Rush Skakel sold the place in 1993 and moved to Florida.

Carroll asks, "Who lives here now, do you know?"

"A younger couple."

"These younger people have so much money these days. They're hustlers." Carroll gazes at the house. "Well, some of it's family money."

We're trundling back and forth in front of the house, pointing, gesturing. Carroll says, "I hope we don't get in trouble."

"Do you know which one was Littleton's bedroom?"

"He was in the master bedroom, upstairs." He points to the side of the house nearest Walsh Lane; Tommy and Martha were last seen on the opposite side of the house, near the brick arbor, out of Littleton's view. "This is three stories high, this house. If you see the third set of windows up there, that's where Tommy and Michael slept. Rushton said, 'Help yourself.' So Jimmy and I went up there by ourselves.

"But we found nothing. Then we had the garbage man, Riccardi, leave out all the stuff he collected here. We went through it at the dump." Carroll shakes his head. "We tried to cover all the bases. We really did. Within the legal limits."

Who the Killer Was

STEVE CARROLL, alone of all the Moxley murder's investigators, has never been shy about expressing what he believed happened to Martha Moxley. Or who he thought did it to her.

"I know Teddy Brosko's told a couple of people I was crazy, because I could get in trouble. But I'm sticking to my guns. I believe it's Tommy Skakel."

And so he begins to explain the steps that led to Martha's murder, as he sees them.

"The camper's up in there," he says, pointing to the Skakel driveway. "It's a good-sized camper. And the Lincoln: they had a maroon Lincoln Town Car, and I believe it's parked right in back of the camper."

"The kids are in the Lincoln."

"In the Lincoln, right, listening to tapes. Martha's in front, between Tommy and Michael. Helen Ix and Geoff Byrne are in the back. Michael told us that Tommy was feeling up Martha's leg, running his hand up and down, and Martha was kind of laughing and brushing his hand away."

"That wasn't in the report."

"Uh, right." Carroll scratches his face. "I was talking to

Frank Garr, who's on the case now. When I said that about the sexual connotation, he says, 'Well, there's nothing in the report.' I think we were probably remiss in not putting that in."

Other cops are annoyed by Carroll's willingness to talk openly about the Moxley investigation—and its errors. Most annoyed is Frank Garr, who once held Carroll in high esteem but now feels he's broken a code of silence that should envelop all active cases. The Moxley case is active, though at this point it is wheezing and limping.

"Still," Carroll resumes, "I don't know how much credence you can put in Michael."

"The kids broke away in pairs. Was there a sense that they should leave Tommy and Martha alone?"

"That's a good possibility. In Martha's diary there are a couple of indications that they had been together in the Skakels' playroom. She said, 'Tommy's going for a home run, but he can't even hit a single.' That kind of thing."

"She was a spirited girl."

"You got it. She was a very outgoing fifteen-year-old. If she were to put on the right clothes, you would have said she might be twenty. She was quite well endowed. Long blond hair. Cute. This is why I say he's trying to get in her pants. And she's saying, 'No way, turkey.' Like that."

We're standing in the yard, trespassing. We'd have been trespassing since we set foot anywhere in Belle Haven's seventy square acres if Jon Lee hadn't given us permission. Nobody's supposed to be allowed in without an invitation, but if you give the man at the booth a hearty wave and a grin, he lets you pass.

A black Mercedes rolls up, slows, and a man with silvery patrician hair and rimless glasses aims a steely glare at us. Then he touches the gas and moves on up the street.

Carroll grimaces.

"Okay, Helen and Geoff go that way, through the backyard. Whereas Martha goes this way"—he draws a line in the air from the brick arbor to Martha's front door—"and she cuts right across the corner of the pool. There's a garbage can out on the lawn. It's a known fact that the boys used to chip balls into garbage cans in the backyard. There are clubs up on the patio.

"The Skakels were saying that maybe the club came from someplace else. 'You could get a Toney Penna six iron any-place.' True. But they had one of those fiberglass mats—that's what they used to chip off of. The mat was still here when we were investigating, so I took the club head and the mat up to the New Haven lab. The fibers on that club put it here."

Carroll and I start back up Walsh Lane, intersecting the path Martha took home as her killer closed in. "I firmly believe in my theory. People say, Well, what about this, that, and the other thing? Okay. Show me how it could change that Tommy and Martha were the last ones together. Nobody else was around. There was no stranger coming through here. For what reason? Was he going to rob them? No.

"As for Littleton. Littleton was physically strapping, about six two, two forty, and athletic. He played football. He wouldn't have used any kind of an instrument. He would have attacked Martha with his hands, his arms."

"Some people say Tommy Skakel wasn't big enough to make that kind of damage on Martha."

"No, no, no. *Contraire.* He was seventeen. I'll bet he was your size right now. No, he was a big boy. Tommy's got to be about six, six one, plenty strong enough. He was very athletic. And easily set off. He'd have these tantrums where his father would actually have to sit on him to quiet him down. Rushton told us that, yeah.

"So Tommy starts pushing and shoving Martha, trying to feel her up. He's getting very frisky. But she's saying, 'No way, no way, turkey.' And she starts home. She's not running home. She feels she has nothing to fear. Tommy goes, 'Aw, come on, Martha, come on back.' He picks up a golf club that was either on the patio or very close. So he's going after her, trying to hook her. It's a playful thing. Now he's on the other side of Walsh Lane, he's on her property."

Carroll is standing in the middle of Walsh Lane, toma-hawking the air with an imaginary club. A big, left-handed hack.

"Is Tommy left-handed?"

"Tommy's left-handed. And he hits just a little too high and a little too hard—*boom*. He hits her in the left temple."

"What happened then?"

"He lost it. Somewhere he lost it."

Blind to Evil

THE TABLOID TELEVISION SHOW *A Current Affair* cornered Ken Littleton in Boston in 1993. The crew appeared to have followed him to Quincy Market, where he was alone, sipping a soda through a straw at an outdoor café. His hands shook visibly.

He added to his version of events a trifling detail. Standing at the front door of the Skakel house, he had heard movement in the brush, as though somebody were dragging a branch through the leaves. It gave him chills. He went back inside.

"I think that's bullshit," Carroll scoffs.

Littleton never mentioned anything about noises and chills. What is stranger: in this account, Littleton finds himself staring out at a lonely darkness. There's nobody anywhere—no Skakels, no Martha, no Helen, no Geoff. But Littleton's memory is suspect now. Who knows what visions it has entertained, what paranoid dreams it has frozen into fact?

Carroll leans toward an earlier version.

"The kids are out horsing around on the lawn, okay? The nanny, Mrs. Sweeney, goes to the stairs to call Littleton: I don't know what she calls him—Mr. Littleton, sir, whatever. He's supposedly unpacking his stuff. And he has *The French Connection* on. But he comes down to the front door and says, 'Hey, guys, knock it off.' And then he goes back upstairs."

We are standing in front of the Ix house, a white colonial resting midway up a gentle slope. The Ixes have never spoken publicly about the Moxley case, with one exception: a letter, written by Cissy Ix, to the weekly *Greenwich News* in the summer of 1993. I was managing editor at the time. Mrs. Ix chided us for implying that some Belle Haven residents were involved in a "cover-up." She went on to report that she and her family had "devoted hundreds of hours" to meetings with police, and while they would not comment on the investigation to reporters, they would "continue to cooperate fully with all officials in their efforts to solve this crime."

The investigators don't seem to appreciate all the Ixes' help. Indeed, they wonder if the Ixes know more than they let on. The family's relationship with the Skakels is rumored to be exceptionally close—as close as blood. And Mrs. Ix has been known to discourage her neighbors from commenting to reporters. "Contrary to what we led people to believe," Carroll says, "there were a number of people in Belle Haven who wouldn't talk to us. Some of the old stalwarts."

When Dorthy Moxley called Helen Ix Fitzpatrick to see whether she held some small, unexplored clue to Martha's murder, Helen replied vacantly, "I don't remember anything." I wonder if Dorthy felt Helen was stonewalling her. Dorthy thought a moment and said, "I did."

Steve Carroll seems almost pained by the reticence of the Ixes. Like them, Carroll is a dedicated Catholic, and so he imagines the Ixes performing somersaults of the conscience. "Bob Ix, he's some big Catholic muckety-muck. Which makes him a real hypocrite."

As if on cue, Cissy Ix crunches down the gravel driveway in a dark-blue Buick. "Cissy Ix," Carroll says, barely containing a sneer. "She's even more of a hypocrite than he is."

Why are they hypocrites? What's an example?

After Carroll left the police department, he drove for hire. Sometime in 1993 he found himself driving the Ix family to Kennedy Airport. On the way, they started asking about the Moxley case.

"It was fairly obvious they wanted to know what I knew about Tommy. Helen says, 'I wish they would just leave Tommy alone.' And I looked at her and said, 'Helen, if the shoe was on the other foot, and you were Martha Moxley, don't you think your father and mother would like to know who did it?' And she just went, 'Hmmph! They should leave him alone.' That's the attitude."

"I wonder how they would react if it were their own daughter."

"I think Bob Ix is the kind of guy who would never let it die."

The wind moves swiftly through the trees. The Ixes and

others remind me of something I read. In *The Death of Satan,* Andrew Delbanco traces Americans' weakening grasp on the concept of evil, even though "never before have images of horror been so widely disseminated or so appalling."

Of the 1947 Lionel Trilling novel, *The Middle of the Journey,* set in a town of whitewashed houses that bears more than a faint resemblance to Greenwich, Delbanco writes:

> Designed in every respect to "refuse knowledge of the evil and hardness of the world," this suburban sanctuary is invaded by sin when the town drunk strikes his child, who dies when a blood vessel bursts in her brain. It happens in church, in full view of the congregation; but despite the invasion, sin and death remain unfit subjects for discussion. At the mere mention of death, Trilling's suburbanites withdraw "in a polite, intelligent, concerted way . . . as if they were the parents of a little boy and were following the line of giving no heed to the obscenities their son picked up on the street and insisted on bringing to the dinner table."

I glance around at the enormous trees and the stolid, freshly painted houses peeking out from behind them and murmur to Carroll, "Sometimes I get a strange feeling in Belle Haven. An outsider feeling."

Carroll laughs heartily. "You're from here, though, right? You're from Greenwich."

"Still."

"Well, I drive for a few people down here, and I get exactly that kind of feeling. I'm always ready with an answer. 'I'm going to see Mrs. McKee, I'm going to drive Dr. Smith.' And I'm a lot older than you. I probably shouldn't have that feeling."

"You get an answer ready in case somebody stops you?"

"Right!"

I'm incredulous. "You, a former cop?"

Carroll grins, shrugs. "Yep. But I would never tell anyone I was a policeman until I really had to."

We edge up to the Ix lawn. We peer up at the windows to see if anybody's watching us. The house has a look of openness and approachability; or maybe it's civility.

All at once Carroll has projected himself back to the night of the murder. "There was a group of us who drove for Dr. Smith, who lives down here. That particular night, I came out of this street here—"

"You were here the night of the murder?"

"Yep. I came out of Meadowwood Drive and turned left to go up Otter Rock. I see all this toilet tissue and stuff in the trees. This is eight-thirty, nine o'clock at night. I was right here. I didn't see any kids. Never saw anybody out that night. Again, it was cold. The circumstances were just so perfect for anybody who wanted to do something. You couldn't have planned it. You could never have planned it so perfectly—the weather, the darkness, the wind, the absence of people. Usually there were a whole bunch of kids hanging out here, rocking against the chain."

"There were only the dogs."

"See, the Ixes' dog came out here—it was a German shepherd—and just started barking. Just stood there and barked. Howled. Came right up to the edge of the yard. Never left the property."

"Helen wanted to go out and get the dog, but the nanny wouldn't let her."

"She said something about the *way* he was barking. But I don't know as you could hear anything. Dogs just sense it.

Even with people screaming at each other, if there's an argument, they sort of sense it."

"The dog didn't come any closer out of fear?"

"Right, right. You know how animals get."

"Do they smell blood, or . . . ?"

"I don't know. I don't think we got into it too much with the animals because it wouldn't have proved anything."

"What, you guys didn't question the dog?"

Carroll gives me a fishy look, and we head back up the lawn to Mr. Lee's Bates Motel. Even on this flawless summer day, the house sits darkly, wearily, as though surrounded by its own bad weather.

I imagine the same bad weather has chased the Skakels through all these years, abating slightly as they travel far afield, hunting for big game in Africa or South America, but thickening again over them like the contractions of a storm, thickening and scattering until the end of their days. Or until the killer is brought to justice. Maybe when the Moxley case is consigned to history, the chain of Skakel misfortunes will also be consigned to the past.

Greenwich Gothic

THE DOOR OPENS. Jon Lee, long hair banded against the wind, steps out into the day. He's wearing faded jeans, a gray sweatshirt, and a day's growth of beard.

Carroll nudges me. "Is that Mr. Lee?"

I introduce the two men, who greet each other and begin to talk of Greenwich history.

"This all used to be Mead property," Lee explains. The

Meads were an old and important Greenwich family, whose number has lately dwindled.

Carroll smiles. "They used to grow potatoes and tobacco, and then they would wagon it down to Greenwich Harbor, and they'd load it on a packet boat bound for New York."

This was in the days when Greenwich was a prosperous farm town, before the real wealth came.

"Before the Golden Ghetto," says Lee.

Lee and Carroll talk of the old Reynolds estate, Quarry Farm, on the western side of the Belle Haven peninsula, now owned by Diana Ross. A man named Peter Voorhis bought the land in 1852 and began blasting stone from the cliffs by the water. Then he sledded chunks of stone—bluestone granite—to the dock at Byram Cove, and Voorhis's schooners would sail down the Sound, riding low with stones that would make the footings of the Brooklyn Bridge, the base of the Statue of Liberty, and several of New York's finest buildings. Then concrete got popular and drove Voorhis out of business. The schooners rotted and sank. Stones lay where they had fallen. But the gutted cliffs made a spectacular backdrop, like a Greek amphitheater, and filmmakers shot movies there. Pearl White's *Perils of Pauline* was one of them. Later an heiress to the R. J. Reynolds tobacco fortune bought the land, which was crowned by a Normandy-style château with small windows and steep slate roofs. It was dark and menacing then, and still is.

"Don't let me take you away," says Lee, excusing himself.

"He's Oriental," Carroll remarks with mild surprise as the door swings shut. Belle Haven is not known for diversity, but things are changing, even though Montel Williams has moved from Walsh Lane to the back country.

"Half Irish," I amend, and this gives Carroll a good laugh on himself.

After a silence, Carroll asks, "Golden Ghetto?"

Whenever the Moxley case is born anew, some rich people imagine it is they who are under attack; that the wild aim of reporters, detectives too, burns them as surely as it burns the Skakels. I explain Lee's full-circle theory, how the destructive power of too much wealth comes to resemble that of too much poverty. The drinking and drugging, the neglect, the dissipation, the suicidal recklessness—they all meet on the far side of the circle.

Carroll nods thoughtfully. "Geoff Byrne. Eleven years old. He had enough liquor up there to run a couple of parties. I still have questions about that. When he's seventeen he dies from an overdose. That was always puzzling to me." The actual cause of death may have been a kind of self-willed suffocation. He gives it more thought and adds, with disgust, "Those Skakels. They've broken more things. Very much like the Kennedys. They've broken more things and taken more things, and the family just pays and pays for it."

It's an echo from *The Great Gatsby*: "It was all very careless and confused. They were careless people, Tom and Daisy—they smashed up things and creatures and then retreated back into their money or their vast carelessness, or whatever it was that kept them together, and let other people clean up the mess they had made."

Rushton's brother George, the one whose plane smashed into a canyon wall in Idaho, was Greenwich's Tom Buchanan, all polo and muscles. It seemed fitting that he died the way he did. "Oh, he was wacky," Carroll hoots. "He put a guesthouse in up at his place on Vineyard Lane. Somewhere along the line he brought home this girl. So he was down in this guesthouse, and his wife, Pat, knew they were down there. She set fire to it and burned it down."

"Whoa."

"Yeah, she set fire to it. He got out."

The guesthouse was eighty feet long. It had a two-story living room with a stone fireplace, a movie screen that dropped down from the ceiling (George loved westerns), a sauna, and a mountain lion set in an African panorama. George had killed the mountain lion himself and had it stuffed by some specialists in New York.

The builder of the guesthouse, James Marzullo, had to rip out a wall to accommodate the mountain lion. When he came to take measurements, he passed by a swimming pool "filled with panties and slippers." After George died, Pat Skakel decided she wanted to rebuild the guesthouse, so Marzullo gathered his old plans and drew up a contract and went to Vineyard Lane one morning to have her sign it. That night she choked to death on the shish kebab. "Hell of a way to lose a job," Marzullo told me.

"George was known to have a lot of women," I say. "Blondes."

"All over the place," says Carroll. "He was a big guy, very athletic, a real world traveler."

We talk of the Skakel curse and how it seemed to run deepest in George's family. At least before the Moxley murder. "Up on Vineyard Lane they had those speed bumps, those silent policemen. The daughter, Kick—this goes back a lot of years—she probably just got her license. There were a bunch of kids sitting in her new Mustang convertible, and she had one kid sitting up on the back. She hit one of those speed bumps, and this girl—I can't remember her name—"

"Hopey O'Brien."

"Right. She got knocked out and killed."

Kick Skakel was sixteen. She'd been playing a game—speeding up and punching the brake, jerking the car along. Other children climbed down into the seat for fear of falling out, but Hopey, the youngest of them at six years old, stayed up on the trunk, her legs hooked down into the back seat. Kick hit the speed bump and Hopey was thrown aloft. She landed on her head and never regained consciousness. She died seven days later.

On the occasion of Hopey's death, Greenwich Police Chief Stephen M. Baran, Jr., spoke out publicly against . . . speed bumps. BARAN DEPLORES ROAD BUMPS AS GIRL SUCCUMBS, read the front-page headline in *Greenwich Time*. Baran was revered as a kind and compassionate man, but one who did not meet controversy head-on. Controversy was to be shunned. Carroll puts it a little differently: "He kind of kowtowed a little, as far as I'm concerned."

Carroll considers the ways of the rich. "Many of these people, they would sponsor Fresh Air kids up here. This was like a penance. There are some that are really sincere. They're not all like the Skakels."

Maybe with the Skakels—the Rushton Skakels—things started to go wrong when Ann died. Maybe things would have been different had she lived.

Carroll tells me Tommy had an especially close relationship with his mother.

"More than the others?"

Carroll nods emphatically. "He more than the rest. We attributed that to the fact that he was slow and the mother coddled him."

"He was slow?"

"He was seventeen and doing the work of a thirteen- or fourteen-year-old."

I had talked to Belle Haven residents who believed the Skakels weren't smart enough to get away with murder. Rich enough, but not smart enough.

"He wasn't retarded; just slow," Carroll says.

"That sounds pretty slow. Could you tell he was slow when you talked to him?"

"Oh yeah. He really wasn't aware of things that were happening in the world. He was always hesitant to answer questions. And slow at it. But not to the point where you'd say he's retarded."

"But," Carroll goes on, "a good athlete. Real good athlete. Maybe the things he really liked he learned well."

You can see Carroll's mind spinning. He's thinking of Skakel contradictions. "But the big thing is that report. Abraham Lincoln and the log cabin. There was no such thing. That was really the only lie we caught him in."

So far.

Chapter Eleven

Revival

A N INCIDENT in 1991—one that bears no direct relationship to the murder of Martha Moxley—lifts the aging case from its slumber.

On Easter weekend, in Palm Beach, Florida, William Kennedy Smith, a nephew of the late president John F. Kennedy, allegedly rapes a twenty-nine-year-old unmarried mother named Patricia Bowman. Bowman claims Willy Smith attacked her on the grounds of the Kennedy compound—pulled her to the grass, reached his hands under her dress, then ferociously raped her—while Senator Edward M. Kennedy slept inside the oceanfront villa.

The Palm Beach incident, true or not, stirs memories of the murder in Greenwich, Connecticut, sixteen years earlier. The Moxley story is similar to that of the alleged rape; the difference is one of degree. Indeed, some fashion of rape attempt seems to have prefaced Martha's murder, but for reasons unknown, the killer abandoned the sexual assault in favor of something worse—as if impotence had been transfigured into rage.

Suddenly it comes to light that the similarities may be more than coincidental. In the spring, less than a month after the alleged rape, a reporter from the tabloid television show *Hard Copy* develops a source who says that Willy Smith was visiting the Skakel house on October 30, 1975.

Could this sensational claim be true? Well, it would explain a few things: why Tommy lied about his Abraham Lincoln report; why Ken Littleton failed his polygraph test; why the Skakels rebuffed the police when things heated up. The Skakels were shielding a Kennedy from scandal.

But it's a stretch. Police had questioned the eight non-Skakels who were at the house that night—Littleton, handyman Franz Wittine, cook Ethel Jones, nanny Margaret Sweeney, Andrea Shakespeare, Helen Ix, Geoffrey Byrne, and Jimmy Terrien—and none mentioned a word about Willy Smith. Besides, police had heard variations on this rumor: cousin Bobby Kennedy, Jr., had been there too—or was it Joe Kennedy or Michael Kennedy or David Kennedy?

The police are nonetheless obliged to check into the matter. They find no information to substantiate the tip, not the faintest glimmer. The source itself chooses to remain anonymous. And yet . . . a collective memory has been roused. People flood the Greenwich police with rumors, tips, memories, theories. Much of the information is nonsense, but there's enough good new data to raise a question in the mind of state prosecutor Donald Browne: *Why didn't we know these things before? After all our investigating, why are all these things coming to us now, sixteen years late?* It's as if the Moxley case is suddenly raised from the dead.

The case had never been closed—only deserted. Steve Carroll had retired from the Greenwich police force in 1977; Jim Lunney teamed with Detective Frank Garr to investigate the growing narcotics trade in town, then left the department himself in 1987; and Tom Keegan, after a rocky tenure as chief—the police union sent forth a vote of no confidence in his administration—retired to South Carolina, where the residents of Surfside Beach elected him to the state legislature. It had been nearly a decade since the Greenwich police actively pursued Martha's killer.

A May 1 *New York Post* headline shouts: FLA. CASE REVIVES PROBE OF KENNEDY KIN IN '75 SEX SLAY. The *Post* notes in a sidebar story that in 1982, *Greenwich Time* hired a first-rate investigative journalist, *Newsday*'s Len Levitt, to delve into the Moxley case. Strangely, though, the *Time* never published Levitt's findings—which are based largely on the police reportage Levitt has acquired after arguing, successfully, before the state's Freedom of Information Commission.

Has undue influence somehow intervened? Was this a cover-up inside a cover-up? Would the paper *ever* run the story?

"We haven't made any decision yet," executive editor Ken Brief reports.

To which a frustrated Levitt answers, "Nine years later, they still haven't made a decision?"

What history does not forget, it amplifies. In the 1980s, while the investigation lay dormant, the murder of Martha Moxley evolved into a kind of myth—a disturbing presence rather than a mere news story. In this heightened state, with high-powered defense attorneys ready to pounce on a journalistic slip, *Greenwich Time* grew timid. It was an instance of a newspaper reflecting perfectly the town it covers.

So other news media began to horn in on the story. The *National Enquirer* reports in May 1991 that a month after Martha's murder, "Kennedy family members" alighted at the Skakel house and in a matter of days, "the family shipped Tommy off to Europe"—though this was actually the funeral.

> A source close to the Kennedy family disclosed: "The way the Skakels handled the murder of that young neighbor was a page ripped right out of the Kennedy handbook. It's just like the way the Kennedys are handling the Palm Beach rape case. Willy Smith has been accused of a felony and weeks later still hasn't had to face questioning by the police."

One month after the *Post*'s hint of a cover-up at *Greenwich Time*, the paper, under fierce pressure, prints Levitt's story. The most exhaustive account yet published on Martha's death, it reveals for the first time the details of the Greenwich police department's investigation—and its less than stellar performance. Suddenly Martha's name is back on everyone's lips.

Three months after the arraignment of William Kennedy Smith on the charge of sexual battery, and days after the appearance of Levitt's *Greenwich Time* story, Donald Browne orders a full reinvestigation of the Moxley case. It is to be led by state inspector Jack Solomon and Detective Garr.

To think it all started in a Florida nightspot. Had William Kennedy Smith not accompanied his uncle and cousin on a late-night jaunt to Au Bar in Palm Beach on Easter weekend 1991, had Smith not convinced a young woman to drive him back to the Kennedy compound, had he not then raped her or caused her to believe she'd been raped—had these events not unfolded a thousand miles away from Greenwich, Connecticut, Donald Browne never would have revived the Moxley investigation.

This is the beginning of a decade in which far-flung events come to influence the case, reviving it again and again.

In July of 1991 an extraordinary thing happens. Rushton Skakel invites Jack Solomon and Frank Garr to his house on Otter Rock Drive.

"Gentlemen," he says, "I want to tell you that back in '75, '76, I was concerned about my children. I didn't know what they had done. I didn't know! Today there is absolutely no doubt in my mind that none of my children was involved in that murder. You know what my problem was? I never should have listened to those attorneys."

The detectives glance at each other, amazed. Skakel shows them around his house. He is a man whose natural inclination is to be friendly, to play host, just as he did in the investigation's first days. "I am going to call my kids, my sons, my daughter. I am going to set up meetings for you with them, and each one of them is going to come in and see you." Skakel holds the detectives with his gaze. "You have my word on that."

They never talk to Rush Skakel again. "The very next day," Garr tells me, "we got a call from his attorney—Tom Sheridan, who represented all of them but Tommy. Sheridan said, 'You don't contact him. If you need anything, you talk to me.' Apparently Rush shared our meeting with his wife, and his wife contacted Sheridan—and that was the end of it."

The Best-Seller

"I KNOW A LOT OF PEOPLE in Greenwich, you see, and they get on the phone, very early, and say, 'Dominick, did you know . . . ?'"

It is a summer morning in the tiny Connecticut River town of Hadlyme. The journalist and novelist Dominick Dunne lives in an elegant yellow colonial overlooking a marshland, a vast leakage from the river. Thickets of wild rice bend in the breeze. Fog blooms softly on the marsh until the sun dissolves it into hues of rose and violet.

Dunne cradles a mug of instant coffee upon his knee. "And this one woman said to me, 'Mrs. So-and-so knows *everything*. Here's her number. She's in Florida.' So I get Mrs. So-and-so on the phone, and she takes this attitude to me. This arch, how-dare-you-call-me attitude: 'I play golf with Rush Skakel! We go to the same parties! We do this! We do that!'" Dunne's face collapses into a frown. "There's an awful lot of that—closing of the ranks. They'd rather whisper about it at tea parties and go for their golf game. Which I find very irritating. I mean, a girl is dead here."

This is in 1993. Dominick Dunne has just published a novel called *A Season in Purgatory,* in which the central act is a lightly veiled rendering of Martha's murder. The killer in Dunne's novel is Constant Bradley, seventeen, the scion of a Kennedyesque clan that is wealthy, Irish Catholic, and politically powerful. His victim is Winifred Utley, fifteen, a pretty girl who is new to the fictional Connecticut town of Scarborough Hill. The murder weapon is a broken baseball bat. A girl cutting through a wooded patch of the Utley estate stumbles upon the bludgeoned body. Harrison Burns, Dunne's alter ego, is the journalist to whom people yearn to tell secrets.

A Season in Purgatory quickly became a best-seller. Dunne went on talk shows and spoke more openly about the Moxley case than anyone ever had spoken before. He hinted darkly about the Skakels and criticized the investigative work—which drew the ire of the Greenwich police. "He is critical of things he knows nothing about," Police Chief Kenneth Moughty told a *Greenwich News* reporter. "He has never called, written, or approached anyone in the police department. This all goes back to people trying to take a shot at the Kennedys and the relationship." Dunne shot back, "If the Greenwich police have pussyfooted for eighteen years, they were not going to cooperate with me. I went in back doors."

Dunne's involvement in the Moxley case was a stroke of immense good fortune. It could not die in the glare of best-sellerdom. And as Dunne made his way around the country, promoting his book, people sidled up to him with secrets of the Moxley case, just as though he were Harrison Burns—or Gus Bailey, the fictional alter ego in Dunne's 1997 best-seller, *Another City, Not My Own,* based on the O. J. Simpson case. These secrets Dunne passed on to Frank Garr and Jack Solomon.

In return, the Moxley case gave Dunne precisely the sort of story that tantalizes him most—rich folk behaving monstrously and then retreating into the maze of their moneyed lives, beyond the grasp of justice. Dunne never directly accused a Skakel of killing Martha Moxley, but most Greenwichites considered his novel a work of journalism more than fiction. "The point was to write a best-seller," he allows. "And having written a best-seller, my secret hope was that it would put a spotlight back on this case. And I think it has done exactly that."

Dominick Dunne's fascination with celebrity, wealth, and murder is a dovetailing of traumatic events in his own life. Before he became a writer, Dunne had been a Hollywood movie producer and fallen prey to all the excesses of that lifestyle. He awoke, as it were, in 1979, when he felt the thud of hitting bottom. "Thank God!" he says in a tone of genuine relief. "Isn't it swell that I did? I could still be in Hollywood if everything went okay. But I screwed up my whole career myself. Nobody is to blame but me."

What happened? "Oh, it was primarily booze. And drugs, dare I say it. And I changed. I became not a very nice person after all those years there. I lost my marriage. I lost everything. Everything! I was married to a fantastic woman. Even with all the things, all the success, all the knowing everybody, I was like a wounded I-don't-know-what. People had stopped inviting me, people I used to know in my life, who had been coming to our house in Beverly Hills, to our parties, for years. It all stopped. I wasn't asked anywhere. Nothing happened.

"One time, at the last minute, I was asked to fill in at a party. Obviously somebody had backed out. It was the kind of party that normally I would have been invited to three weeks ahead of time, before my downfall out there, and they obviously couldn't get anybody else. Do you know what I mean, when you're asked at seven-thirty to be there at eight-ten? I went. It was at the home of Mrs. Jack Benny. I'll never forget this. I realized I was nothing. I was just somebody to sit in the gold chair. That's all. It had nothing to do with the fact that I knew all these people. I realized, *This is over. You're never going to get back.*

"The next morning I got in the car and drove away. I was like this whipped dog leaving town. The old Mercedes was long gone. I had this little two-door Ford, the cheapest one they make. And I drove and drove and drove, all the way to Oregon. I'd never been there before. I was in the Cascade Mountains and my car broke down there and I had to stay the night while they fixed it. I stayed for six months in this little place, Camp Sherman, Oregon.

"For almost three months, I didn't talk to a single soul. I didn't know anybody. I used to walk every day to a country store, which was several miles from my house. I didn't know how to cook, either, by the way. I lived on roast beef hash. You get these little cans of it and you fry it.

"Finally, after a couple of months, this woman came to my door and she brought me some elk stew. She said, 'They tell me all you ever eat is roast beef hash.' Elk stew, she made. I thought it was the kindest thing.

"I started seeing a few people up there. I never talked about my own life, ever. I would get into their lives. Sometimes they talked about stuff they read in the papers. And sometimes they talked about people I knew. I never said a word. I remember one time they were talking about Elizabeth Taylor, and they had it wrong about her marriage or something like that. I never said a word. I kept telling myself, 'It doesn't matter, it doesn't matter.' And it doesn't. It doesn't matter. Each time I let something pass, it was like one more string was cut from the puppeteer above."

The second thing that drew Dunne to the Moxley case gives him an almost mystical connection to it. On Halloween Eve of 1982, seven years to the day after Martha's murder, the actress Dominique Dunne was strangled to death on the lawn of her West Hollywood home. She was twenty-two and had just made her major motion picture debut in *Poltergeist*. She was the daughter of Dominick and Ellen Griffin Dunne.

In a jealous rage, her ex-boyfriend John Sweeney, head

chef at the exclusive West Hollywood restaurant Ma Maison, took her by the throat and squeezed the life out of her. For this act he served three years in prison.

"I can talk about my daughter's death now, but I also have been able to write about it. My books have helped me a great deal. How awful to have to keep it in! Do I still have rage? Yes. I must still have it. After Sweeney got out of his ten-minute prison sentence, for a while I had private detectives following him, getting reports and all this shit. And then one day I was with my two boys and I said, 'I don't want to live like this. This can't be what my life is about—revenge.' I felt, *God will deal with this man.* And I believe that."

The theme of justice—beating down as insistently as rain in Dunne's books—stems from the justice denied his daughter. The latest to be skewered on his quill is O. J. Simpson, judged criminally innocent of double murder despite a mountain of evidence. The Simpson case combined Dunne's preoccupations in ludicrous potency—the celebrity, the murder, the getting away with it. It is difficult to imagine Dunne will ever again find a subject so suited to his gifts and mind-set. But of the three murder cases that have touched his life most deeply—Dunne, Simpson, and Moxley—a sense of resolution, however feeble, has graced only two of them.

The Moxley case is the odd one. A trial is like a line in the dirt that, once crossed, tells a person he must get on with the business of living a life. There is before and there is after. Dorthy Moxley lacks the benefit of that ritual. On nobody's face can she pin her anger—it is diffused, undirected. "I call it an open wound," Dunne says. Any peace that Dorthy has been able to find has come from a strength of spirit arrived at quietly, over time.

Meanwhile, Simpson and Sweeney roam free, as does the

man who killed Martha Moxley. Dominick Dunne believes that justice, in its infinite forms, will visit us all. But it is of murderers he speaks when he says, "I don't think anybody gets away with it. There are always consequences. Always. Nobody has a bad life and dies happy."

The Private Eyes

WON'T IT EVER GO AWAY? Reeling from the fallout over the reopening of the Moxley case and then Dominick Dunne's novel, Rushton Skakel, through Tom Sheridan, hires a private investigative firm. His stated intention is to clear the family name.

Skakel sits down for lunch one summer day at the Belle Haven Club with former New York City detective Billy Krebs, an investigator with the Long Island–based firm Sutton Associates. Skakel tells him, "If my kids didn't do it, I want my family's name cleared publicly. If they did do it, I want to prepare the best possible defense."

I've heard bizarre rumors about Rush Skakel over the years. One has him in the emergency room of Greenwich Hospital, covered with blood, the morning of the afternoon Sheila McGuire discovered Martha dead. Another says he went up to Canada with a girlfriend to dispose of the Moxley murder weapon. A third says he orchestrated a cover-up with a battery of Kennedy lawyers—this in anticipation of a run for the presidency by Senator Edward M. Kennedy.

But Skakel goes ahead and hires Sutton Associates. This means he really doesn't know what happened to Martha Moxley. He wouldn't have hired Sutton if he did. "I think the entire family would have kept it from him," Frank Garr remarks. "You see, he's made motions toward cooperating now and then. He wouldn't do that if he knew. So my guess is that while he may have some personal doubts about his kids, he really doesn't know one way or the other."

The people of Greenwich see Rush Skakel's earnest effort at resolution as a farce. *Of course* he won't turn in his own boys, if it comes to that. Meanwhile, when the heat from Dunne's novel is at its hottest, the normally reticent Skakel lawyers get defensive. "We don't think this matter should be dealt with in the newspapers," Emanuel Margolis, Tommy's lawyer, snaps at a *Greenwich News* reporter. "*A Season in Purgatory* by Dominick Dunne has been receiving all kinds of publicity generated by the publisher and the author, and we don't intend to take part in that. We have maintained our silence and our composure despite ridiculous statements that have been appearing here and there in connection with that book. It's not only fiction, it's fantasy."

Tom Sheridan assails Solomon and Garr. "All they do is knock the brains out of the Skakel family. They thought this was going to be an open-and-shut case. A little hard questioning, push Tommy Skakel pretty hard, he'll break down. He never broke down. All they've done is tear him apart for seventeen years."

Sutton Associates begins by building a case against Ken Littleton. They compile a list of bludgeon murders of young women and match them to Littleton's movements. Predictably, they come up with four or five killings in Florida and Massachusetts that—based on proximity alone—Littleton (and thousands of others) could be responsible for. The investigators make him out to be a serial killer.

Sutton investigators interview Belle Haven residents, but

some residents quickly doubt their sincerity. Joan Redmond says that when an investigator called on her, "All he did was look at his watch. He was due at the Skakels' house for lunch. He seemed a lot more interested in what he was going to eat for lunch than what I had to say about Martha's case." Dorthy Moxley talks with Sutton investigators in May, by phone, and comes away disheartened. "They didn't ask me one single question about Martha. Can you believe that? Not one question! All they told me was how they could prove without a doubt that no one in the Skakel household had committed the murder."

This is news. More and more, the Skakel investigators—and lawyers—drop hints of total exoneration. What do they know? How can they be so certain? "Manny Margolis is claiming his client is innocent," Jack Solomon says angrily. "If he's so sure he's innocent, and says he has evidence to prove it, then by God, my doors should be coming off the hinges. Why isn't he coming in here to speak with us? You don't have to be a rocket scientist to figure it out."

The proof of innocence never materializes. The case sinks into another lull. A brief one. Soon enough, Len Levitt will uncover damning information—at least for the Skakels—and this information will come from none other than Sutton Associates.

Opening Old Wounds

THEN THE FOCUS of the investigation shifted back to Ken Littleton. Peter Coomaraswamy, the only person in this story outside the police who knows the Moxleys, the Skakels, and

Littleton, arranges for John Moxley to meet with Littleton in Boston in 1993. The police are dead set against it. John tells me, "They seemed to think, 'We're the police, we investigate. You're the victim, you go home and cry.' I said, 'Look, I'm going. So why don't you help me know as much about him as I can?' And eventually they acquiesced."

There's a laying out of conditions with Littleton's lawyer, Carole Ball. The meeting would take place in her office. She would be present. As they discuss this on the phone, John asks, "What happens if Ken breaks down and admits guilt?" A long silence. Then Ball says, "I don't know. We'll cross that bridge if we get to it. But we won't get to it, because he didn't do it."

So John Moxley sits down with the man who several forensic experts believe to be his sister's killer. "He's a strange guy. Just is. I came away not knowing if he was crazy because he did it or because he was a suspect in something of incredible magnitude. I came away with more questions than answers."

Littleton shows John many sides. The sorrow, the stubbornness, the paranoia. He spoke of a softball game on Nantucket back in the 1970s. The third baseman had asked Littleton and his girlfriend if they wanted to go do some coke. "Why me out of all the people on the team? Why me? I think I was being set up to take a fall. They hooked me on cocaine and set me up to take a fall."

There are details about Littleton that John cannot square. His unwillingness to cooperate with the police, for one. "I'm not going back to Connecticut for that naked-lightbulb treatment," he had said. So John asked him, "Why aren't you able to convince anyone that you weren't involved in this? Your life is a mess. There are all sorts of people who would like to hand you over to the police. It's ruined your marriage. What are you doing?"

Littleton started to sob. He said, "You know, I haven't seen my kids. I'm not growing up with them." And through the shedding of tears, he seemed to arrive at a sort of catharsis. He began to seem happy. When the meeting was over, he walked John out of the building, showed him where to catch a cab, and ended up hailing the cab himself. "And you're standing there thinking, *Oh my God, this could be the guy who killed my sister.*

"After meeting with him, you just saw how screwed up his mind was. He was an impossible guy to benchmark. I had the impression that he was crazy enough to do anything. I just didn't know what had made him crazy."

A Weary Dr. Lee

"I DON'T HAVE MAGIC WAND! I don't have chrysto baw! People expect me to have chrysto baw! 'Here, Dr. Lee, have a look, who done it? Who done it?'"

I first met Henry Lee in 1994, when he was at his most luminous. Connecticut's chief criminalist was no mere forensics man; he was a conjurer, a magician, a seer who unlocked mysteries of Holmesian complexity.

The Woodchipper Murder brought him national attention. When a flight attendant named Helle Crafts had gone missing, police in Newtown, Connecticut, suspected her husband, Richard, of murder. But they lacked a body. Curiously, though, a man had seen Richard Crafts driving a woodchipper across Silver Bridge in a snowstorm.

A woodchipper in a snowstorm? Hmm, thought Dr. Lee. He ordered a search of Lake Zoar. Hauled up from its depths was a chain saw with its serial number filed off. Lee brushed bone, teeth, hair, and fingernails out of the blade. He took the grisly evidence and came up with Helle Crafts's blood type and nail polish. He traced the bleach in the hair to the salon she frequented. Carefully applied acids revealed the chain saw's serial number. As for the Brush Bandit woodchipper: Crafts had rented it with a MasterCard. "Moral: Don't use credit card," Lee says, beaming.

Lee put it all together: Crafts had killed his wife at home, took her apart with a chain saw, and fed her remains through a woodchipper into Lake Zoar. He was convicted of murder in 1989, almost wholly on forensic evidence.

When Lee was not using his genius to convict criminals in Connecticut, he was spending time getting the accused off the hook in other states. One was William Kennedy Smith. To show that no great struggle had transpired on the lawn of the Kennedy compound, Lee compared the state of Patricia Bowman's dress and panties—pristine—to that of a handkerchief he'd wiped on the lawn—grass stained. Prosecutor Moira Lasch asked Lee why he hadn't conducted his experiment with panties. "Usually I do not carry panties," he answered. "I carry handkerchief."

I met Dr. Lee at an Italian steakhouse in Stamford, where he was giving a talk to a society of chemists. Afterward, I cornered him and told him of my interest in the Moxley case.

"Ah! Interesting, interesting," he said to me. "Story without end."

He said he'd give me a tour of the new forensics lab that his fame and influence had won for the state, and then he'd lay out for me the special problems of the Moxley case. The case had sunk again into a brief slumber. I was thankful for this. Those who knew its intricacies let down their guard only in these drowsy intervals; when things flared up, as they always did, caution and fear ruled the day.

But fate did not align me well with Dr. Lee. Shortly after we agreed to meet, I read in the newspaper that O. J. Simpson's defense team had hired him. I groaned. Lee was already among the busiest humans on earth. He rose in his beachfront home at four-thirty in the morning and, after a full day of work, labored in his own third-floor forensics lab until well after midnight. Lee was quoted in *Connecticut* magazine:

> My neighbors say, "Henry, you haven't stepped on the beach for a year." I'm struggling in front of my computer, or working at my upstairs laboratory, and people didn't understand. Like in the middle of the night they call me, "Respond to crime scene." I go out. Nobody is driving in the street. Everybody is sleeping. The moon is shining. You are by yourself. Everything is quiet. You say, "What you doing this for?" A normal person supposed to be asleep. Tomorrow you have to work. But you can't stay home like other detectives. They can take a day off, or the second shift take over. I don't have a second shift. I am second shift. I am third shift.

Lee's presence on the Simpson defense team should have bathed the former football star in halo light. If the great Henry Lee was stepping up for the Juice, then surely Lee had turned up something critical. Would Lee risk his aura of sainted genius for a scoundrel and a murderer?

Alas, he might. Lee never pronounces on guilt or innocence. In theory it does not really matter whether he's working for the prosecution or the defense, because he calls the evidence as he sees it. He concerns himself with blood spatter and fiber and DNA. Lee is considered the world's reigning expert on DNA, the genetic coding we leave on almost everything we touch. O. J. Simpson's DNA was found at the crime scene and again at his own house, mingled with that of Ron Goldman and Nicole Brown Simpson.

Lee said nothing about DNA at the Simpson trial.

That he steered clear of the DNA evidence raised eyebrows: Henry Lee believes in DNA, preaches DNA, and now there was nothing to say about it? This said more than all of his expert testimony.

What Lee did say: the blood spatter at the crime scene suggested a prolonged struggle, contradicting the prosecution's assertion of two quick kills. Detectives had failed to dry blood swatches before storing them in evidence folders, suggesting sloppy work. This too contradicted the prosecution; asked to explain, Lee replied, "The only opinion I can give under these circumstances is something wrong."

"Something wrong," became a catchphrase, a sound byte.

Lee's big forensic discoveries in the case were a bloody print on Ron's jeans and another on a piece of paper lying on the ground; these could be shoeprints other than Simpson's "ugly-ass" size twelve Bruno Maglis, Lee said carefully. A *second* pair.

FBI experts' testimony rebutted this. The prints were merely cement texture created by the mason's trowel, they said. Lee felt stung. He held a press conference in Connecticut. "Mason, trowel, tool marks. What to do with my testimony?" he asked. "I only show I found two imprint, one could be shoeprint. No more, no less." David Margolick wrote in the *New York Times* that this left Lee, "a man often canonized in law enforcement circles, in two unusual places; in the crossfire and on the defensive. . . . Like so many participants in the Simpson case, he has been singed by its hyperintense flames."

After the Simpson trial, Henry Lee seemed less funny, less patient. His face showed strain. Reporters now put him on his guard. "Publicity can hurt you," his new wariness prompted him to remark.

To reclaim something the Simpson trial had taken from him, Lee rang in the New Year in Bosnia. He traveled to mountain towns near Sarajevo to identify the remains of war dead who had been buried in a mass grave under dirt and rock and snow.

The bodies were badly decomposed. Their DNA had all run together. Yet people craved the knowledge: was their daughter, their mother, their son, buried in the grave—or had the one they sought slipped away from the shelling and turned up in a refugee camp in a distant town? Lee, working with other doctors, identified nine hundred fifty of those thrown into the mass grave at Kupres.

I caught up with Henry Lee again in the summer of 1997. Driving up to his office in Meriden, Connecticut, I switched on the radio: there had been an explosion at a Meriden building site that morning. Somebody was dead. Lee's day had begun in chaos. I was ushered into a conference room to wait for him. On the wall were color photographs as big and bold as abstract art: a blood-splattered mattress, with a decomposing shoulder in the bottom of the frame; the hand of a dead man, lying like an upturned crab in the weeds; the shirtsleeve of a state trooper killed by a truck on the highway, and next to it the rounded edge of the truck itself, which Lee had dusted to reveal the clear imprint of the trooper's shoulder patch.

Henry Lee was born sixty years before near Shanghai, China, a sprawling city at the mouth of the Yangtze River. In 1943 the Lees fled the war-ravaged mainland and went to Taiwan. Ho-Ming Lee was the father of thirteen children and a wealthy businessman. He stayed behind for a while, then set sail for Taiwan. His ship went down under communist fire and he was killed.

Chang-Yo Lee (as Henry was then known) entered Taiwan's Central Police College at eighteen, graduated at the top of his class, and was promoted to the rank of captain at a precocious twenty-three. Some aspects of the job, however, did not agree with the softhearted police captain. It was not in his nature, for instance, to bully suspects.

In 1962 Lee married Margaret Song, from Borneo. In 1963 Lee got stabbed on the job, prompting him to abandon police work and settle briefly on newspaper reporting. In 1964 Henry and Margaret left Taiwan for Malaysia, and the following year they emigrated to the United States, settling in New York. Lee worked as a waiter, a stockboy, and a kung fu instructor while attending John Jay College of Criminal Justice at the City University of New York. He was on his way.

Lee's office is cluttered with weapons and pictures of corpses laid on his desktop. He smiles distractedly and mentions the explosion, the formidable workload.

"I'll try to be quick," I say.

"No problem; just some other pressing—"

The intercom buzzes. Lee does not take the call.

He is eager to tell of the new crime lab, a low-slung brick building with a bright copper roof. It is full of equipment that examines fingerprints, handwriting, rug fibers, paint chips, hair, blood, and bone. These devices have names like "gas chromatographs" and "atomic absorption spectrophotometers," and it's a safe bet that Connecticut would have neither the building nor the equipment without the famous Henry Lee.

"First time I visit laboratory, in 1978, I was pretty shock, okay? It was literally pathetic! The serology section was in men's room. As a matter of fact, the john still existed—they just put a piece of board over it—and whole laboratory had only one microscope." So it is clear that forensic science had little hope of solving the Moxley murder in its early stages.

The new lab cost two million dollars to build, and it is a forensics palace. Thirty criminalists work inside it, operating forty million dollars' worth of equipment. If they can't solve the Moxley murder here, then it probably can't be solved, at least by forensic science.

Lee spent hours on the case, reached some confidential conclusions but no solid answers. This is when he starts talking about his crystal ball. The Moxley case has stumped even him.

If the murder had happened today, Henry Lee almost certainly would have solved it. He would have descended on the crime scene in minutes, rather than the next day, as Elliot Gross had. "At crime scene we going to look at pattern of evidence. Her body appeared to be dragged. Quite a long distance moved. Anytime you have physical contact you going to have evidence. An individual carry her body, drag her body, he have to walk. So you going to have shoeprint. You going to have her hair. Going to have trace evidence. All of these you have to try to recover.

"Of course, I have no idea how other people search. I wasn't there! No information about it! But the location of her body, it's sort of a wooded area, right? Behind some bushes—"

"Under a tree."

"—which means somebody familiar with the environment. However, you can see this hesitation: one spot, another spot, another spot. This hesitation indicates that this individual have mental and psychological condition."

"What sort of condition?"

Dr. Lee leans forward and makes a steeple with his index fingers. He's preparing a roundabout answer. "When you investigate a case, you always look at same thing: motive, opportunity, and means. Motive, that's a psychological issue. It is not easy to commit a crime. Only few serial killers in this is lucky. Those serial killers basically preplanned it, it's not normal. Now, ordinary people, like you and me, even if we get into traffic accident we feel pretty upset about it.

"So to kill somebody—we are not talking about cold-blooded killer here. This case somehow develop to that situation. If at the scene you can read that, you can try to build psychological analysis of possible suspect. Maybe can develop some crucial lead."

"You believe strongly in psychological profiling?"

"I believe strongly in physical evidence. If I find you have some scratches—okay?—if I find your hand have some bruises or cuts—"

"Like O.J.'s?"

"—if I find your shirt have small amount of bloodstain, if I find your shoes have blood splatter, those you can use for advanced reconstruction."

The intercom buzzes. "Excuse me. I have Andy on the phone."

I stop the tape and park myself in an adjoining room. The windowsill bustles with tokens from appreciative towns all over America. The bookshelves are stacked with loose-leaf binders about blood and semen and fingerprints. I can hear

Lee going "uh-hum, uh-hum" in the next room. A woman has been murdered, and the man on the phone apparently utters some facts of the crime and wants to know whether Lee thinks the boyfriend did it.

Lee listens a long time, sighs, and says, "Problem is, not enough love in the world. Not enough love."

I am summoned. "Whoever kill Martha should have sufficient amount of bloodstain and maybe other biological fluid. First day, second day, we can search for those things. I did revisit the scene. Of course, it's many years later, what can you find? Nothing. If I was called to the scene right away, going to be a different investigation."

Lee wrote a lengthy report of his findings, but will say little about it. He asks that I speak to other officials, who say nothing about it. Lee's work on the case, however, did not put detectives much closer to a solution. Lee cannot conjure what evidence does not exist.

"Say I am famous chef, okay? If you don't give me ingredients—rice or vegetable or meat—I can't cook you a whole meal. See what I mean? If you just give me couple potatoes, all I can do is make side dish of potato.

"I didn't have crime scene. I didn't have all the physical evidence. I didn't have body. Some of the evidence, nobody knows where it is."

A side dish of potatoes. I wasn't going to get much more out of Henry Lee.

I tell him one investigator, Steve Carroll, believes the killer to be left-handed, as Tom Skakel is. Lee shrugs. "Well, basically that's interpretation. People say if you see blood spatter go one way, that's left hand. How about a back right hand? Do you see what I mean?

"But we do know there's a lot of strength involved, okay?

Because it is brutal, brutal murder, and you need a lot of strength."

I nod. But later it becomes apparent to me that Dr. Lee has probably not tested the destructive power of a golf iron. Hefting one fills you quickly with a new understanding. It is a crushing weapon. It cuts like an ax. Brute strength would not be required to crack a human skull. Perhaps Dr. Lee is distracted and tired and trying to hurry me along.

Martha Moxley was murdered in the forensic dark ages. Had the killing occurred a year or two later, scientists might have tried to lift fingerprints off her body with iodine fuming; when heated, iodine gives off a vapor that adheres to oil secretions on the skin. A year or two after that, they might have tried silverplate transfer, which entails the additional step of pressing a special plate to the victim's skin and waiting for the iodine to etch a print into the silver.

Even if they had done these things successfully, however, they might have learned nothing, unless the prints were wrapped around Martha's neck or hips or legs. Outdoor killings are problematic for forensic scientists: condensation creeps up from the earth and destroys trace evidence. So do changes in body temperature and the dragging of a body from one place to another and the presence of insects.

Could Lee learn anything from exhuming Martha's body? I feel tasteless asking the question, and his answer is no.

Lee tells me there are four good reasons to conduct an exhumation: cases of misidentification, in which a badly damaged corpse is buried under the wrong name, as happens in war and airline disasters; to reexamine the manner of death, as when a suicide proves to be a homicide; to double-check the cause of death—heart attack or snake venom?; and to solve paternity disputes.

"Identity, basically that's Martha. Cause of death pretty simple. Manner of death pretty simple—murder, okay? And nobody claims Martha is not Mrs. Moxley's daughter. What can you get by exhume body, except publicity?"

Henry Lee looks at me a little strangely. "You know, we did find some hair." Lee lifted it from a pair of jeans that Michael Skakel had thrown in the garbage. Some of the hair was microscopically similar to Martha's, and other hair was dissimilar—possibly that of a white male. But that's all his crew was able to learn. "We did our best we can do here. They took the hair someplace else. Do other advanced test."

For now, Lee's work on the Moxley case is done. He's examined every speck, fiber, and dust particle available to him, without the big break only his wizardry could produce. "Let's say they find another piece of evidence, want me to examine. By all means, I will do that. But they don't have any new physical evidence."

"So you're at a dead end?"

"Not really dead, no. I never in my life take a case as a dead end." He recalls a police commissioner from long ago who kept a file box full of his unsolved cases dating to the 1920s. "He say those cases he took with him when he retire always bug him. He say, 'Finally I have found somebody who can solve them. Can you take a look?' I take a look. Some of those cases only one page. How much can you do with one page? Did I give up? No."

But the commissioner did. After handing over his file box, he committed suicide.

"So many cases in this world. So many mysteries. And Moxley, this just one of those many."

Levitt's Big Break

ON NOVEMBER 3, 1995, twenty years and four days after the murder of her daughter, Dorthy Moxley brings together police, state investigators, journalists, and a few of Martha's friends for a dinner at the Belle Haven Club.

There is some apprehension at the outset of the evening. The night is much like the one on which Martha was killed, and here we are, twenty years later, yards away from the crime scene. Will it seem macabre? Will it seem too much like a wake? Things go unsaid. Looking out at the black water—it is incredibly dark out there—many of us can't help running the scene through our minds: the murderer dispatching his weapon into the Sound with a quiet *plunk*. Just beyond range of these lights.

Soon everybody's holding a drink, and the line between the journalists and the police softens—it's a relief, finally, to meet in a social setting. There's a crowd around Henry Lee, plying him with O. J. Simpson questions. Don Browne approaches Steve Carroll, but Carroll turns away, still smarting from their contretemps two decades ago. Martha's friend Christy Kalan quizzes Jack Solomon on the case's recent developments. People joke about the absent Dominick Dunne: "What, he has a Los Angeles party instead? He's too big for us now?"

There's Len Levitt in a rumpled brown suit, arms folded across his chest, flanked by Steve Carroll and Jim Lunney. The former detectives are leaning in, listening intently. Levitt is the buzz of this party. He's working on a big story—it could be the biggest break yet in the Moxley case. Levitt tells me, "You'll definitely know who was with Martha at the time she was supposed to have been killed. There will be very little doubt about what happened."

"A bombshell, then?"

Levitt grins. "A bombshell."

The makings of Levitt's scoop begin in 1992. In that year, Tom Sheridan, Billy Krebs, and Jim Murphy—the ex-FBI agent who heads Sutton Associates—go to Levitt and ask him for copies of the Moxley police reportage made public under the Freedom of Information statute.

They claim the Greenwich police department refused to hand over the reportage, even though they're obliged to by law.

"If you help us," the men say to Levitt, "we'll give you our final report, which will clear Tommy Skakel in this."

This all happens when the focus of the police investigation has shifted heavily to Ken Littleton. He's failed the polygraph yet again, in 1991, and forensic psychologists are telling police that Littleton is not only Martha's murderer but possibly a serial murderer. Murphy, Krebs, and Sheridan believe the state is on the verge of prosecuting him, and their forwardness with Levitt is colored by this belief.

Levitt tells me, "They felt I didn't have any agenda here. They felt I was straight down the middle. I said, 'Okay, I'll Xerox my reports,' and we established a relationship."

Jim Murphy tells Levitt, "Sheridan never believed Thomas committed the crime, and he wanted to gain as much knowledge of it as he could, should Thomas be called as a witness."

The Sutton investigators, in their pursuit of Littleton, hire some ex-FBI behavioral scientists who have formed a private company called the Academy Group, in Manassas, Virginia.

Their profile of the killer, however, does not align with Ken Littleton. The scientists say the killer knew Martha; the severity of the beating suggests personal animus; and the source of that animus may well have been sexual rejection. What's more, they note, Martha Moxley had an absence of defense wounds—no injuries on her hands or forearms—which further suggests victim and killer knew each other and that the victim was taken by surprise.

And then Levitt learns—through someone he calls a middleman, who we can reasonably guess has links to Sutton Associates—that Tommy and Michael "are telling a different story."

Sutton investigators Billy Krebs and Richard McCarthy have interviewed Tommy Skakel twice in the law office of Manny Margolis in Stamford. Noting the discrepancies in his story, Krebs and McCarthy plan a third interview, but Sheridan wards them off; he also says a forthcoming report analyzing Tommy and Michael's apparent lies won't be necessary. It begins to sound as though the Skakels aren't on the side of truth after all.

Levitt receives this potentially combustible news in 1993. But the middleman says to hold on; Levitt will see the report one of these days—but not yet. Levitt, meanwhile, doesn't know what to make of the tip, but some law enforcement friends warn him he'd better be careful; his sources may be giving him a bum steer. Levitt's gut knowledge of things rarely fails him, though, and this time, in his gut, he feels the tip is good.

The Sutton report finds it way into Levitt's hands, as promised, in 1995. The bombshell drops on November 26.

Levitt reports in *Newsday* that both Tommy and Michael Skakel lied twenty years before when questioned by Greenwich police. They've given Sutton Associates an entirely new version of what happened the night Martha Moxley was killed—with lots of lurid teen detail.

After his flirtatious shoving match with Martha Moxley, Tommy said, he did indeed go back inside his house at nine-thirty—briefly. But he'd already arranged a tryst with Martha. She waited for him in the cold. Tommy met her out on the edge of the Skakel property, by Walsh Lane, right across the street from her house. Then they fell to the ground and masturbated each other to orgasm. The encounter lasted some twenty minutes—until about nine-fifty, Tommy said.

Based on the panicky barking of the Ix and Bjork dogs—and the Bjork dog's fearful interest in something on the Moxley lawn—the detectives' best guess is that Martha was killed between nine-fifty and ten o'clock. If that is correct, then Tommy has placed himself with Martha at just about the time of her murder. Tommy maintained that when he left for home, Martha Moxley was alive and well, fresh from an experience of ecstasy.

Michael Skakel's new story is equally strange. He told the Sutton investigators that he went to Martha's house after returning from Sursum Corda, at about eleven-thirty. Presumably Martha had already been attacked by this hour. But Michael, not knowing this, climbed a tree outside Martha's room and threw pebbles at the window. Then he climbed down from the tree and started home, passing the pine where Martha lay dead or dying.

Tommy's new version raises more questions than it answers. First, why did Tommy go back inside and leave Martha waiting for him? Did he have to get something—a condom, maybe? Can we believe that minutes after Martha rejected Tommy's advances in the Lincoln, and then again outside, she was now prepared to engage with him in a sex act?

And what happened when the supposed encounter was over? Did Martha stay out in the cold, waiting for the real murderer, lurking in the bushes? Why did Tommy tell Dorthy Moxley, on the night Martha went missing, that he'd last seen the girl at nine-thirty? Why didn't he just say about ten o'clock—unless he already knew something had happened to her? Why didn't he tell police the truth twenty years before? And how did he trump the polygraph, having lied so liberally about the events of October 30, 1975?

Most puzzling of all, why did Tommy Skakel put himself closer to the murder? One of Levitt's unnamed sources suggests that Tommy concocted the story in mortal fear of new scientific tests. Would Dr. Lee use his million-dollar gadgets to match a pubic hair, God forbid, or DNA left from saliva or semen, to the hair sample Tommy gave Greenwich police on December 13, 1975?

Until Levitt's revelations, police had never considered Michael Skakel much of a suspect. Years before, they learned that Michael was perhaps the most unbalanced of the precarious brood, compulsively scattering light mischief in his wake. The two truly disturbing anecdotes had him "whacking the heads off of squirrels" as one detective put it, and collecting a bag full of birds that he'd killed. And Steve Carroll notes, "Michael would have been prime," more so than Tommy, had he been on the scene and not up at Sursum Corda. Now he has himself on the scene, living up to his wacky billing—and perhaps hearing Martha in her death throes.

But to cast Michael as the killer you have to rearrange the

time line of the killing: it took place not around ten o'clock, but after eleven-thirty. It's possible that the murder occurred later than ten o'clock. (The autopsy report is no help in this: Elliot Gross put the time of death between 9:30 P.M. and 5 A.M.) Once you change the time line, you have to figure out where Martha spent the hour or more between leaving Tommy and getting killed, and you also have to discount the reports of disturbed dogs. Still, why would Michael place himself at the murder scene after years of escaping detection?

One thing is clear: the Skakels have done a lot of lying about the night Martha was murdered. They've spent hundreds of thousands of dollars "clearing the family name," only to see it sink intractably into mud.

Lone Ranger

FRANK GARR IS the only investigator still working the Moxley case; it is he who would arrest the accused, if that made-for-TV moment should ever come to pass. In January 1998 Inspector Garr believes he is closer to that moment than ever before.

But he's saddled with a small public relations problem. Garr knows more about the Moxley case than anyone alive (save possibly the investigative reporter Len Levitt and Inspector Jack Solomon, who left the state's attorney's office in 1995 to become a small-town police chief) but cannot tell what he knows. So it *seems* nothing's happening. Blame for the lack of progress tends to fall squarely on his shoulders.

He says this does not bother him. Not even when people murmur confidentially, "C'mon, Frank. You know who did it,

I know who did it, why don't you do something about it?" Or, "Get real, Frank. You're never going to solve this thing." After seven long years of this, he's grown a tough skin. "Well, it bothers me when people feel that way—that we'll never be able to clear this case," he allows. "But I can't blame them. Look how many years have gone by, and we still haven't solved it."

Born in Port Chester, New York, the run-down little city just west of Greenwich, he wanted to be a detective from an early age. But first came the war in Vietnam: he spent 1966 in country and has little to say about it. He shrugs. "Nineteen years old, they send you, you go. I wasn't one of these political types. I got drafted and I went. Sure there were some scary times. But you got through."

Now Garr's silvery hair is mostly gone from the top of his head but curls down his neck and over the collar of his well-made suit. After twenty-eight years on the Greenwich police force, nineteen as a detective, Garr left in 1994 to join the state's attorney's office. There he continued his work on the Moxley case.

I visit him in his tiny, windowless office on the second floor of a courthouse and state building in Bridgeport. He greets me warmly and helps me hang up my coat. "Jack isn't here anymore. He's chief of Easton. I'm sort of like the Lone Ranger. I'm the last one."

Discussing the Moxley case is a tricky business for him—he wants you to have *some* information—and at certain moments you even sense a desire to talk freely about what is, in effect, his life's work. He never does. As soon as you ask specific questions of evidence—was Martha stabbed before death or after? what exactly is being tested at the FBI lab?—he says, politely, "I'm not comfortable talking about that."

No detective who has worked this case will say much about it, except for Steve Carroll. Carroll has broken the code of silence surrounding active cases, feels it's time *somebody* did, but he's drawn Garr's scorn. "You know that old saying 'Close your mouth and be thought a fool, open your mouth and confirm it'? That's Steve Carroll. Steve Carroll to a T."

Garr's frustration with Carroll is a minor annoyance. He reserves all-out fury for the Skakel family, hiding behind its brigade of lawyers. "Manny Margolis says the Skakels cooperated in the beginning. I don't care what Manny Margolis says—they didn't cooperate with us. Ever! Because they lied. It's all bullshit, because they lied back then and they're lying now.

"I'm sure that once Rush Skakel got back from his hunting trip—once all the attorneys assembled—I'm sure there was a major meeting about how they were going to proceed. A young girl, somebody's baby girl, was murdered. *The way to proceed is to try and help in any way you can.* Period. Period! 'We're gonna help in any way we can, because there's a girl who's been brutally murdered next door to my house. What do you want us to do? What do you need?' That's how you proceed. You don't cut that off.

"Now, you fast-forward to Len Levitt's stories, and Tommy and Michael are claiming they lied. Why would they lie? *For what possible reason would they lie?* Well, I can come up with one reason."

Mention of the Sutton debacle brings to Garr's face a bemused grin. The scope of the mistake, the irony of it, backfiring like that! As Garr understood it, Rush Skakel had planned to share the results of the Sutton investigation with police no matter what. If a Skakel turned up guilty, there would be medical treatment and the best legal defense money could buy.

"That's the original story. Well, obviously that didn't happen. What I think happened was, these guys were out doing the investigation they should, but things weren't turning out the way they expected—"

"They expected Littleton?"

"Apparently. And as soon as things didn't look the way they expected, they shut down. That's my impression—just shut down."

Garr does tell me that he discounts the theory that Martha's murderer has somehow blocked it out of his mind. "I think the killer of Martha Moxley knows exactly what he did, and lives with it every day—but is able to."

"That's chilling."

"I think they have no problem with it because I think these people are so self-centered and self-absorbed that it doesn't matter."

"Could it happen again?"

"I don't think Martha's killer was a serial killer by any stretch of the imagination. I think something went wrong and something got out of hand and Martha died. Now, could it happen again? Sure it could. But I don't think we should all be fearful that these persons are going to go out and do the same thing again. But I believe the killer knows very well what he did. He thinks, 'She's gone, I can't bring her back.' Rationalizing it like that. That's what I think. I'm not a doctor. I'm not a psychologist. I'm nothing but a cop. But if you want my opinion, that's my opinion—that the person who killed Martha Moxley don't give a shit."

Garr reflects on the remarkable history of the case in which he is now the Lone Ranger. It's a case that should have died quietly in the 1980s, when no one was looking. In almost any other American town that's exactly what would have happened. Then along comes a Willy Smith. Then a Dominick Dunne. Then a . . .

"It's like an omen. Whenever we reach a wall, whenever there's nowhere else to go, whenever we think, *That's all she wrote*—something happens. The phone rings. We start again. Another inch, another foot. And it's always been that way. That's the reason this thing is still alive and breathing."

The Prosecutor

"I'M NOT GOING to discuss suspects in this case. I want to make that perfectly clear. Some people come to see me and they seem disappointed. They think I'm going to lay out all the evidence and who I think are the prime suspects. Things of that sort."

Donald Browne, the state's attorney for Fairfield County, is going over a few ground rules before I meet him. He's a thorough fellow. I ask him, "You'll shut me down if I get into prime suspects?"

"I will do that! I've done that with other people in the past. I'll do it with you, if need be. This is still a pending case. It's not a closed case. I believe it's still a *solvable* case. I just don't discuss evidence or suspects with anybody."

Steve Carroll told me, "When you go see Don Browne, bring your dancing shoes. Oh, he'll waltz you! You can tell him I said that, too." But it seems I won't even get on the dance floor. Without suspects and evidence, there's not a whole lot to discuss.

Browne's office, down the hall from Frank Garr's, could belong only to a prosecutor. Volumes of *The Criminal Re-*

porter fill the bookcase, issues of a journal called *The Prosecutor* sit in foot-high stacks on the floor. On the wall hangs a cartoon of a jury chatting and yawning as the prosecutor strains vainly for their indulgence.

Browne is a vigorous man of sixty-four. He's dressed in gray slacks, a snug white short-sleeve shirt through which his T-shirt is plainly visible, and a cool purple tie with warm purple stripes. His language is weirdly formal—"In nineteen hundred and sixty-five, a gentleman who . . ."—and often backfires on him: "The judges of Fairfield County invited me to assume the position."

He is notoriously mute on the subject of the Moxley case, drawing his wide mouth shut against the escape of pertinent information. He'll "no comment" you even on softball questions like "Do you feel there are people out there who know what really happened?"

It is Browne who decides whether the Moxley case goes forth to a grand jury. His failure to convene a grand jury in 1976, when the Skakels started hindering the investigation, and again in 1995, when Len Levitt exposed the Skakel lies, has been roundly criticized. (Some journalists on this story have even wondered—not in print—whether Browne has been "paid off." They note that, strategically, he'd be the right man *to* pay off, since he holds the power to keep the case in abeyance. But it was Browne who decided to reinvestigate the Moxley case in 1991.)

Why didn't he convene a grand jury in 1976? He can't remember, but suspects the state lacked a strong enough case. And police were still gathering evidence. What about 1995? Still premature. "I still believe that scientific procedures can and will produce valuable evidence."

Legally, Browne is an extremely cautious man. He's convened only two investigative grand juries in twenty-four years on the job. There are those who are anxious to see him retire for this reason alone: maybe a less cautious prosecutor will spur action in the Moxley case.

But the grand jury issue is a knotty one. State law has changed since Martha was killed. Gone is the old, eighteen-citizen grand jury system, under which jurors would return "a true bill" if they believed the evidence warranted an arrest. In its place is a probable-cause hearing, conducted by a single superior-court judge. The judge, in effect a one-man grand jury, reviews evidence, hears testimony, then decides whether to recommend an arrest. If he does, it's the prosecutor—Browne—who sets the specific charge.

I've heard that Donald Browne considered applying for a probable-cause hearing after the Levitt stories. I've also heard he is contemplating an investigative grand jury, whose chief purpose in this case would be to compel Skakel friends and relatives—perhaps even the Skakels themselves—to testify. Early in 1998 the grapevine is thick with rumors of an imminent grand jury, in one form or the other—but, of course, we've heard it all before.

I mention how monstrous in its complexity the Moxley case has grown: the more you know about it, the cloudier it gets. Browne nods vigorously. "Your statement is true and appropriate! We'll get part of the picture, but not the whole picture. But we still get pieces. From the strangest sources, we get pieces. The interesting thing, Tim, is these pieces never stop arriving."

Browne will retire in a matter of days. So what he says next surprises me. "I'm going to stay on as a special assistant state's attorney for one purpose and one purpose only—prosecuting the Martha Moxley homicide."

Chapter Twelve

Mark Fuhrman's Redemption

IN THE SUMMER OF 1997, the man who became infamous for saying the word "nigger" and then lying about it is sighted on the streets of Greenwich. He alights at police headquarters to pick up the modest stack of police reportage on the Moxley case. The cops recognize him and try to freeze him with glares. But Mark Fuhrman is accustomed to far worse than this. Three years earlier, he was the third-most-reviled man in America, after Timothy McVeigh and the Unabomber; hated even more, it seemed, than the ex-football star standing trial for double murder. The Simpson trial had turned into the Fuhrman trial.

One man infuriated by the charade was Dominick Dunne. Dunne was covering the Simpson trial for *Vanity Fair* magazine, in which he published lucid, gossipy articles about the evolving travesty. Dunne and Fuhrman struck up a friendship.

At some point in Los Angeles, Dunne told Fuhrman of a bizarre unsolved murder case back east, and Fuhrman, intrigued, read the popular novel Dunne had based on it.

Fuhrman himself would soon brave the literary currents. His book on the Simpson case and his remarkable role in it, *Murder in Brentwood*, quickly vaulted up best-seller lists. Fuhrman was indeed a riveting character. Perhaps Americans wondered how a man could survive such a ferocious condemnation; perhaps there were those who felt, as Dunne felt, that a good detective's career had been unjustly destroyed in the service of evil; or perhaps a silent contingent of Fuhrman sympathizers shared the detective's scorn for the "low-class" people he believed were ruining America.

The prevailing view of Fuhrman, however, had not changed much since the revelation of the infamous "Fuhrman tapes" made by aspiring screenwriter Laura Hart McKinny: he was a pariah, an outcast, a symbol of cretinous oppression.

All of which made him the ideal subject for a grand experiment: he would test Americans' capacity for forgiveness. And his instrument, he hoped, would be one of the most stubborn murder cases in modern memory—the Moxley case.

Dominick Dunne cleared the way. One day Dunne called Dorthy Moxley and said, "Dorthy, have I got a writer for you! Now, don't blow me off when I tell you who it is."

Dorthy was perplexed. But she had always been generous with reporters, feeling strongly that they might succeed where police had failed. Certainly reporters, not police, were making the most headway these days—as far as anyone knew. And in Fuhrman she would have both a top detective and a best-selling author. Dorthy agreed to meet with Fuhrman.

When they did meet, Fuhrman told her he planned to investigate the case himself—he firmly believed it was solvable, even at this late date—and then to write a book revealing his findings.

Dorthy found the former detective charming and intelligent. For all his travails, he still exuded a particular swagger she associated with talented cops. This, she judged, was exactly what her daughter's case needed.

In the fall of 1997, Fuhrman and his ghostwriter, Stephen Weeks, book rooms at the Homestead Inn, a lovely old place set amid oaks and maples on the edge of Belle Haven.

Fuhrman wakes some mornings and unobtrusively jogs past the scene of the murder. The Moxley house is owned now not by Jon Lee—he moved last year to north Stamford—but by an investment banker named Jim McEntee. The place looks bright and full of life. Three black labs romp about the yard. A plastic cow grazes on the front lawn. It does not seem a house where the ghost of a murder could exist.

Those who recognize Fuhrman can't quite place him, despite the former ubiquitousness of his image. The bridge between a Los Angeles courtroom and quiet Belle Haven is too far to cross. He's a big, good-looking man with an easy stride. Perhaps a television actor—haven't they seen him on TV?—recently moved to town. They were all moving to town.

Greenwich at large learns of Fuhrman's presence on September 30, when *Greenwich Time* runs a story headlined FUHRMAN MAY PEN BOOK ON MOXLEY. Some residents react almost viscerally, as though they've been kicked in the stomach. One woman who lived in Belle Haven at the time of the murder shakes her head and says to me, "Poor Dorthy. She'll grasp at anything now."

Greenwich never did take well to interlopers. The town character has always resembled that of a wealthy nation-state: sovereign, superior, shining with cool pride. Ever since

Greenwich tried without success to escape the clutches of Puritan New England, the town has struggled to repel plundering hordes. The most dramatic instance of this—one that is paradigmatic of the conservative Greenwich soul—unfolded in the early months of 1946.

After World War II, the Allied victors set to creating a new world order, with the United Nations Organization as its centerpiece and unifying theme. The UNO did not then have a world headquarters, and cities all over America—San Francisco, Boston, Philadelphia, and New York—vied for the honor. What city could resist playing host to the world?

The UNO site-selection committee did not choose any of those cities; it chose instead a vast swath of Greenwich back country, gorgeous land upon which reigned the estates of Henry R. Luce, Joseph Verner Reed, Rhea Reid Topping, and Lewis Rosensteil. An airport would be built upon Tamarack Country Club. Gone too would be the venerable Round Hill Club, the Stanwich Club, and the Greenwich Polo Club. The proposed UNO site was so wide that it spilled into Stamford—and the estate of boxing legend Gene Tunney—and also into Westchester County—and the estate of John Sterling Rockefeller. Upon all this land would stand a twelve-story office tower, a hotel, a four-lane highway and a railroad spur, churches and schools, a power plant, and the UNO's own courts and police force.

The town did not consider itself honored. Rather, it was horror-stricken. Some town fathers mobilized the forces of wealth and influence in an effort to fend off the UNO's advances. One of them was the moderator of Greenwich's Representative Town Meeting, Prescott Bush, father of George, who laid out a seven-point plan on the front page of *Greenwich Time*. For a while, it looked as though Greenwichites would have to fall prostrate before the demands of the world, as it were.

A point man for the Greenwich opposition was a Missouri-born advertising executive named Amedee Cole. The situation looked bleak when Cole received a snooty letter from a State Department official—none other than Alger Hiss, whom Richard Nixon would later ruin with charges of espionage—which read: "The United Nations site committee has been given a blank check by us to take whatever land they want."

The good news, according to the UNO report, was that residents whose land fell in "Unoville" would be permitted to stay on temporary leases "to cater to the requirements of international residents."

Greenwich's snubbing of the UNO drew ridicule around the world. The London newspapers portrayed Greenwich as a pampered, selfish town with thirty servants staffing every mansion. The *London Daily Express* said the town is "so particular about who lives there that you almost have to produce your birth certificate to buy a house."

But Greenwich stood firm. In March the town held a referendum: 73 percent voted against the UNO plan, and with that the site-selection committee backed off. But the opposition, though general, was not universal—and that is how the sentiment ran when Mark Fuhrman came to town a half century later.

Between the Moxley and Simpson murders there had already been cross-pollination. Almost enough of it to endow the linkages with a mystic sheen. It began, of course, with Dominick Dunne, who turned each case into a best-selling novel. The Simpson defense team's forensic experts, Drs. Henry Lee and Michael Baden, each had beamed their much-publicized genius on the Moxley case, to little avail.

I myself had interviewed O. J. Simpson, when he was still

married to Nicole, out on the Stanwich Club golf course in back country Greenwich. I found him a charming and candid subject, even though he constantly referred to himself in the third person, as "Juice." He would say, for instance, "That's a hell of a shot! That is why they call me Juice, babes," or, after a lousy shot, "Juice! How could you do that?"

At one point Simpson resolved to pick up his game. "All right, I'm starting right now. This is the Juice that you've all grown to know and loathe," he said presciently. Simpson stood over his ball, sticking out his tongue and waggling it from side to side. It was a little nervous thing he did. "Now my daughter does it," Simpson remarked. "I say, 'Sweetheart, you look so stupid doing that.' And she says, 'Daddy, you do it all the time.'"

Simpson smacked a towering drive that cut the fairway in two. His golf partners applauded. But the good feeling was short-lived. Simpson dumped a short approach shot over the green and down a hill. "Oh, Juice," he said. "Oh, no, Juice."

Another in his group sighed and said, "God help us."

I asked Juice why he had switched from tennis to golf. Did that mean he was getting older? "That means I'm married," he answered. "At home, your wife can nag you. She can't do that out here." Later he gave me further counsel on the art of marriage: "Women are attracted to humor. I can certainly say it's never gotten in the way of any relationship I've had. In fourteen years of marriage you're going to have some tough times, and the ability to look at those times humorously, satirically, has helped us through."

With Fuhrman's arrival in Greenwich, the Simpson-Moxley connection began to seem almost dreamlike, as though separate planes of reality had got stuck back-to-back. Fuhrman was a celebrity now—an *O.J.* celebrity—and he could not help bringing a touch of the Simpson circus with him. But Fuhrman is, in his own right, a man who relishes being in the center ring. "I'm the key witness in the biggest case of the century," he boasted in July of 1994. "And if I go down, they lose the case. The glove is everything. Without the glove—bye-bye."

All through October, he occupies the Moxley case's center ring too.

The police do not hide their scorn for Fuhrman. Dunne calls Frank Garr to see if he will go over the case with Fuhrman, and Garr refuses. "Dominick became of the opinion that Mark Fuhrman was made somewhat of a scapegoat. I don't know if I totally believe that. I think Mark Fuhrman made Mark Fuhrman exactly what he is by the way he behaved on the stand. So I guess the two of them discussed it and decided, 'Okay, let's give it a whack,' and they contacted me. I didn't see any need to sit down with Mark Fuhrman to help him write a book on a case he knows nothing about. I mean, where does Mark Fuhrman get off writing a book about the Moxley case? So I declined, which I think pissed Dominick off a little bit."

Garr's rancor is nothing compared to that of Peter Robbins, the new Greenwich police chief. Robbins is a slender man with sad blue eyes and a soft voice that carries much authority. He is a Vietnam veteran who did not shrink from the violence of that war: his favorite duty was the dangerous job of helicopter door gunner. The son of a much beloved Greenwich police chief of the 1950s, he determinedly carved his own path: depending on your point of view, he was either very brave or very mad. Once, he stormed a room where an intoxicated gunman was holding a cop hostage and wrestled the gunman to the ground. Another time, he leaped on the back of an armed man who had been told he had a brain tumor and had made what sounded like a suicide threat. In bringing the man down, Robbins struck his back on a curb and blew out a disk. When Andrew Wilson appeared at Greenwich police headquarters in 1993 and announced he had just shot Jack Peters, it was Robbins who raced up to the Peters place and dived into the pool to try to rescue the mortally wounded man.

More temperate these days, he is still passionate about police work. He demands a great deal of his officers and runs his ship with military attention to detail. Mark Fuhrman is exactly the sort of cop who would offend his deepest sensibilities.

The two of them wage a war of words in the newspapers:

Robbins: The way he came in here demanding information was an exact representation of the way he acted on the stand during the O. J. Simpson case—and I watched every minute of it.

Fuhrman: I'm rather shocked by Peter Robbins' attitude. He can't stand me! He won't cooperate with me but will cooperate with Tim Dumas. I don't know Tim, but I do know he is not a detective.

Robbins: Neither is Mark Fuhrman.

Fuhrman: I have a hundred times more police experience than anyone on this case. Peter Robbins appears not angry but scared I'm going to find something that solves this case or about how they investigated it.

Robbins: In my opinion, Fuhrman isn't here to solve the Moxley murder. He's here to make money. . . . I am not going to cooperate with Mark Fuhrman. And as far as credibility, I personally can't stand the man. He did more damage to the credibility of the police force than any other man in America.

Fuhrman: In May of 1998, people are going to know the Greenwich police department and the state's attorney's office for one of two things. Either they really don't care about who killed Martha Moxley, or they were just too damn busy.

Things do not go much better for Fuhrman in Belle Haven. On October 3 the townspeople are greeted with the *Greenwich Time* headline, running across the top of the front page, FUHRMAN FOILED IN BOOK RESEARCH.

Yesterday, [Fuhrman] managed to give Greenwich police the slip after they were called by security guards in the private Belle Haven section of town, where Fuhrman allegedly trespassed at the former Moxley residence on Walsh Lane. . . .

According to Robbins, private guards in Belle Haven denied access to Fuhrman twice Thursday, turning him away from a guard shack on Field Point Road. The second time, he said, the former detective "peeled away" in a rented Chevrolet Corvette.

This is only part of the story. Fuhrman, in the passenger seat of Steve Carroll's pickup truck, does drive unchecked into Belle Haven that day. Fuhrman and Carroll pull up in front of the McEntee house, seeking permission to photograph the place where Sheila McGuire found Martha's body. Mrs. McEntee denies them access. Cissy Ix, across the street, has advised the McEntees not to cooperate, and as she explains this, Mr. McEntee speeds into the driveway.

"I know who *you* are," he says to Fuhrman, and then points to Carroll. "Who are you?"

Carroll explains who he is—a retired police detective who investigated the Moxley case at its inception.

Then Jim McEntee says to his wife, "Did you call the police?"

She nods.

Carroll keeps trying to explain that Fuhrman wants only to snap a couple of photos, but McEntee does not entertain the request.

"Get out," he says.

"Would you like us to wait until the police get here?" Carroll asks finally.

"Get out," McEntee repeats, and the former detectives shake their heads and drive away, Fuhrman muttering, "This goes in the book."

Mark Fuhrman believes such encounters have nothing to do with his reputation; instead resistance is bound up with the secrecy that surrounds the Moxley case like an Atlantic fog.

Probably both are true. Greenwichites snicker when they read of Fuhrman's rented Corvette. Nobody who has the money to drive a Corvette would be caught dead in one. Fuhrman's choice of car not only reinforces his status as an outsider—a *West Coast* outsider—but also serves as a piquant character clue: the Corvette fits perfectly with our image of the man. It's a muscle car. Just the sort of conveyance you might expect Mark Fuhrman to peel away in.

Only there never was a Corvette. Fuhrman's car was a sufficiently Greenwichy Ford Explorer.

What is less well articulated is the idea that a man of Fuhrman's reputation breaking the Moxley case would constitute a cosmic injustice, especially after so many men with excellent reputations (personal, if not professional) tried and failed. In this scenario, Fuhrman plays Mozart to their Salieri:

the man judged unworthy receives heaven's gifts and good fortune.

Sometimes things work that way.

Meanwhile, the longer Fuhrman stays in town, the more apparent it becomes that he has fans. Doug Miller, a reporter and editor at the weekly *Greenwich Post,* tells me the paper's getting calls from residents who want to escort Fuhrman around town, buy him pizza and beer. A *Greenwich Time* reporter says to Fuhrman that his mother, suffering from cancer, is an admirer, and Fuhrman pays her a visit. A town gadfly I've known for years calls me with a not very hot tip about a golf club handle. He says, "I'm trying to get this information to"—his voice drops to a reverent hush—"Detective Mark Fuhrman. But since I know you, I'm giving it to you too."

Steve Carroll, in a letter to the *Post*, writes, "Let us not make Mark Fuhrman out to be a villain. . . . I find it very difficult to understand why anyone would not cooperate with an investigator attempting to resolve this case, whether or not it is for financial gain." People whom Fuhrman interviews describe him as charming and polite; one notes how nicely his suit hangs on him; another speaks of his "cop charisma." But would he be able to crack the case?

FUHRMAN: MOXLEY WEAPON AT SCENE. This is the lead headline in the October 23 edition of *Greenwich Time*. One of the jokes circulating around Fuhrman's arrival in Greenwich was that he was sure to find the bloody glove of the Moxley case—the Skakel golf club handle. In a sense, that's exactly what Mark Fuhrman did.

The *Time* story reveals that Millard Jones and Dan Hickman, the first officers to arrive at the Moxley house on October 31, 1975, recalled seeing a piece of golf club embedded in Martha Moxley's skull. Hickman has told *Time* reporter J. A. Johnson, Jr., "What really blew my mind—I remember seeing a shiny object impaled through the skull and it came out the other side. It obviously was the shaft of a golf club."

Jones seems no less certain. "I'm almost positive that thing was sticking through her head. You could see the leatherette or vinyl grip. And my wife swears that's what I told her I saw when I came home that night."

Fuhrman crows, "I can't imagine how you can lose a murder weapon. I'd like to think there's an innocent explanation. Maybe it was lost at a hectic crime scene. Or maybe someone took it. What I do know is the Greenwich police department, the Connecticut state's attorney's office, and other law enforcement agencies have spent twenty-two years searching for a piece of evidence that was already there at the crime scene."

All of Greenwich is dumbfounded. None of the cops who arrived just after Jones and Hickman saw it. None of the crime scene photographs show it. Sheila McGuire and Joan Redmond, who saw Martha's body before *any* cops arrived, didn't see it. Hickman? I interviewed him twice, for a total of three hours; when I asked him to tell me what he saw, he said nothing about a shaft of metal impaled in Martha's skull.

I think of Henry Lee's phrase: "Something wrong."

Hickman says to Johnson he never told this story to anyone before; apparently he "blocked it out." But when Fuhrman's ghostwriter, Stephen Weeks, sat Hickman down for an interview, all the gory details came flooding back. Hickman, now a Baptist minister, gives himself a public flagellation: "I thought I was a professional police officer, but up until now, I just went blank." Millard Jones didn't tell anyone of the impaling, either—"because no one asked me." No one asked him? In his two-and-a-half-page report on his and Hickman's actions that afternoon at the Moxley house, he makes no mention of a leatherette or vinyl grip.

I reach Hickman at his home in Norwalk, and it is evident that Fuhrman's bombshell has left him shattered. "Last night I was tossing and turning, couldn't sleep a wink. I want to be clear in my mind. Did I say the right things? Did I *see* the right things? I'll tell you what I'm going to do. I am going to find a nice quiet place and pray for clarity."

"You mean you're not sure you saw it?"

"I thought I did."

"Are you sure?"

"I don't know."

Millard Jones is no help. "I'm not talking to anybody, unfortunately," he says, and hangs up the phone.

Joan Redmond confirms for me that she saw nothing protruding from Martha's skull. Could the thing have been buried beneath the collar of Martha's parka?

Supposedly it was plainly evident. The piece was at least a foot long and, according to Hickman and Jones, had been jabbed into Martha's skull, not her neck.

Sheila McGuire was at first shy with me in describing Martha's wounds. I had dreaded asking her about them almost as much as she dreaded telling me. Now I ask her again, pointedly. Sheila tells me that she had a clear view of the back of Martha's head; her face was pressed against the pine needles. Her head appeared somehow misshapen—the skull had been bashed in—and there was blood caked in her hair. But nothing was impaled in her skull. Of this Sheila is certain.

Fuhrman's tape recorder, however, has captured the voices

of two ex-cops who remember differently. Good men who have no reason to lie. It's Fuhrman's big break.

Still, both Garr and Carroll say flatly that it never happened. Even the reticent Keegan sends a letter up from South Carolina, refuting the story. So what happened? Is it a simple case of flawed memory—details melding together over time? Were the questions put to Hickman and Jones designed to elicit a fantastic response? How else could *both* men come up with the same story?

Fuhrman's discovery gives Greenwichites another reason to disparage the police. That is the immediate impact. In the long term, the consequences could be far graver. If the police ever do arrest anyone for the murder of Martha Moxley, the disparity in the accounts of so important an issue could leave the prosecutorial waters fatally roiled. There could be reasonable doubt.

Late in October, just before the twenty-second anniversary of Martha's murder, Mark Fuhrman flies home to Idaho. But he leaves behind this letter, which the *Greenwich Post* printed on its front page: "I would like to thank everybody who made my stay in Greenwich both enjoyable and productive. And to those who did their best to frustrate my search for the truth, you will not be forgotten."

The Sutton Reports

IN 1997 a second drama involving the famous Sutton reports unfolds. On September 30 Len Levitt—the only reporter known to have seen the reports up to then—writes in *News-*

day that the reports have landed in the hands of Dominick Dunne.

Dunne reportedly received them in 1996 from a Jamie Bryan. Bryan, a twenty-one-year-old employee of Sutton Associates, wrote the reports using interviews, psychological profiles, and available evidence. But he was also an aspiring screenwriter, and everyone knows it's a bad idea to trust writers with confidential information.

It is unclear what Bryan expected to gain from Dunne in return. I've heard—confidential sources—that Bryan wanted to write an article for *Vanity Fair* magazine, in which he would paint Michael Skakel as Martha's killer. In any case, Dunne handed the reports over to the state's attorney's office. And then he gave them to Mark Fuhrman.

When Levitt calls Dunne for confirmation, the celebrated author says, "I am out of this story," and Levitt says, "Sorry, you're in the story." Soon after, Levitt's phone rings. It's Mark Fuhrman. When Fuhrman came on the scene, he called Levitt and asked to meet with him. Levitt invited him over for lunch. But now Fuhrman says, "I hear you've been making phone calls."

"So?"

"I don't think you should be putting Dominick Dunne in your story."

It dawns on Levitt that Fuhrman would look more heroic if it seemed he turned up the Sutton information with his vaunted detective skill.

Then Fuhrman says, "Timing is all. Timing is payback."

Levitt says, "Get the fuck off this phone right now."

* * *

Len Levitt shows me the Sutton reports in January of 1998. They're gripping. What the reports make most clear is that the events of the night Martha Moxley was murdered are far more intricate than was previously believed.

One comes away, especially, with new suspicions of Michael Skakel. Could it be, as Ken Littleton intimates, that Michael did *not* go with his brothers Rush and John to take Jimmy Terrien home? Littleton is guarded and sometimes cryptic in his interviews with Sutton investigators; often he hedges on critical questions. It is difficult to determine what he knows and what he suspects, but he casts suspicion upon himself when he answers the question "Who do you think killed Martha Moxley?" with "No comment."

The reports confirm the horror story that his life became. An assault and battery arrest, a shoplifting arrest, numerous drunken driving stops. Once, police (the reports don't say where) stopped him driving the wrong way down a one-way street where prostitutes worked. A drunken Littleton mumbled, "I have to speak to the Kennedys." Littleton tells the Sutton investigators of a time in Hull, Quebec, in 1982 when he was mugged and badly beaten—"left to die." This was, he tells them, a Skakel "hit."

Littleton's contempt for Michael Skakel is palpable. He believes the boy was a cocaine addict. He brings up the old story about how Michael once "bludgeoned" a squirrel during a golf outing. And then, the day after Martha's body was discovered, the Skakels went hunting in the woods up in Windham: Michael wantonly shot his high-powered rifle at small animals, Littleton says. There seemed to be a total lack of regard for life.

Could Michael have shown the same lack of regard for Martha's?

Michael placed his stone-throwing episode at the Moxley house between 11:40 P.M. and 12:30 A.M., after his return from Sursum Corda. When he heard no response, he masturbated in the tree, then walked back along the driveway and out to the road. Under the streetlight he "felt a presence" near the tree where Martha lay. Then he shouted "into the darkness" and threw stones at the tree. Hearing only some "noises," he became frightened and bolted home.

But the investigators wonder: could the "presence" have been Littleton? Curiously, they note, Littleton believes Martha's murder occurred later than the police detectives' estimation of 10 P.M.—sometime after 10:30 P.M. Littleton places the murder after 10:30 because of the chase scene in *The French Connection*. Tommy entered the master bedroom, where Littleton was watching the movie, before the chase scene, which began at 10:23. Tommy seemed unruffled—not like a young man who had just committed murder. After the chase scene ended, at 10:32, Tommy supposedly went to the kitchen for some food, then to his room to work on what Littleton calls Tommy's "infamous" Abraham Lincoln report. But, Littleton says, Tommy could have gone anywhere.

Tommy places the time of his tryst with Martha at 9:30 or 9:35. It happened out on the Skakels' back lawn and lasted about twenty minutes, he tells the Sutton investigators. After they masturbated each other to orgasm, Tommy watched Martha "hurry away across the rear lawn" toward home—the last time he saw her.

It was also at about 9:30 that Nanny Sweeney asked Ken Littleton to check out the "fracas," which these reports suggest was the barking dogs. Littleton walked out the door, stood amid some cypress trees, and heard only "rustling" behind some bushes in the backyard. He did not investigate. Was this the tryst in progress—or perhaps a sexual assault?

Then things turn really muddy. Steven Skakel tells investigators that he heard the laughing girl—"Helen or Martha"—out behind the swimming pool at about 10:30 P.M., not the previously reported 9:30. Julie Skakel, interviewed under hypnosis, recalled looking out the kitchen window and seeing a sizable man, perhaps hooded, crouching in the backyard. He had "a bundle" clamped under his arm. Then the man stole across the back of the house, across the driveway, and into some bushes. This, she says' was around 10 P.M.

Julie's "man with a bundle" prompts the Sutton investigators to consider Charles Morganti's 10 P.M. sighting of a mystery man—the man who disappeared between two houses across Otter Rock Drive from the Skakels'. Was it Littleton? Sutton investigators think not: Julie reports chatting with Littleton in the kitchen at almost the same time as her crouched-man sighting. The investigators conclude that Littleton couldn't have been everywhere at once.

The Sutton reports make riveting use of the Academy Group's findings. The behavioral scientists' portrait of the killer does not remotely fit Ken Littleton. But it fits the Skakel boys perfectly—the young and sexually inexperienced killer who knew his victim well, and may have killed her after she rejected his advances. The Academy Group scientists go on to say the killer lived within walking distance of Martha; had sexual fantasies about her; was a voyeur; and was of a "high class"—at least of the same socioeconomic class as the Moxleys. This sketch fits both Michael and Tommy, but Michael a bit more, given the masturbation, the voyeurism, and his sexual immaturity. (Michael told the Sutton investigators that he would stand outside a window and watch a certain Belle Haven woman walk around her house naked.)

Whether Michael did or did not go to Sursum Corda, he seems to have been absent for a stretch of time. It is most likely that he went with his brothers to the back country. On his return, did Tommy taunt Michael with his "conquest"? Did Michael then storm over to the Moxleys' house and lure Martha out? A problem: this scenario requires Martha to have *slipped home* without attracting Dorthy's notice. Dorthy had painted the mullions on the master bedroom windows until about 10:30, took a shower, and started to watch the eleven o'clock news, when she fell asleep. Martha would have come home from the Skakel house well before 10:30, by Tommy's version of events.

But maybe Tommy's version bears little resemblance to the truth of that night. Maybe Martha Moxley did not leave the Skakel estate when he said she did, and unknown scenes—blowups, cleanups, vows of secrecy—played out until the morning sun glowed through the trees. Maybe the secrets of that night sit in Tommy and Michael Skakel (and in who else?) like some mortal affliction, destroying them by degrees.

One hard detail of Martha's murder I hadn't known until now: the girl suffered a broken nose. In order for the Sutton investigators to know this, Steve Carroll thinks, they must possess the carefully guarded autopsy report. How on earth could this be? "This sounds dirtier and dirtier," Carroll says. "You got money, you can get whatever you want."

In any case, the Sutton investigators believe, based on the bruising in the canthus of Martha's eyes, that she was struck in the face with a fist. It's a detail I find enormously intriguing. Did Tommy try to force himself on Martha after everyone had left? Did she resist—bite him or kick him—only to see

Tommy's fist flying at her face? Did Martha pick herself up off the grass and sprint for home? Did Tommy then race up to his patio, retrieve a Toney Penna six iron, and overtake Martha beneath the willow of her own front lawn? Did he raise the club in the faint beam of a streetlamp and set the dogs to their furious barking? *Did he . . . ?*

Chapter Thirteen

And Life Goes On

MOST OF THE PEOPLE in this story have left town. Rush Skakel sold his estate on Otter Rock Drive in 1993 for three million dollars. He moved to a gated community called Loblolly Pines in Hobe Sound, Florida—or "Snob Sound," as a realtor I met in Vero Beach labeled it.

I go down to Florida and call Rush Skakel, hoping to meet with him. The man who picks up the phone says something like "Hobe Sound Interiors," and I say, "Sorry, I was looking for Rushton Skakel. I must have the wrong number." The man says quickly, "No, no, no, you've got him. How can I help you?"

I tell him how. He begins to stammer. He says, "M-m-my wife won't let me talk about it. It's a family problem." Which is an interesting way of putting it. He hangs up. I drive down to Loblolly Pines, but a guard with a military bearing turns me away. It is the perfect place for Rush Skakel to live.

I call Michael Skakel at his home in Cohasset, a suburb of Boston. I've heard he got his life together after a fearful substance abuse problem. He married a woman he met in rehab, graduated from college in his thirties, and, after a scant professional history, went to work for his cousin, the late Michael Kennedy, at Citizen's Energy Corporation.

Skakel reportedly suffered a mental collapse after getting entangled in Kennedy's baby-sitter sex intrigue. He had been a confidant of the girl and supposedly talked her mother down from the roof as she contemplated jumping.

Right after his alleged collapse is when I call him. After a few rings, the message machine picks up, but a man's voice cuts in with a breathless "Hello."

"The Moxley murder? Hmm. What's that?"

"You're saying you don't know?"

Long pause. "I'm a cousin from California," he says at last, laughing a little. "Michael's not home."

Michael remains a suspect in the murder of Martha Moxley.

Tommy Skakel lives in Stockbridge, Massachusetts, the pretty little town in the Berkshire Hills where Norman Rockwell lived and painted. Tommy attended Ithaca College in upstate New York but never graduated, and afterward he traveled the world, indulging his passion for hunting. At some point, in Mexico, he reportedly contracted malaria. Later he worked for Helen Downey, a family friend with a tony real estate firm in New York City.

In the spring of 1989 he married Anne Gillman at Christ Episcopal Church in Greenwich, with Ethel Kennedy in attendance. The Skakels moved from Pound Ridge, New York, to Windham, to Stockbridge. Tommy seems to be living a

Rockwellian life there: he and Anne are raising two small children; they joined the Episcopal Church; and Tommy serves as a volunteer fireman. One report even has the Skakels running a bed-and-breakfast. Another source tells me, more reliably, that he's a venture capitalist.

Len Levitt interviewed Tommy briefly in 1984. "Like who the hell are those people to judge me?" he said, speaking of Greenwichites. "What gives them the right?"

Ken Littleton is the most psychologically damaged person in this story. In 1991 Jack Solomon and Frank Garr convinced Littleton to come to Connecticut and once more try to clear his name. The State of Connecticut wined and dined him and put him up in a hotel. They had the United States Army's foremost polygraph expert waiting for him. After unhooking Littleton from his machine, the expert announced to the investigators, "We've got him. This is your man."

In 1993, on the power of a warrant, police took Littleton from his home to an undisclosed place, where they compelled him to give up hair and blood samples. Yet there is still no reason to be certain that Ken Littleton ever laid eyes on Martha Moxley. Carole Ball refused to let me interview him. But she sent me a statement, which reads in part:

> It is not in his best interest to contribute to the media frenzy now surrounding this case. It is no exaggeration to say that his mere presence in Greenwich, Connecticut in October of 1975 has ruined his life. He is in danger of being made a scapegoat here. His only comment is that the prime suspect is a person of influence, prestige and financial resources who has been able

to frustrate the investigative efforts of the authorities who are under tremendous pressure to make an arrest.

Littleton married, divorced, drank heavily, and was diagnosed as a manic depressive. He was in and out of the psychiatric ward at McLean Hospital in Belmont. At McLean he met a Smith College graduate who had been a belle of the campus. A year after she graduated, she suffered a nervous breakdown. The woman moved in with Littleton, and they've been together ever since. "They're like two wounded lambs," someone who knows them both tells me. "But every time there's a new development in this case, Ken goes on another bender. It really did ruin his life."

William Edward Hammond lives at a good address in Manhattan and practices business law. He found his legal calling rather late, earning his degree in 1990, but finally he works at a job that he loves, and his drinking is more than a decade behind him. He is married and has a young daughter. But the ghost of the Moxley case still haunts him—especially when journalists call to remind him of the strange and troubled young man he once was.

"I wish to God I'd seen or heard *something* that could have helped the police figure out what happened to that poor girl. But I didn't, and I became a suspect. I have to live with that every day of my life."

Frank Garr keeps pressing the case, alone. The last time I talked to him before finishing this book, in January 1998, he said the state was considering convening a grand jury. Though he does not say so, I'm convinced he's targeting Tommy and Michael Skakel.

In 1997 Tom Keegan was reelected to the South Carolina state legislature. Jim Lunney, who described himself to me as "a gypsy," recently moved back to Greenwich. Steve Carroll never left. He occupies the same well-tended house that he's lived in for the past forty-two years. Carroll is willing to publicize Martha's case whenever he gets the chance.

Martha's friends went on to live their lives. The Fuchs family moved to another part of Greenwich a year after Martha's death. Today Tori Fuchs is the advertising director of the *Greenwich Post.* Christy Kalan lives in New York City and works for a student travel company. Peter Ziluca, Martha's boyfriend, runs his own yard-maintenance company in town. Helen Ix and her husband moved from the nearby town of Darien back to Belle Haven. They built a new home at the corner of Walsh Lane and Field Point Road, just up the street from where her parents still live.

Somewhere in her future, like leaves, like snow, Sheila McGuire imagines there will come a trial.

It will be a circus.

She will have to push through the cameras on the courthouse steps, enter a packed and airless courtroom, and fight the panic. Will she be strong enough?

Sheila will mount the stand, take the oath, and describe the horror. The accused man will sit at a long table, in a fine suit, his hands clasped so tightly in front of him that his knuckles go white. There will be a pitcher of water. He will keep filling his glass and drinking the water to keep his mouth from going dry.

His eyes. What about his eyes? Will they stare down at the table—or up at her? And will these eyes be the eyes of a man she knows?

Everyone will wait to hear the adjectives. It was dark. Maybe the killer himself does not know the adjectives.

And so when the hour comes, Sheila will stare down her demons. She considers the silent people of the town, people who might come forth with a piece of the puzzle but instead sit locked behind their walls, stony, resistant. "I am angered by anyone who has not been as forthcoming as I have been. I didn't exercise any right not to be. We're grown now and we're parents. I just pray that these people who weren't helpful don't have an experience when they, or their children, need the support of friends and don't get it. Because they would be living the legacy they left Mrs. Moxley with. I believe that hell is absolutely living with who you are. I'm content with who I am. I'm not perfect, I need to grow in a lot of ways, but I'll do what I have to do."

I mention Jon Lee's contention that Martha is bad publicity for Belle Haven and for all Greenwich. A shocking thought.

"How easy to say, 'Keep it out of Greenwich.' Okay, when your child gets stolen, you're going to be content with a couple of news clippings? And then the neighbors will say, 'Get over it,' because they don't want this kind of thing? What is really the point? I don't get it. Someone's child was brutally murdered in a town. All the earth is the same sphere, Greenwich or Istanbul or anywhere. A crime was committed against a child; justice should prevail. I don't understand anything else than that."

*   *   *

John Moxley has prospered in the field of commercial real estate. From his office on the twenty-second floor of a towering black building, he gazes out over the tip of lower Manhattan and wonders, from time to time, where Martha would be today. "Would she be a managing partner in Morgan Stanley, making a million dollars a year? Would she have five kids and a French gynecologist for a husband?"

Then his musing turns more serious. What would it be like if a man accused of Martha's murder ever came to trial? "It would be terrifically hard. In Dominick Dunne's book *A Season in Purgatory*, the hardest thing for me was the trial. Because with Martha's case, you know it would be a circus like that. It wouldn't be just cut-and-dried. It would be a long, drawn-out ordeal that would take a terrific personal toll. It would be like going to the dentist to have all your teeth removed. It would be terrifically painful—for everyone involved."

Dorthy Moxley lives in a spacious brick home, painted white and framed by blossoming fruit trees, in a small New Jersey town called Chatham. John and his wife and two young children live in nearby Short Hills.

"Everything in my life was so perfect," she reflects. "I had good, solid parents who loved us, I went to college, I met a wonderful man, I had two beautiful children—and then my life fell apart."

In New Jersey, she has glued it back together, insofar as this is possible. She has her grandchildren to sustain her. She has the Methodist Church. A new community of friends. "It feels like I belong here," she says. But Martha, and the endless speculation surrounding her death, is unavoidably at the center of her existence. Dorthy appears often on television—

Unsolved Mysteries, American Journal, Hard Copy, Today—
to discuss her daughter's case. These dealings with TV people
and print journalists and detectives have given her a shrewd-
ness that I would not have thought possible of her the first
time we met, in 1993, and that she mostly hides behind the
more natural Dorthy—the gentle, mothering Dorthy.

She would like to have been a simpler woman. "I was
cleaning out my freezer the other day, and you know what I
found? Fifteen jars of jam! Can you imagine? Fifteen?" Her
voice grows very tired. "I don't know. Sometimes I think I
ought to have been a Michigan farmer's wife, going to the
state fair with my jams and jellies."

Instead she is haunted. What haunts her most, for the moment, is her memory of the voices. The voices of agitated
young men down in her yard. One of them must have been the
voice of her daughter's killer. Why did she shut out the voices
for so long? Dorthy marvels at what a curious organ the brain
is—protecting her from evil the way it did. Now she says,
"You know, I may be the only witness to Martha's murder."

Those who have spent time with Dorthy know that the passage of twenty-two years has not buried the raw nerve of
Martha's death. And so she breaks into tears as she says, "I can't
comprehend why anybody would kill Martha. I don't think she
had an enemy in the world. Why would you want to kill Martha?
What did she ever do to them?" Dorthy stops to level her voice.
"It must have been sex. She was so . . . so . . . *appealing.*"

Belle Haven returned to its former grandeur. Workmen's ham-
mers ceaselessly beat out the rhythm of the new wealth, the
sound of shining new palaces rising in place of the old. The
owners of these palaces—in Belle Haven and all over town—

are mostly youngish Wall Streeters who are beginning a cycle of wealth like the captains of industry a century earlier.

"Regular" families who bought houses on the peninsula in the 1950s and '60s could never afford to do so today. In 1997 the average price of a house in Greenwich surpassed one million dollars, and that average is roughly tripled in Belle Haven. "I can't afford the Belle Haven Club anymore," one resident complained to me. "Belle Haven used to be a real nice family place, and now it's just stuffy, stuffy, stuffy—all that New York money."

There is something to say about Belle Haven trees. I have mentioned the toppled willow in the front yard of the former Moxley property. "This is so eerie," Cynthia Bjork says. "The pine under which Martha's body was found then started dying from the ground up, branch by branch." This pine and a sister pine, she tells me, began listing toward each other after Martha's death; then the one pine died, then the other, and eventually both were removed. (I am unable to find out whether Mrs. Bjork has the correct trees in mind; but tall pines do still exist on the property near the place where Sheila McGuire found Martha's body.)

There is one redemptive tree in Belle Haven. Not long after Martha's death, Tori Fuchs went around raising money for a tree and a plaque in her friend's memory. Eventually she collected enough for a small cherry tree and a brass plaque that reads: MARTHA, YOUR SMILE WILL ALWAYS BRING HAPPINESS AND LOVE TO ALL YOUR FRIENDS. *1975*. Today the tree stands in a grass circle beyond the Belle Haven Club tennis courts. It is tall and full and beautiful. Shortly after the tree was planted, however, an incensed neighbor called Barrie Fuchs and yelled, "How dare you plant that tree there! You didn't get permission!"

*   *   *

As for Greenwich itself? It still fends off the jeering of out-siders. Though, admittedly, opportunities for jeering abound.

Five Greenwich High School seniors encode the message "kill all niggers" in the 1995 yearbook and, as punishment, are sent to a boot camp run by black men. In the wake of that scandal, the tabloid television show *A Current Affair* sends in reporters to study the town's real estate practices. Their hid-den cameras show some agents trying to steer black couples to Stamford ("You can get more for your money there"), while making no such pitch to white couples ("Regrettably, they have a very large black population").

A truck hauling four thousand dollars' worth of lobsters over-turns on I-95. Greenwich firefighters extricate the driver, whose leg will soon be amputated, then make off with his cargo, the crates strapped to the backs of their fire trucks. A Greenwich in-vestment banker flying home from Buenos Aires is refused drinks and defecates on the first-floor food cart. This sorry ex-ploit makes international news—and David Letterman's Top Ten List. The town cannot seem to keep out of the news.

Meanwhile, inside Greenwich, the natural world goes qui-etly berserk. The deer population explodes. Deer have fewer places to roam since the mansion building continues apace, and my father jokes about swatting them away with the news-paper as he walks out to get his mail. A buck slams through the window of a Japanese restaurant on Greenwich Avenue. A baby doe strolls into the Ann Taylor shop on the Post Road, thrashes around a bit, and has to be carried out on a stretcher.

The Canada goose war reaches its apogee. The geese befoul Greenwich's ponds, parks, and beaches. The *New York Times* calls them "the nemesis of the barefooted beach-goer." Frank

Keegan, head of Greenwich's parks and rec department, calls them "rats with wings." The town tries everything to shoo them off: fake swans, low-amperage shock fences, blank-shooting cannons ("That really scares the feathers out of them," Keegan says), and border collies from an outfit called Goose Busters. But the efforts of anti-geese activists sag after one of their leaders beats a gosling to death with a stick.

Coyotes have come to the back country, and sometimes you hear their plaintive howls rising up from the woods. A girl on Lower Cross Road in the back country is brushed or bitten by a silver-haired bat and dies of rabies.

A nervousness has crept into Greenwich life. In the winter of 1996, a dermatologist who has built a new house on Beechcroft Road commits the mortal sin of clear-cutting his trees, and a few of the town's as well. The neighbors go for blood, as if venting a frustration they do not clearly understand. Motorists scream obscenities as they drive past the desecrated lot. A neighborhood woman confesses to feeling so heartsick over the trees that she reroutes her morning walk. The dermatologist gets harassing phone calls, anti-Semitic abuse, even death threats. As Christmas draws near, a sad little sign, hand lettered, appears on the doorstep of his naked house: "In the spirit of the holidays, please do not try to chase us from our home or steal our property." And finally the dermatologist closes his practice and moves away.

This man's story is a kind of Greenwich parable. It reflects the anxiety of a town defending itself against the cultural backhoe, the vast gray sameness overtaking life in America. Greenwich need not fear. The mansions rise, the walls grow taller, the money pours in, the heart hardens. Through these defenses only ghosts can pass.

Epilogue

A COLD AUTUMN wind sweeps coffee cups and failed Lotto tickets through the streets of Bridgeport, the largest and most depressed of Connecticut's cities. It is here that the Moxley murder case, known for its connection to wealth, power and exclusivity, will see its official resolution.

The Fairfield County Courthouse, bland and bureaucratic, stands in the center of downtown Bridgeport. On this day—September 24, 1998—a man jingling change in a cup and a knot of lawyers stall on the courthouse steps, watching cameramen wrestle gear out of their vans. The news crews are on the lookout for a man whom investigators believe could be a pivotal witness before the Moxley grand jury—if he would cooperate. But the man is strenuously resisting his subpoena on grounds of client privilege, and claims he remembers nothing about a murder anyway.

A white stretch limo with Maine license plates (cost: $600; courtesy of the State of Connecticut) pulls up to the side of the courthouse and parks under a tree that has harpooned a fluttering plastic bag. Nobody sees the limo arrive. When the reporters discover it, a chauffeur is leaning against the fender. "Is this Joe Ricci's car?" someone asks. The chauffeur nods. "He went in about five minutes ago."

The reporters hustle inside and take the elevator up to the fifth floor. Joe Ricci stands outside the courtroom, huddling with lawyers. He's a fat, pink-faced man with thick brown hair, clad in a black dress shirt and pastel tie depicting a panther on the prowl. He's a former heroin addict from Port Chester, New York, who struck it rich in Maine. He owns a horse-racing track there, Scarborough Downs, and he ran twice for governor, though that was a bit like Norman Mailer running for mayor of New York City: more spirit than substance. In 1970 Ricci founded the Elan School for seriously screwed up kids, in the town of Poland Spring. Michael Skakel spent two nightmarish years at Elan, from March 1978 to February 1980. Now the nightmare has come back to haunt him.

It was at Elan, prosecutors allege, that Michael confessed to the murder of Martha Moxley.

Two weeks after the hardcover edition of this book appeared in stores, in April of last year, prosecutor Donald Browne abruptly quit the case. As his reason he cited "the Dumas book." On page [252] I recount, in a parenthetical aside, how some journalists had speculated that if anyone had been "paid off" in this case, it was probably Donald Browne, since he held the power to drive the case forward or let it languish. He did the latter—though in his own mind, I believe, he was waiting for the absolute clincher, the stone-solid piece of evidence that was unlikely ever to materialize. I also suggest that the rumor of Browne's being corrupted makes no sense, as it was he who ordered the reinvestigation of the case in 1991. Indeed, the prosecutor had a reputation for diligence and honesty. He was not known, however, as a bold man. "He's a chicken," said his old adversary Steve Carroll.

Browne's intrepid replacement, Jonathan Benedict, wasted no time in applying for a grand jury. Such applications are rare in Connecticut—about fifteen in the last decade—and are granted only half the time. The panel of judges responsible for hearing grand jury applications, when presented with an outline of the evidence, must be convinced that a grand jury is likely to find probable cause to arrest.

This panel was convinced.

And so, less than two months after Donald Browne's departure, the state appointed an investigative grand juror. Dorthy Moxley thought she might be dreaming: "I've been going around pinching myself to see if it's really happening," she kept saying, and it was as though something oppressive, some private, defeatist whisper, had left her.

The grand juror was George N. Thim, a Superior Court judge and former public defender of impeccable reputation. Behind the closed—and locked—doors of Courtroom 3C, Thim would listen to subpoenaed witnesses tell the secrets of the Moxley story, and ultimately decide whether to recommend the arrest of Michael Skakel.

A flurry of subpoenas issued from the state's attorney's office in the summer of 1998. Thim heard his first witnesses—Dorthy Moxley, John Moxley, former officer Dan Hickman, and the woman I call Joan Redmond—on July 10. Others followed in short order: Sheila McGuire, Helen Ix, Tom Keegan, Steve Carroll, Millard Jones, the Reverend Mark Connolly, Cissy Ix. The sequence of witnesses suggested the grand jury was tracing the case's chronology: Martha's disappearance, the discovery of her body, the arrival of the police, the first days of the investigation . . . things would spread out from there.

On August 4, a nervous, hulking figure appeared at the courthouse, declining reporters' solicitations. Ken Littleton. He looked weathered and strained and his hair had gone gray. He disappeared into courtroom 3C but did not stay long. He emerged after a few minutes among a small herd of lawyers and officials and walked directly across the hall into open court. Littleton had asserted his Fifth Amendment right, Jonathan Benedict explained, and declined to answer any questions of substance. Benedict asked Judge John Ronan to order Littleton to testify.

So ordered.

Now, this was intriguing. Littleton had two choices: one was to disregard the order and face contempt proceedings; the other was to testify. By testifying under order, according to state law, Littleton automatically triggered "transactional immunity"—that is, he could no longer be prosecuted for the murder, even if he turned out to be its perpetrator. (This is why prosecutors deem it pointless to subpoena either Tommy or Michael Skakel.) But simply by requesting the judge's order, Benedict had declared his belief in Littleton's innocence. And, just like that, his years of torment were over.

That left only Thomas and Michael Skakel on the suspect list. The pressure on Michael had become particularly acute. It first began to escalate in 1995, when Len Levitt broke the story about Michael telling the Sutton investigators that he'd been all over the Moxley yard on the night of Martha's murder, had even masturbated in one of the Moxleys' trees. Frank Garr began publicly referring to Michael as a suspect. Garr had long felt that Michael merited deeper investigation, and now he had a nice wide avenue. But the Sutton report was just the beginning.

On February 16, 1996, *Unsolved Mysteries* aired a report about the Moxley murder. The popular television show may sport a cheesy look, with its clumsy reenactments and *Dragnet*-style voice-overs, but it is factually scrupulous, and has an impressive history of breaking cases. It even made a nice clean crack in the Moxley case.

Though most of those who called with "tips" were viewers with strong opinions, psychics who seemed off-track, and people who knew the Skakels glancingly, one tip stood out above the others. It was from a Phil Lawrence, who lived on Florida's west coast. He'd cooled out at Elan in the late 1970s, the same time as Michael. *Unsolved Mysteries'* internal report of Lawrence's tip reads, in part: "Caller said that . . . Michael admitted to people there that he did it with a golf club . . . Caller said that Ricci has this on tape. Caller said that Michael told a lot of people there about this. . . . Michael said he did it because he was drunk. He told them this in group therapy. . . . Caller said it was unusual that it was not brought up in group therapy again. . . . [Michael] said that he would often have drunken blackouts."

If Michael told people that he'd killed a girl, then surely other witnesses could be found. As the grand jury wore on, Joe Johnson and I kept vigil outside the state's attorney's office, waiting for unfamiliar faces to announce themselves for Frank Garr. Gradually the faces showed, about seven in all, a mixture of residents and counselors.

We imagined Frank Garr was beginning to get a well-rounded picture of Michael's alleged confession. But without that picture, reporters were left to wonder about context: Did Michael say whatever he said to be tough? Did he say it for kicks? Did he say it sarcastically? Was it beaten out of him? If he spoke sincerely, how did he word the confession—did he say vaguely that he was involved, or did he say, unmistakably, that he was the killer? Do the accounts of the witnesses agree? All we knew for sure was that some people witnessed what they believed to be Michael's confession of murder.

He denies making a confession of any sort.

Adding to Michael Skakel's distress was the publication in May 1998 of Mark Fuhrman's book *Murder in Greenwich: Who Killed Martha Moxley?* In blunt prose, Fuhrman stated his case for Michael as Martha's killer, and propagated his theory on all the TV talk shows. Suddenly Michael's name was everywhere.

What must he have thought? He'd managed to reverse the course of his chaotic life, he'd married a lovely woman, and she was pregnant with their first child. Now, with a couple of books out and a grand jury in progress, he was being vilified across the land. Newspapers and magazines were calling his home in Cohasset. Reporters turned up on his doorstep.

Something had to be done.

One day in June, Michael walked out and hammered a small wooden sign into his front lawn. All it said was "NO." Not long after, the windows were dark and the furniture was gone. Michael and Margot Skakel had moved to Hobe Sound, Florida, where they took refuge with Rushton behind the pretty walls of Loblolly Pines.

As the grand jury wore on, a presumption of Skakel innocence became harder and harder to maintain. Team Skakel did let Julie, John and Steven Skakel appear before Judge Thim without quarrel, as well as Skakel cousins Georgeann Dowdle and Desneiges Terrien. But soon the sounds of resistance could be heard from Nantucket to Colombia.

The most dramatic fight occurred in Martin County, Florida. Rush Skakel Sr.'s lawyers were contending that their client should be excused from grand jury participation for two reasons: he wasn't home when Martha was killed, rendering him immaterial; and he was incompetent to testify because of psychological problems, not to mention physical infirmities.

The first reason was patently ridiculous: Rush didn't have to be home to know a thing or two. The second was less ridiculous, for Rush was behaving oddly. At a competency hearing in October 1998 in Stuart, Florida, a psychiatrist testified that Rush suffered from degenerative dementia. Dr. Alvin Rosen, of North Palm Beach, said Rush would pick food off strangers' plates in restaurants; moon a woman who lived next door; growl like an animal; and greet men he did not know by bumping bellies, and women by rubbing noses. Lately he had become anxious and fearful, double-locking his bedroom door and sleeping with a loaded gun and a hunting knife, added neurologist Mark Stafford. A priest at Rush's church, Aidan Hynes, said he'd met Rush in 1993 and quickly decided he was "mad." (This did not stop Father Hynes from dining at the Skakel house five times a week.) To make matters worse, a radical prostatectomy had left Rush impotent and incontinent. "His personal hygiene is disgusting," Anna Mae Skakel said as her husband looked on. His toenails were so long they put holes in his shoes; he refused to change his Depend undergarments when he soiled them; he would not shower or brush his teeth.

In spite of all this, Rush *could* seem quite sane. He'd seemed lucid, basically, in 1997, when he described the Moxley murder to me as "a family problem." Cissy Ix said he appeared to be fine, and a family member admitted the same. A *Palm Beach Post* reporter asked Rush in 1998 who he thought killed Martha Moxley, and he guessed Ken Littleton—showing a soundness that witnesses claimed was beyond him.

But the fight dragged on.

Joe Ricci exits Courtroom 3C red-faced, head slanted forward. He's declined to answer grand jury questions, citing privilege, and now there'll be a hearing, a lengthy one, in open court to determine whether privilege applies.

During a break in the proceedings, I find Ricci down on the courthouse steps, smoking a cigarette. He smokes at every opportunity. "First Kenneth Starr, now this," he grumbles. "It's lunacy! If this gets breached, kiss treatment goodbye. Nobody will want to go get treatment."

I ask Ricci if he's using the privilege issue to protect Michael Skakel. He gives a "yeah, right" look and exhales a cone of smoke. "Look. At no time did anybody say to me that Michael Skakel committed a murder. At no time did I *overhear* anybody say he committed a murder. Michael never *admitted* to committing a murder. Whoever is spreading this stuff ought to be investigated, and I'll bet I know who it is."

He names a name that is not Phil Lawrence's. I say maybe, but that's not who I heard. He has given a name and gotten nothing in return. He is visibly irritated.

"Who the fuck is this mystery person? I mean, at Elan we had people who are attorney generals now. Big executives. And we had people who the program didn't work out for. Who's to say this person wasn't sipping a bottle of vodka when he dialed *Unsolved Mysteries*? Who's to say he's not a heroin addict?" Court documents say there's more than one witness. Ricci scoffs. "These are people, a lot of people, who had severe emotional problems. And twenty years later they have a pang of conscience?"

Ricci does not seek privilege just for himself; rather, he wants to draw a shade around the whole strange little world of Elan, to protect its "twenty-four-hour therapeutic environment" from the reckless reach of the law. This is what Ricci told "that banana Garr" when Garr carried out a search warrant at Elan in the fall of 1997. (Garr came away with school records, but no therapy records—those are purged every seven years.) Now lawyers for Michael Skakel and Joe Ricci are asking Judge Edward Stodolink to draw the shade for them—to bar, in effect, the grand jury testimony of anyone who might have witnessed certain words fall from the mouth of Michael Skakel.

After all, everything was therapy. Even a confession of murder.

On December 10, after seven days of hearings spread over two months, Judge Stodolink made his ruling: a double victory for the prosecution. Not only did the judge allow the testimony of former Elan residents—that was the big one—but he also ordered Ricci himself to testify before Judge Thim.

Over the years, so much suspicion converged on Tommy that Michael went largely unexamined. But little clues had begged attention: the gardener, Franz Wittine, noticing how Michael's siblings treated him "as if he knew something" and "were being exceptionally nice" to him after the murder; Cissy Ix's telling Dorthy Moxley she didn't think Tommy capable of the crime, "but Michael—I'll give you Michael any day" (she claims to have no recollection of saying this); and, most disturbing, Michael's obsession with torturing and killing small animals.

Who was the real Michael Skakel? Friends from the seventies remember a Jekyll and Hyde character, extravagantly generous on one hand and mindlessly cruel on the other. This speaks of alcoholism's anarchy. Michael turned heavily to the bottle at about age twelve, his best friend at the time told me. He habitually raided his father's wine cellar. Rushton tried to thwart him by padlocking the door, but Michael used some Skakel ingenuity to get past the snag: he pried the door off its hinges. The friend, whom I'll call Frederick, said Michael shot his dog (not fatally) with a pellet gun. Frederick didn't see the shooting, but he knew that only Michael Skakel went around picking off live creatures with guns. One day after school, Frederick walked over to the Skakels' to find Michael inside a shed in the back yard, baiting birds with bread crumbs. He'd toss the crumbs onto the grass and slaughter the birds as they landed outside his blind. Michael was laughing; he thought it was funny.

The other Michael Skakel, Frederick said, had a measure of charisma. No other Skakel boy had it. Where Michael was spirited and full of ideas, his brothers, the teenaged ones, were remote and even dull. On jaunts to Greenwich Avenue, his pockets full of his father's cash, Michael would offer to buy his friends gifts of bicycles and baseball gloves. He also took friends skiing to Colorado aboard the Great Lakes Carbon corporate jet.

Michael made many friends outside his extended family. One of them was Martha Moxley. Frederick said Michael was infatuated with her, and had kissed her several times during the summer of 1975. Though Martha had let him do it, the affection was clearly one-sided. On October 31, the day Sheila McGuire found Martha's stabbed and beaten body, Michael went over to Frederick's house and told his mother, with great excitement, "Somebody killed Martha and they're trying to pin it on Tommy." Strange, because nobody was trying to pin it on Tommy yet. That afternoon Frederick came home from soccer practice and, as usual, walked across the street to the Skakel house. He was intercepted at the front door by an unfamiliar man in a dark suit. The man turned Frederick away with an ominous sentence: "You won't be able to talk to Michael for a while."

After that day, Frederick's friendship with Michael—well, what exactly happened to it? It suddenly seemed not to exist anymore. Perhaps this was because of what Frederick told me next: "I always believed, in my heart of hearts, that Michael killed her."

We come to March of 1978. Michael's episode in Windham—crashing into a telephone pole after a police chase—had brought his frenzied life to the brink of ruin. Instead of dying or going to jail, he went to Elan.

The eighty-acre compound at the end of a long dirt road in Maine must have seemed to him like the ninth circle of hell. "Life there was *not normal,*" said Chuck Seigan, who arrived at Elan three weeks before Michael. "It was noisy. There was confusion. It was fifty-two-card-pickup every day. Nothing was normal—confusion was normal. The whole purpose was to stir shit up in people."

There was much to stir. One boy went to Elan for raping a seven-year-old girl, sticking pins in her heart, and burying her body under some leaves. Another hoisted a black boy up in a tree by his legs and blew his head off with a shotgun. Still another stomped a three-year-old to death. And the worst of the crowd weren't even kept at Elan proper. They lived at a maximum security branch called Parson's Field, up in the mountains, an hour and a half away. This is all according to Seigan and another Elan contemporary of Michael's who asked me not to use his real name. I'll call him Arthur Conrad. "They were a bunch of crazy idiots," Conrad said.

Joe Ricci and Dr. Gerald Davidson, a now-deceased friend of the Kennedys, oversaw this rough preserve. Dr. Davidson gave Elan official standing, being the only licensed doctor there, but his presence was as thin as a ghost's. A resident would meet him on entering and might see him once or twice more before leaving. The staff were "a bunch of ex-heroin addicts," Conrad said, some not even twenty years old.

Ricci, though, was an impressive and complicated character. "He was God," Chuck Seigan said. "When he walked into the room, he was like a movie star. But he could make your life miserable if he wanted." That was how he thought of him then. Today the best he can say is, "I don't believe he's a *completely* evil man." Arthur Conrad said, "He's a loser. A *big-time* loser. He's fucking nuts."

Ricci admits the Elan of yesteryear was experimental, even controversial. "Elan was hardcore like football was hardcore in the days when they played without helmets," he told me without irony. Ex-Elan residents speak of "surviving" the place as though they'd been away at war. "Put yourself in our place, Arthur Conrad said. You're far from home, you're afraid, and your parents bring you in and sit you down in front of Dr. Davidson. He tells you how great you are, how great the program is, how much it's going to help you.

"Then they walk you over to the house and reality crashes down. Complete culture shock. There are people in cages. People wearing signs around their necks. People in dunce caps. It was a fucking circus. Like being thrown into the lion's den with a bunch of ya-yas." The days unspooled like a surrealistic nightmare. Kids were made to dig holes in the dirt with spoons. Made to live in Dumpsters for a week. Motorcycle gangster Mike C. earned the most serious form of attitude adjustment, a "cowboy ass-kicking." That's when a room full of peers, maybe ten of them, pummel you senseless. "We beat the crap out of him," Conrad confirmed.

"Joe's theory was, if somebody acts bad, you treat him as bad as he acted," Conrad went on. "The point was to break you down and build you back up. But in the midst of breaking your spirit, some people broke down for good."

All this for only $18,000 a year.

In the land of Elan, Michael Skakel was something of a wallflower. "He kept to himself and he was real quiet," Chuck Seigan said. "He was well liked. He didn't antagonize or provoke anybody."

Seigan reflected, fished out a memory. "There was a girl named Sarah M. She and Michael were inseparable. They were just friends, I think, but it was like he was protective of her. She had long blond hair, a beautiful face. Now I see, from the pictures, that she looked a lot like Martha Moxley."

"Michael *was* quiet, Arthur Conrad said. He never put himself in the spotlight, except for at a couple of general meetings. That was because of Joe. If anything, Joe Ricci put him in the spotlight." Conrad added, "Joe Ricci hated Michael—and everything he stood for."

"General meetings" may sound as innocuous as homeroom, but they were actually occasions of misery and terror. Usually they were directed at a single person—Elan's version of the stocks. Without warning, that person would be interrupted from his duties as the cry of "general meeting" resounded through the house. He would be held in an office while residents collected in the dining room and sat quietly with their hands folded on their laps, eyes fixed straight ahead. They would wait in silence. Then, like a circus barker, staff members would start whipping them up—not their curiosity, but their anger: "So-and-so thinks he can do whatever the fuck he wants! Just like the day he came here!" When the residents were sufficiently worked up—jeering and stamping their feet—the transgressor would be "stood up" for ridicule. Sometimes meetings would go on all day and into the night. "It could be real intimidating," Chuck Seigan said. "People just storming up at you, jabbing their fingers at you, spit covering your face because they're yelling and screaming at you."

Michael Skakel was stood up at one general meeting that nobody in attendance would ever forget—nobody, apparently, but Joe Ricci. It occurred in November of 1978, after the first of Michael's two escapes. (Ten or fifteen people fled every week, despite head counts every quarter hour. "They were running from themselves," Ricci explained, and ex-residents do not entirely disagree.)

Arthur Conrad remembers the meeting like this: "Everybody's sitting there, not saying a word. Joe's pacing around the room, he has a real sense of presence to him: 'Does anybody know why Michael's here?'

"'No, no.'

"Joe says, 'Skakel, get the hell up. Let me tell you why Michael's here. He's here because of the murder of Martha Moxley. His family's got money, that's why he's here instead of jail.' Michael's there in total shock. *Total* shock. Joe says, 'Anybody want to let him know how you feel?' And then everybody raced up and yelled at him."

However arresting that meeting may have been, the alleged confession apparently did not happen during it. Seigan and Conrad could not address the confession issue, at least not directly, for fear of drifting into forbidden territory, which is to say grand jury territory. But Conrad allowed, forcefully, "He's as guilty as the day is long."

Michael left Elan in February 1980, but this wasn't the end of his Rehabilitation Road. In 1987, Michael found himself at Father Martin's, a country-clubbish rehab campus on the Chesapeake Bay in Maryland.

"He scared the hell out of me," said Steve Dougherty, a recovered heroin addict who knew Michael at Father Martin's. "I could forget almost everybody in rehab, but not Michael Skakel."

For one thing, Michael's physicality was imposing. "You should have seen him hit a volleyball. I thought he'd pop the damn thing. He busted my finger. I took a spike and he telescoped my middle finger." Michael would play croquet as if driving golf balls down a fairway: "He used to slug the thing. He used to send that thing right into the bay."

Michael never said anything about killing a girl. But one day he and Dougherty were fishing off the pier, and the subject of weapons arose. "I caught a fish, and it was flopping around on the dock. I said, 'Quick get something to kill it with.' He said, 'What we need is a golf club, kill it with that.' And I'm thinking, 'Golf club? Why not just get a knife?' That's how it came up. He said he used to kill small animals with golf clubs. Cats, squirrels, groundhogs—things of that nature. Anything on his estate."

Dougherty happened to be watching *Unsolved Mysteries* on February 16, 1996, when he heard something that made him sit up straight. A murder with a *golf club*? *Michael Skakel* was a suspect? What the hell . . . ?

Dougherty picked up the phone.

In July of 1998, two weeks after George Thim heard his first witnesses, Michael hired noted defense lawyer Mickey Sherman. Sherman's presence amplified the Moxley case's sense of inwardness and circularity: he grew up in the working-class Pemberwick section of Greenwich, four houses down the street from Frank Garr.

These days Sherman travels in glamorous circles. He's got Johnnie Cochran's phone number on his speed dial. His best friend is the singer Michael Bolton. He was sitting poolside with Paula Barbieri, at the Mirage in Las Vegas, when she got the news that her ex-boyfriend's ex-wife, Nicole Brown Simpson, had just been murdered.

Earlier this year, I went to Mickey's office in Stamford.

"If these were real confessions—bonafide, effective, credible confessions—we wouldn't be going through this exercise right now." The grand jury exercise, that is. "They would have taken statements from these people, applied for and received an arrest warrant. And then they would've arrested Michael or Tom or whoever. That's why I don't believe these confessions are the real deal."

Shortly before I met with Mickey, a fellow named Ben Works emerged as a Skakel family spokesman. Perhaps the Skakels were sick of the steady critical drumbeat, and sought a few contrapuntal notes. And so there was Works on *The Montel Williams Show* (on which I was also a guest), claiming to be "99.5 percent" certain the Skakel boys had nothing to do with Martha's murder. And there he was in *Greenwich Time,* asserting that the Elan confession, or whatever it was, came from kids "beating the pulp out of Michael" in the boxing ring. "Because this was under duress—what was essentially torture over time—whatever they thought was a confession they wrung out of Michael is absolutely meaningless."

Might this be a preview of the defense—Michael coughed up a few words in order to stop the beating? Mickey Sherman nodded. "It's a rational explanation as to why Michael would make any such utterance. And again, I don't believe he ever said, 'I did this.'" Mickey wouldn't say, however, whether Michael claimed he was beaten at Elan. "I don't want to confirm or deny that. Let's just say this was not Camp Grenada for him."

"Michael was never beaten. I'll tell you that right out front," Chuck Seigan asserted. "They knew who his father was, and they didn't want to mess with his father." When I mentioned that the "torture over time" supposedly took place in the boxing ring, Seigan gave a dry laugh and said, "Yeah, they would say that."

The boxing ring, like the cowboy ass-kicking, was one of Elan's many attitude fixers. If someone broke one of Elan's three Cardinal Rules (no sex, no substances, and no violence—"pretty ironic, considering the punishment," Seigan said), Joe Ricci might, at a general meeting, throw down the boxing gloves and say, "Who wants to join this punk?" Peers would encircle the culprit to form a ring. One at a time "hitters" would enter to do battle; by the third or fourth hitter the culprit—scared, exhausted, a little beat up—was sufficiently demoralized. "It wouldn't last long, maybe five minutes," Seigan said.

"It humbles you really fast when you get your ass kicked in front of ninety people."

Michael had a turn as a ring victim during one general meeting—not the infamous one—and was never touched again. Neither Seigan nor Conrad considered it anything like a beating. "Don't get me wrong, there was physical abuse at Elan," Conrad said. He added with a sardonic chuckle, "But Michael was never beaten in his life."

Mickey Sherman admits he's in the minority when he says he thinks his client won't be arrested. The state's case is weak; why would they bring forth a case they can't win? Indeed, legal experts do give Sherman the edge if the case goes to trial, since the murder happened long ago, memories have proved contradictory, police and forensics work left much to be desired, physical evidence is supposedly scant, and (according to Sherman) the circumstantial evidence is of poor quality. "I've always felt that if they have some statements which mildly resemble a confession, then it might be enough for probable cause to arrest," he said. "But I also believe that the state's attorney's office is wise enough not to make an arrest, if that's all they have. If all they're dealing with are these alleged, flimsy, shaky, mock confessions, I don't see that as proof beyond a reasonable doubt to a jury."

(Frank Garr, who by February was answering questions in the fewest possible words, said, "This is not a weak case.")

By the way, how was Michael holding up, down there in Hobe Sound? Sherman said he's lived with this for so long that he was "numb" to the idea of being arrested. "He's obviously very uptight. But I think he's a little relieved that there'll be a resolution. The cloud will go away, somehow, some way. And he's ready to accept whatever happens to him."

In November 1998 I went back down to Hobe Sound, Florida. I didn't have much of a plan. I knew that Rushton attended Mass at St. Christopher's Church; perhaps Michael and Margot would be there with him. What would I do if I found them? I took care of the problem by oversleeping. When I got to St. Christopher's the last service was emptying out and Cadillacs and Lincolns, white and powder blue and pale yellow, were humming off to brunch.

I decided to walk across the street for pancakes and coffee. But first I went to a payphone and dialed a number I had reason to believe might be Michael's. A mechanized male voice picked up and I left a message. I had hoped he'd join me for pancakes—not because

I expected him to address the facts of the Moxley case, but because I wanted to see whether he would add to or subtract from the rather sorry portrait that had begun to emerge. No luck.

(When I got back to Connecticut, I ran into Mickey Sherman. "Heard you were in Florida," he said.)

I then headed up to Stuart, the Martin County seat. Though I showed up without warning, assistant state's attorney Bob Belanger agreed to see me. It was Belanger who was trying to get Rush Skakel to comply with the grand jury subpoena from the Florida end. He pointed to a bulky file resting on the floor next to his desk. "All that work because Rush Skakel's trying to get out of testifying."

Belanger sat me down in a quiet room to peruse the file: "Florida has pretty friendly sunshine laws." I'll say. In a matter of seconds I was leafing through medical files marked "confidential." The earliest, from March of 1991, is a list of symptoms recited to a therapist by Rush's wife, Anna Mae. They don't seem all that serious: gets upset easily, spits, often says silly things, calls people names, pinches women, feigns sickness when advantageous, wears mismatched shoes, puts jacket on backward and thinks he's entertaining.

Rush had always been odd. Now it seemed the oddness in him was more pronounced, and a little volatile. Perhaps there were the beginnings of serious trouble: he'd forget the names of close friends, babble incoherently, take powerful tranquilizing medications and cadge sleeping pills from the maid. Something was amiss, clearly, but it was hard to say what. As one psychiatrist wrote to another in 1992, "Rush remains a bit of a puzzle. On the positive side, I did see him while I was in [Florida] and he appears to be doing as well as he ever has."

An evaluation from July 1991 gave a clearer window into the muddle of Rush's psyche. The examiner, Dr. Joseph Richman, began: "Although cooperative, he complained constantly about the demands I placed upon him, saying for example, 'Why are you so tough? Why do you do these things? You're a Popsicle.' He also asked if my sleep is troubled, apparently because of my sadistic nature. . . . Later, I asked why he seemed to find the use of his mind so unpleasant, and he replied, 'I've not been well.' " (Dr. Richman's tests indicated a recent psychotic break. Consider the timing: three weeks before Rush's examination, *Greenwich Time* had published Len Levitt's detailed account of the Moxley investigation.)

Dr. Richman found the Rorschach test results especially intriguing. In response to Card V, sometimes called the self-image card, Rush gave an almost poetic rendering of defeat. He saw in the inkblot "an extraordinarily big moth that has just come out of the sky and landed on the ground. Its wings are covered with whatever it formed in the air. Looks like mud. They all look like mud." Richman wrote: "Such imagery, of flying high and coming down covered with mud, has a strong manic-depressive, or grandiose-defeated, quality."

On November 10, 1998, Judge John Fennelly ordered the King Lear of Hobe Sound north, to Bridgeport. Rush's lawyers appealed, and at this writing no final decision had been reached.

Just before Halloween 1998, I drove up to Stockbridge, Massachusetts. Even with the focus trained so sharply on Michael, certain questions about Tommy persisted: What had happened around ten o'clock on the night of the murder? What was the disturbance that so agitated the neighborhood dogs at that hour? Must not Tommy have been nearly in the middle of it, since his own account had him trysting with Martha at almost precisely the moment of the barking dogs?

I had found Tommy's 1990s version of his actions hard to believe—and not only because of the seeming unlikelihood of Martha engaging him sexually. The story smacked of ass-covering. By this time, Henry Lee had started examining evidence with his magic machines, and Tommy knew that someday he might be called upon to account for whatever Lee turned up—like the presence of semen.

Still, the tryst story helps Tommy's case in one crucial regard: it unwittingly creates a motive for Michael. What meaner brotherly trespass could Tommy have committed than to encroach on Michael's love interest? How would the emotionally precarious Michael have reacted? Consider that the behavioral scientists said the nature of the attack on Martha was personal, that the killer knew Martha and fantasized about her, and that he was a voyeur. (Michael told Sutton investigators he was a habitual window peeper, and had peeped on the very night of the murder.) If Michael was indeed the killer, then the scientists had sketched a stunningly accurate portrait of him.

Though I had hoped Tommy would provide some point of enlightenment about the night of Martha's murder—any new detail that could erode the mystery—I wanted, at the very least, to come away with a sense of the man Thomas Skakel had become. People said he was a loving father of three daughters. That he was a good neighbor. And that he manufactured, of all things, golf clubs for a living,— which is true.

A man wearing a mechanic's jacket saw me roaming around Main Street. He asked what I was looking for, I told him, and he pointed to a small, faintly lavender house across the street. There were friendly Halloween decorations in the front windows—Mickey Mouses, Caspar the Ghosts, rubber bats and spiders—and Indian corn on the door.

The house was dark.

I left a note with a neighbor and went for a drive in the Berkshires. When I came back, I saw a well-worn four-by-four parked out in front. I used the brass knocker and waited. A pale hand flashed in a window pane, seeming to wave me away, but I wasn't sure, so I pressed my face to the glass and peered inside. Uh-oh. Tommy was on the phone. The police would surely come screeching in at any moment. What else did they have to do in Stockbridge? As I was walking away, anxious for the shelter of my car, I heard the door open behind me.

Tommy called my name.

He stepped out onto his front lawn, staring at me quizzically. He wore khakis, a blue oxford-cloth shirt and moccasins. What remained of his hair was cut very short and his eyes were enormous and blue. I don't know why he did not order me off his grounds instantly, considering that he had read the hardcover edition of this book. He pointed out something I had gotten wrong—Steven was the youngest Skakel brother, not David—and seemed slightly offended. But he was never less than polite. He asked me not to quote him, I agreed, and then we talked for about fifteen minutes.

He said nothing that sheds light on Martha's death. He said nothing new about the specifics of the case. He did say, in response to my question, how he would go about my business if he were me. His answer, not surprisingly, involved Ken Littleton.

Soon our discussion turned to small talk—his house, the town. As I watched him and listened to his words, Tommy did not strike me as dim-witted. He did not show signs of a life colored by tragedy and suspicion, nor a trace of the sloppy, hot-tempered boy he once had been. That was someone else. Here in Stockbridge, Tommy Skakel was a contented man living a steady and uneventful life, save for intrusions like this one. Humdrum familial peace, some hunting and some golf, were all he seemed to want.

As our meeting wound down, a beautiful dark-haired girl, about six years old, appeared in the doorway. She bounced impatiently on her toes. "Daddy! Come here."

"In a minute, sweetie," Tommy said, and turned back to the

stranger on his lawn. Even after the girl disappeared into the house, though, I could not stop thinking about her. By the time she turned fifteen, the old "family problem," as her grandfather had so oddly put it, would be settled. Her uncle Michael probably would have stood trial for the murder of Martha Moxley. Her father—still a suspect at this writing—would have been vilified too, since his role in the crime, if he had one, would remain a topic of intense speculation.

One day the girl would understand why her family was under attack, as it were, and this grim epiphany would begin to make scars. For Michael's baby, born around Thanksgiving of 1998, the consequences would be graver: at worst, there was the prospect of a father torn away from him to live behind bars. And so the family problem descends to a generation of innocents, sounding a fiery Old Testament note.

Ironically, in the end, the Skakel money may prove to do nothing more than extend and amplify the nightmare. If Michael Skakel did have something to do with Martha's murder, a prompt confession could have, in effect, saved his life. He probably would have been a free man by the time he turned twenty-one—given his age in 1975 and the relatively benign judicial climate of the time. Instead, nearly a quarter century later, the family's legal bills are mounting precipitously (at one point, they retained ten lawyers in three states), Michael is unemployed and unemployable, and the story in which he finds himself appears to have no blue sky beyond the gloom.

Now it was late afternoon. The sun slanted through the trees. I shook Tommy's hand goodbye and looked past his shoulder to the cozy frame house on Main Street. A happy house. So unlike the sprawling, chaotic one of his Belle Haven boyhood; so unlike the jaw-dropper of his father's youth. It was as though Tommy had renounced his own family history in order to construct a new future—one that would rest upon a small foundation, to insure intimacy, balance and humility. But rejecting the past does not erase it. So I could not help thinking, *Now that he's got it put together right, it's all going to come apart*—just as it had for the Moxleys a quarter century before.

—February 22, 1999